WEAVING
THE NEW
CREATION

WEAVING
THE NEW
CREATION

Stages of Faith and the Public Church

James W. Fowler

HarperSanFrancisco
A Division of HarperCollins*Publishers*

FIRST EDITION

Library of Congress Cataloging-in-Publication Data

Fowler, James
    Weaving the new creation : stages of faith and the public church / James W. Fowler.—1st ed.
        p.   cm.
    Includes bibliographical references and index.
    ISBN 0–06–062845–6 (alk. paper)
    1. Faith. 2. Church. 3. Theology.   I. Title.
BT772.F68   1991
230—dc20   90–46148
                                              CIP

91 92 93 94 95 MART 10 9 8 7 6 5 4 3 2 1

This edition is printed on acid-free paper that meets the American National Standards Institute Z39.48 Standard.

Contents

Gratefully dedicated to

The members of C.E. 379, Spring 1990, Candler School of Theology

and to

The Ecclesia Class, Glenn Memorial United Methodist Church

Who nurtured, called forth, and enriched
the ideas, themes, and passion of this book
and its author

Preface

Once I visited the medieval palace of the schismatic popes in Avignon, southern France. One enters the palace from a wide cobblestone square marked by fluttering banners and flags. The interior, in my memory, is like a series of large and smaller rooms connected by rather dark and cavernlike hallways. The large rooms—especially the dining rooms, council rooms, and papal bedrooms—have windows that illumine their stone walls. Some smaller chambers have line drawings and simple paintings on their walls; others have narrow frescoes around the wall just under the ceiling. The striking thing in my memory, however, is the tapestries that hang on the large walls in the main rooms of the palace.

Woven on commission in the Netherlands, they exhibited magnificent spread and impressive artistry. Some of them told, in unfolding narrative, events from Greek or Roman mythology and history. Others portrayed the movement and drama of biblical stories. As I pondered these tapestries it occurred to me that, unlike oriental rugs whose complex pattern is established and repeated by the weavers, these narrative tapestries required a designer to work closely with the weavers in order to compose the forms and colors that would capture the details of the whole. I can imagine the artist-designer experimenting as the work proceeds, finding that some planned strategies succeed and that others don't and have to be modified. I can also imagine that in the execution of the design the artist discovers new depths of the action and new dimensions of the characters to be portrayed, thus requiring the design to be revised as it is being woven.

The composing of this book has been like weaving a series of such tapestries. Each chapter is a tapestry in its own right, telling a story and requiring careful weaving and blending of color and form. But then the whole collection of tapestries has been woven, as it were, to be placed in a circular space from the center of which an observer can see and enter into them all. Themes in the separate chapters link up to form a circular room of interrelated meanings and perspectives.

You will see blemishes and rough places in these weavings. Artistry and knowledge falter at points. The perspective required by the weavings alters subtly at times, requiring the observer to accommodate and work to discern the weaver's intentions. The entire gallery challenges viewers to let the pattern of the whole take form as they focus successively on the separate weavings. The tapestries are offered now, with skylights for good visibility, in the hope that they will intrigue, involve, and reward those who make the effort to enter into their room and ponder their patterns.

The weaver has acknowledgments and gratitude to express. Earlier versions of chapters 1 and 6 were presented at Moravian Seminary in Bethlehem, Pennsylvania, as the Weber Lectures, and at Alaska Pacific University as part of the Everett Palmer Lectures. Parts of chapter 2 were presented at a conference on the twentieth anniversary of the deaths of Thomas Merton and Martin Luther King, sponsored by the Aquinas Center of Theology, Emory University. A version of chapter 4 first found voice at the Episcopal cathedral of Houston in a lectureship there. An insistent invitation by the New England Association of United Church Educators to address the problem of gender inclusiveness in theology led to my discovery of the poetry of Brian Wren. Parts of chapters 5 and 6 were delivered at a conference on Care and Discipline in the Congregation at Christian Theological Seminary, Indianapolis, Indiana. Early versions of chapters 3, 5, and 7 took form in preparing for a conference of Episcopal religious educators at Kanuga Conference Center. It was for that occasion that I found the title and theme, "Weaving the New Creation," and the inspiration to try to weave the whole into this book. I am grateful for the hospitality and lively discussions that were part of each of these events. Especially do I thank Doris Blazer and Gus Boone, designers and leaders of the Kanuga event, for their challenge to elaborate a practical theological vision of public church for religious educators. It has been encouraging to me to remember faces, eyes, and dialogues from all these occasions in the lonely early morning hours when these pieces have been rewoven for this circle of tapestries.

Several conversation partners over the years have helped nurture my turning toward some of the themes and concerns of this book. Especially important among these are Sharon Daloz-Parks, Jan Campanella, Christine Wenderoth, Susan Shutt, Susan Parsons, and Jürgen Moltmann and Elisabeth Moltmann-Wendel. For their friendship and loving criticism when I needed it, I am grateful.

In the spring of most intense writing on this book I had the privilege of working with an unusually engaging group of our students at the Candler School of Theology. Thirty-two men and women enrolled in my first-time course Toward Christian Religious Education for the Twenty-first Century. Their investments in that course—their adroit co-teaching of it—stimulated immeasurably the process of this writing. It was with them that chapter 3, a dialogue with Sallie McFague, took form and insisted on being written. I dedicate the book, in part, to them. The other group to whom it is dedicated are the members of the *Ecclesia* class of Glenn Memorial United Methodist Church in Atlanta—the "young singles class." Though I am neither single nor young, they have allowed me to be part of their remarkable fellowship for the past three years and have given me a number of occasions to share and test some of these forming thoughts with them.

For help in reading and improving this text I am grateful to my friends Bill Everett, Pat Chamberlin, Lurline Fowler, Lewis Mudge, and Karen DeNicola. My editor, John Shopp, did what editors are supposed to do: he gave me a constructively critical but encouraging reading, which helped in the revising and strengthening of the book. To each and all I am grateful.

Let us begin to spread the tapestries.

Emory University   James W. Fowler

Introduction

At century's close—at millennium's ending—radical changes in human consciousness and in geopolitical relations are under way. This brewing, yeasty time of falling walls and paradigm transformation arises out of a combination of many factors. Among these I am especially conscious of the following:

1. Worldwide movements for liberation, with the resulting pluralization of voices and standpoints that must be counted in;
2. Our global telecommunications linkages, which enrich the humming stimuli of everyday consciousness and imagery with data that arrive simultaneously from all parts of the globe;
3. The reimaging of Earth as fragile ecological spaceship, requiring interdependence with and care for *all* life;
4. International economics, with the connectors and civility it requires, in which even political enemies have a common stake in the economic stability of the world's systems; and
5. The intercultural awakening to spiritual cosmology, involving solidarity with Earth and an expanding universe of pulsing matter.

This book records the jottings of one author's efforts to think, to talk, to pray and act, and to help form faith and church for the new era opening around us. I am conscious that what I have written comes from *within* the process of transformation toward new paradigms. I have no perspective above, beyond, or out front of the birth processes of this new era. I am at least partially aware that much of what I have written here and the ways I have written it reflect the way our minds—both personal and collective—seem to operate in this era. The chapters of the book are not linked together by a linear logic that attempts to move the reader from one place of departure to a sure destination already fully seen and formulated by the author. Rather, the chapters, and the elements of narrative, discourse, exposition, and autobiography that make them up, relate to one another in circular fashion, with lines of connection flowing across the circle to and from each other, while each pursues some specific dimension of a larger, emerging whole.

The use of the term *weaving* in the title is intended to communicate that in writing about church and faith, I am trying to evoke a sense of participation in dynamic patterns of action and being. These patterns of action and being include

1. The finding and making of meaning, both corporate and personal;
2. The shaping and forming of community, both ecclesial and secular;
3. The interpretation and transformation of tradition, both theological and cultural; and
4. The discernment and relation to God's provident involvement in these transforming times, both theoretical (scientific) and practical (theology, ethics, life).

The weaving proceeds in this book without a clear, fixed, closed-ended design. Rather, it selects threads and strands retrieved from the indispensable patterns and colors of earlier art and interlaces them with themes and colors newly emerging. In the weaving of the book there is a sense in which the author's own tapestry of conviction and expression, of vocation and faithfulness, is also being rewoven for a new decade, and perhaps a new millennium.

For readers who want a map and appreciate a path, here is an overview of the weaving of each chapter. The book begins with an evocation of images of the twenty-first century. In teaching and lecturing about these matters I have found that audiences become engaged by the invitation to offer their images of the new millennium to one another. As we enumerate the conditions to be anticipated in this decade and the new century, we usually find elements of both hope and dread, promise and peril. In chapter 1, I offer my own version of the promises and perils of the coming era as a backdrop for asking what kind of faith, what kind of church, we are called to in the twenty-first century. Toward the end of this first chapter I introduce the concept of paradigm shift in cultural consciousness and employ stages of faith as a framework for focusing on the paradigm shift in which, I believe, we are currently involved.

Both chapter 2 and chapter 3 engage in constructive theology. Both are concerned with trying to depict and evoke awareness of what I call the divine *praxis*—the underlying patterns of God's action and being in relation to creation and human history. These chapters approach their topic in quite different ways, however. Chapter 2 approaches the characterization of God's providence through biography and narrative. It considers the lives and teachings of Martin Luther King, Jr., Thomas Merton, and Carlyle Marney in the effort to discern disclosures of the *praxis* of God. A concluding story of a contemporary woman in vocation offers a distinctive view of God's astonishing weaving.

Chapter 3 takes a more systematic theological approach. There, in dialogue primarily with Sallie McFague, I explore possibilities for a metaphoric transformation in our depictions of God's involvement in the processes of an evolving, expanding universe. For me this marks a moving away from my long-time reliance on the metaphor of God as sovereign toward exploration of a reconfiguration of my earlier expressions of God's *praxis* in the action metaphors of creating, governing, liberating, and redeeming. Though the convictions underlying those earlier metaphors have deepened, I believe that we must find metaphors to express and commend those convictions that are more resonant with an ecological, nuclear, religiously pluralistic, and gender-inclusive era.

In chapters 4 and 5 the reader will find what I have called "Two Stories of Faith." In these two chapters I have tried to depict the dialectical dance at the heart of faith development. The dialectic is the interplay between the gradual process of development in faith depicted by the stage theory of faith development, and the conversional, transformational dynamics of faith as life lived in commitment to God in Christ. Chapter 4 offers the most recent description of faith stages. In their formal description of the journey of faith the stages are offered as a kind of "everyperson's story." Interwoven through this chapter are the stories of several distinct persons, depicting through their experience the process—and the pain—of stage transition and fixation.

Chapter 5 focuses on the life of Christian commitment in terms of vocation. In partnership with the poetic theology of Brian Wren, it then retells the narrative of God's *praxis* and human responsiveness that constitutes the Christian story and vision. Linking with chapters 2 and 3, Wren's poetry employs many of the metaphors developed in the dialogue with Sallie McFague. (Wren has been deeply influenced by McFague.)

The final two chapters offer and explore a vision of church for this decade and the twenty-first century. Under the rubric "public church," chapter 6 sets forth the characteristics of communities of faith that can hold together both deep Christian commitment and a principled openness and effective contribution to the common good in a pluralistic and increasingly crowded world. This chapter draws upon research in progress with my colleague Thomas E. Frank and a research team we have led. Tom has agreed for me to lift the lid on our findings in this project and to sketch some preliminary impressions in this chapter. He and I together are working on the fuller and more complete volume that will publish the rich results of that work.

Chapter 7 explores the normative bases, in scripture and tradition, for *ecclesiogenesis*—the rebirth, the rebuilding of the church from within and below and from outside its established structures. This term, taken from Leonardo Boff, points up the process of ecclesial (re-)formation to which we are called in the coming era. A "semiotics" of ecclesiogenesis begins the chapter. Then the multiple dimensions of ecclesial *praxis* underscore a holistic approach to formation and re-formation. The themes explored in this final chapter deserve their own book. In descriptions that are clear enough, however, it sketches some of the ways by which congregations can get from where we are today to something more nearly approximating public church modes of being, ministry, and mission. Here you will find the outlines of a systemic, comprehensive approach to *paideia* for congregations that discern their calling to lie in the direction of public church. A final section gives an overview of the special implications of stages of faith for Christian *paideia* in public church congregations.

Several themes constitute warp and woof in this weaving. The first centers in the recognition that faith and consciousness involve dynamic processes of construction and interpretation. In the book this theme finds development at several levels—personal, ecclesial, societal, and cultural. An underlying assertion of the book is that the Enlightenment of the eighteenth century opened an era marked by "procedural knowing"—approaches to inquiry and knowing that made themselves accountable for methods, use of evidence, and the justification and verification of conclusions. In more familiar terms, the Enlightenment institutionalized and made normative the "procedural knowing" that constitutes modern science.[1]

It happens that the Enlightenment emphasized what Belenky and her colleagues call the "separative" form of procedural knowing—knowing through objectification of the known, through detachment and disinterested inquiry. More recently the voice of "connective" procedural knowing has made its claims, with its concern for a "knowing in rapport," a participative attention through methods that employ the disciplined subjectivity of the inquirer. This book suggests that the paradigm shift in which we are currently involved draws us beyond procedural knowing toward what Belenky et al. call a "constructive knowing."

In my own terms, constructive knowing involves pursuing forms of inquiry and construction that combine procedural care with multiple perspectives on the known. It employs the self-aware use of metaphorical and imaginal modeling to make possible the communication of multileveled knowing about matters of great complexity and moment. Throughout this book appeals are being made to perspectives that require constructive knowing. The chapter on stages of faith helps us see that the conjunctive stage best fits with the art and rigor of constructive knowing.

A second theme woven throughout the book is that of vocation. As chapter 5 suggests, whenever I try to speak or write about persons and communities living faith in conscious and committed relation to God, I draw upon the concept of vocation, or calling. By vocation I mean the response a person makes with his or her total life to the call of God to partnership. I believe that humans have evolved for ontological vocations of partnership with God—in co-creation, co-sustaining, and co-healing and rectification of the "world." This ontological calling is not limited to Christians. My formulation of it I take to be a Christian formulation of a universal vocation. Throughout the book this assumption and this theme play a fundamental role.

The third theme of which I am conscious in the book centers in the effort to retrieve and reconstitute—in different metaphors and imagery—what the church has meant when it has testified to the sovereignty of God. In chapter 3 I make clear why I no longer find it helpful to employ this key organizing metaphor directly. I also try to make clear, however, that the conviction that metaphor expressed is of deepened importance to me. Throughout this text I try in a variety of ways to express the "spread" and pervasive presence of God throughout the universe and throughout all of life. This is one key strand of what the sovereignty metaphor intended but had difficulty expressing. I do not intend to *reduce* God to God's involvement in nature and creation. God's priority in being, value, power, and agency are, I believe, consistently affirmed in this writing—and they are crucial parts of what sovereignty tried to convey. But the power and influence of God, as depicted here, are meant to be more pervasive, more participative. I offer a God more integral to human and animal suffering, and more intimately loving and confirming of the worth of human beings and all creation. I am trying to learn to speak of and image a more vulnerable, yet transcendent and all-powerful, God.

Finally there is a theme of deep hopefulness. This hopefulness does not find its grounds in a romantic optimism that overlooks the jeopardy to humanity and all animate life represented by the nuclear threat and our ecological abuses. Rather it finds its grounds in the discernment of God's presence and *praxis* at so many levels and in so many subtle yet transformative ways in our corporate and personal lives that we have difficulty accounting for it.

When Jesus reached the outskirts of Jerusalem, prepared to enter the city at the beginning of Passover week, his followers and the aroused people of the city set up a loud clamor of hail and hosanna. Officials of temple and empire arrived on the scene to keep the peace. They directed Jesus to quiet the crowd. Jesus told them in response that if he tried to close off this clamor, to damp down this acclamation and welcome, the very *stones* would cry out (Luke 19:40). For those who have eyes to see, today—in communities all around our nuclear-threatened, ecologically jeopardized, endangered planet—the very stones are crying out in rising tides of consciousness and determination to be part of a new and renewed creation. The themes of this book, especially the effort to set forth ways of seeing and responding to the hope-grounding *praxis* of God in our time, are offered here prayerfully as one contribution to that chorus of stones crying out to be counted in the divine weaving of the new creation.

NOTE

1. The term *procedural knowing* I take from Mary F. Belenky, Blythe M. Clinchy, Nancy R. Goldberger, and Jill M. Tarule, *Women's Ways of Knowing* (New York: Basic Books, 1986).

Every day we find a new sky and a new earth
with which we are trusted like a perfect toy.
We are given the salty river of our blood
winding through us, to remember the sea and our
kindred under the waves, the hot pulsing that knocks
in our throats to consider our cousins in the grass
and the trees, all bright scattered rivulets of life.

We are given the wind within us, the breath
to shape into words that steal time, that touch
like hands and pierce like bullets, that waken
truth and deceit, sorrow and pity and joy,
that waste precious air in complaints, in lies,
in floating traps for power on the dirty air.
Yet holy breath still stretches our lungs to sing.

We are given the body, that momentary kibbutz
of elements that have belonged to frog and polar
bear, corn and oak tree, volcano and glacier.
We are lent for a time these minerals in water
and a morning every day, a morning to wake up,
rejoice and praise life in our spines, our throats,
our knees, our genitals, our brains, our tongues.

We are given fire to see against the dark,
to think, to read, to study how we are to live,
to bank in ourselves against defeat and despair
that cool and muddy our resolves, that make us forget
what we saw we must do. We are given passion
to rise like the sun in our minds with the new day
and burn the debris of habit and greed and fear.

We stand in the midst of the burning world
primed to burn with compassionate love and justice,
to turn inward and find holy fire at the core,
to turn outward and see the world that is all
of one flesh with us, see under the trash, through
the smog, the furry bee in the apple blossom,
the trout leaping, the candles our ancestors lit for us.

Fill us as the tide rustles into the reeds in the marsh.
Fill us as the rushing water overflows the pitcher.
Fill us as the light fills a room with its dancing.
Let the little quarrels of the bones and the snarling
of the lesser appetites and the whining of the ego cease.
Let silence still us so you may show us your shining
and we can out of that stillness rise and praise.

Marge Piercy, "Nishmat"

Nishmat Kol Chai (The Soul of All Living Things) is a Jewish ritual morning prayer.

PRELUDE

1. The Church and the Future: Images of Promise and Peril

In my estimation, all that we suffer in the present time is nothing in comparison with the glory which is destined to be disclosed for us, for the whole creation is waiting with eagerness for the children of God to be revealed. . . . We are well aware that the whole creation, until this time, has been groaning in labor pains. . . . The spirit . . . comes to help us in our weakness, for, when we do not know how to pray properly, the Spirit personally makes our petitions for us in groans that cannot be put into words, and the One who can see into all hearts knows what the Spirit means because the prayers that the Spirit makes for God's holy people are always in accordance with the mind of God.

ROMANS 8:18–27, NJB

You have already been told what is right and what Yahweh wants of you. Only this, to do what is just, love mercy, and walk humbly with God.

MICAH 6:8, NJB

"May you live in interesting times" says an ancient Chinese curse. As we claim entry into the last decade of this tumultuous twentieth century it seems likely that we will continue to experience this curse/blessing. These are, indeed, roiling, dynamic, fermentative, *interesting* times. This book sets forth a vision for the future of faith and the church intended to guide the shaping of personal and public faith for interesting times.

As a way of approaching the question of faith and the church in the 1990s and the twenty-first century, I have found it useful to reframe the present by looking at both past and future. This exercise, more subjective than objective, gives us an opportunity to step back from the unfolding present and see it from the distance of past memories and future projections. In what follows I am inviting you to enter into some of my memories of and reflections on the recent past and some projections and imaginings for the near future. I do this to inspire you to your own reflections and remembering, your own projections and imaginings for the future. I do this to focus on the question, What kind of church is God calling us to be and become in the 1990s and the twenty-first century? What kind of presence and witness are we called upon to be and give in a future that seems so full of portent and possibilities, so brimming with promise and peril? As a way of beginning to think about the future, I invite you to accompany me in a brief review of the drama of change in the five brief decades of my life in the twentieth century.

REFLECTIONS ON THE LAST FIFTY YEARS: 1940–1990

Born in 1940, I entered history on the cusp between the economic dislocations of the depression era and our global mobilization for the conflagration of World War II. Rationing tokens, blackouts, and air-raid wardens, frightening news film of fire-bombed cities and emaciated prisoners liberated from death camps, and the death of friends' fathers and big brothers swirl in my earliest memories. Ringing the church bell in celebration and thanksgiving for the end of that terrible war, my father turned the bell over with his exuberant pulls on the rope, and we had to go up into the belfry and right it.

Three short years later news films of the blockade of Berlin and the heroic airlift that guaranteed that city's survival entered my memory as a seven- and eight-year-old. Today these memories symbolize my felt sense of the beginnings of what we have come to know as the East-West cold war. To me, everything in Europe in those years seemed gray, bleak, and tragic. On the horizons of my imagination the world I lived in exhibited a cloud-line of depression.

The boyhood pleasures of a small-town coming-to-awareness in the early 1950s mingle with images of troops dying in Korean snows, Eisenhower's heart attacks, and his troubles over vicuña coats, U2 flights, and the Suez Canal blockade. I tried to make sense of the charismatically bitter Wisconsin senator Joseph McCarthy and the crime-fighting FBI director J. Edgar Hoover, who made the crusade against communism a matter of religious fervor against godless, demonic, and uncannily dangerous subversives. In church I sometimes fantasized armed troops breaking in and confronting us with the possibility of a martyr's death if we clung to our Christian faith in face of their demand that we become communists. A jeweler on Main Street had the name Stallings. As a youngster I watched his store carefully and pondered his possible connection with the arch-demon of communism, the hard-eyed, menacing dictator of the Soviet Union, Joseph Stalin.

In an early-fifties Saturday afternoon film, a grade B spy movie, an eleven-year-old's consciousness first entered the nuclear era in a personal way. In the black-and-white somberness of this film a man asked a teenager what he wanted to be when he grew up. The lad, referring to the devastating power and menacing presence of the atomic bomb, responded, "You mean, *if* I grow up."

Later in that decade years of preparation and frustration catalyzed the beginnings of a new era when Rosa Parks refused to relinquish her seat on a Montgomery city bus and a young Ph.D. Baptist pastor emerged into his public destiny. As the forces propping up the rotting wall of racial segregation burned their crosses, a small bleeping satellite marked with the red star shifted the battle front in the cold war from espionage and atomic-armed B-52s in perpetual flight to the science and math classrooms of American schools.

The opening of the 1960s found me in student politics on a major university campus in the south. As *in loco parentis* died, fifty miles away the first lunch counter sit-ins began. We picketed restaurants and movie theaters and fought for a charter for the NAACP on campus. We rejected the idea that steam tunnels under the campus should be converted to bomb shelters. We thrilled at Kennedy's election and early promise and agonized through the disastrous Bay of Pigs invasion.

The Cuban missile confrontation came when I was twenty-two and engaged in graduate theological study in the New York area. Khrushchev banged his shoe on a table at the United Nations while Malcolm X brought steely new tactics and the threat of black counterviolence into northern cities. I participated in the summer 1963 March on Washington. We thrilled as the coalition of the Kennedys and King seemed to promise meaningful and permanent legal change toward racial justice. Then there came the first Kennedy assassination, the heady, grief-inspired triumphs in civil rights legislation, LBJ's Great Society, the affirmation "black is beautiful," and the cries for "black power." These developed during the rapid escalation of our involvement in the small Vietnam initiative Eisenhower and Kennedy had begun.

During the last half of the 1960s my family and I lived in Massachusetts. Graduate study in religion and society framed my involvement in anti-Vietnam politics. In April of 1968 an assassin killed Martin Luther King, Jr. Months later Robert Kennedy's violent death closed the books on Camelot.

In the early 1970s I finished my doctorate and launched a teaching and research career. The painful winding down and withdrawal from Vietnam, the opening of relations with China, and then the protracted agony of Watergate and presidential impeachment hearings provided the backdrop against which I worked with an exciting team at Harvard on fundamental research leading to the faith development theory. Black, feminist, and Third-World liberation theologies began to reveal the ideological entrapment of our dominant theological models. Liberation and the empowerment of oppressed minorities moved toward center stage, while persons like E. F. Schumacher, Garrett Hardin, and the Club of Rome gave voice to the need for population control, monitoring and moderating our use of nonrenewable resources, and care for our endangered biosphere.

Toward the end of the 1970s, as my place of work shifted to Atlanta and Emory University, the strident voices of what came to be known as the New Religious Right had begun to call for a renewal of the moral bases of American society, to be grounded in their versions of fundamentalist Christian ethics. Joining the potency of telecommunications with well-financed legal battles fought over school prayer and "secular humanism" in textbooks, and over abortion, they combined entertainment with effective fund-raising and for a time succeeded in electing, appointing, or otherwise influencing political figures at national, state, and local levels. Yet, throughout the Reagan years the number of teen pregnancies continued to increase, drug use and the drug economy expanded dramatically, HIV infection and AIDS took on epidemic proportions, and Wall Street scandals threatened the integrity of this country's corporate financial structure. Meantime, the controversial effort to create a nuclear guard-all shield in the "Star Wars" defense initiative buttressed a peacetime economy while siphoning off vast amounts of money badly needed for renewing the nation's infrastructure, for education, health care, and healing the environment. As deficit spending continued, making the United States the largest debtor nation, the Iran-Contra scandal confirmed a sense that the nation was dangerously adrift. Against this backdrop scandal-ridden TV evangelists have faded rapidly, some into prison, some into indebted oblivion, others into desperate retrenchment and the closing of major divisions of their missions. The fundamentalist mentality and power bloc, however, remains in firm control of some large Christian denominations. And at the new decade's opening the struggle over the complex of issues identified with the phrase "right to life" continues in legislatures and in the courts.

In these same years there emerged a new leader in what President Reagan had called the "evil empire." In 1985, at age fifty-four, Mikhail Gorbachev was the youngest member of the Politburo when he was tapped to become General Secretary of the Communist Party. Realist and idealist, bold and imaginative, with his intelligence and charisma he has encouraged revolutionary changes within his nation. At the same time, his initiatives toward nuclear disarmament and his manifest readiness to allow the breakup of the Warsaw Pact and the democratization of Eastern European nation-states have led, at this writing, to a series of utterly unexpected new beginnings there. The dismantling of the Berlin Wall and the hastening of German reunification are the most vivid symbols of the end of the cold war.

IMAGES OF THE FUTURE

It is a notoriously difficult and dangerous thing to try to gaze into a crystal ball and predict what conditions we can expect less than a decade from now as we enter a new century. Indeed, at the close of this fateful twentieth century we not only mark the turning of a new hundred-year cycle, we also anticipate the turning of a new millennium—the third of our "common era."

Nothing in my background or training qualifies me to be a crystal-ball gazer. Nonetheless, I offer some suggestions about what we may expect as we approach the twenty-first century. You will readily see that the vectors toward the twenty-first century that I'm pursuing are extensions of trends that you too will have recognized around us. I will examine a set of promises that the new century and new millennium seem to hold. In each case, however, I invite you to consider the dark side, the perils, that accompany what seem to be positive possibilities.

The first set of promises can be identified as *expanded choices.* Our era has been characterized as one of "overchoice." From automobiles to vinegar, from TV channels to religious denominations and groups, from life-styles to leisure-time travel, we have opportunities and choices to make that are unprecedented in history. Because of continuing technological developments and the need for economic growth, it seems likely that our range of choices will continue to expand. Anyone who has bought a car recently, in addition to being shocked by how much it cost, was perhaps stymied for some time by all the options available. I am told that there are at least 124 different kinds of compact automobiles one can buy in the American market alone. I anticipate that we will continue to experience enhanced opportunities for choice and for individual expression through our choices. This seems to be one of the promises of the next decade and of the twenty-first century.

The peril that goes with expanding choice may be characterized as *homeless minds and hearts.* The phrase "homeless mind" belongs to Peter Berger and his coauthors of a book by that title.[1] It points to minds and souls that are no longer attached or connected to particular places, communities, or traditions that provide standards and guidelines for the exercise of choice. Another author has characterized our time as leading to "the vertigo of relativity," the dizziness of relativity. Too many options, too many choices, too many ways of seeing things—this leads us to develop what the philosopher Carl Jaspers called "cipher skepticism." We are exposed to too many models of reality, too many perspectives on values and meanings. How shall be commit ourselves to *one* in the midst of the many that appeal to us? In his academic best-seller *The Closing of the American Mind,* Professor Allan Bloom of the University of Chicago asserts that the one thing we can be certain that undergraduates will have learned by the time they come to college, as a result of their elementary and high school education, is the *dogma* that all values are relative.[2] It is the task of a good liberal arts education, he says, to try to shake up that dogma and to demonstrate the possibility of grounding values and ethical principles on something more solid than subjective personal preference or solipsistic meanings. As we consider the peril side of expanded choices we are reminded of the lines from "The Second Coming," by W. B. Yeats: "The best lack all conviction, while the worst are full of passionate intensity."[3]

A second set of promises portended by the twenty-first century can be identified as *increased global awareness*. We are all mindful of the ways in which telecommunications media are revolutionizing our awareness of what is going on on this increasingly small planet we call Earth. The Polish poet Czeslaw Milosz, in his Norton Lectures at Harvard, reflects on the impact of this globalization of consciousness upon the poet:

> The unification of the planet is not proceeding without high cost. Through the mass media poets of all languages receive information on what is occurring across the surface of the whole earth, on the tortures inflicted by man on man, on starvation, misery, humiliation. At a time when their knowledge of reality was limited to one village or district, poets had no such burden to bear. Is it surprising that they are always morally indignant, that they feel responsible, that no promise of the further triumphs of science and technology can veil these images of chaos and human folly? And when they try to visualize the near future, they find nothing there except the probability of economic crisis and war.[4]

None of us will ever forget the remarkable experience of transcendence provided by that view from the moon of our globe that we came to call Earthrise. The radiant blue-green planet against the dark background of space gave us a perspective on ourselves and our interdependence with all other beings on this terrestial sphere that we could not have gained any other way. I believe we will continue to experience a widening of global awareness.

And yet, there is a peril that goes with this expansion of awareness: *fractured relationships and identity*. As we become really aware of those with whom we share this globe, we are aware in heightened ways of the strained relationships in the human family. Speaking at the microcosmic level, we are painfully conscious in our society of the betrayal of covenants between marriage partners, between parents and children, and in business and in government. We see how people working to the hilt in their occupation leads to neglect and abuse of even financially privileged children. And then we see millions of children on this globe dying or crippled from malnutrition. Recently I got a picture of hell on earth from a young woman psychologist from Los Angeles who has been doing research on infancy and early childhood in a region of that city where most of the children are the offspring of teenage mothers. Many of these young mothers (and fathers) are involved in substance abuse. As she studies the children she collects the painful data that show how their early signs of brightness and responsiveness, by about age four or five, begin to flicker and dim, until soon the child's little light effectively goes out. She says it is unlikely, in most cases, that it can ever be lit again. This year the first waves of "crack cocaine babies"—the children of addicted parents, who were born addicted—are entering the public schools. They seem to bring serious deficits of attention span and to be subject to frequent and sudden mood swings. They begin with real handicaps that raise grave questions about whether they will be able to prepare themselves for a place in this society. Fractured and broken relationships and identity represent the dark side, the peril side, of increasing global awareness.

A third set of promising factors for the twenty-first century have to do with continuing developments in *medical and technological mastery* of human disease and frailty. Every evidence suggests that we will continue to advance the quality of virtuosity in medical practice to which we have become accustomed over the last five decades. Some time ago I bought the fifteenth edition of the *Merck Medical Manual*. Compared with the dozen-year-old fourteenth edition it has an additional four hundred pages. It includes descriptions of operations, procedures, syndromes, and approaches to treatment not even on the horizon of thought in 1976. We have become accustomed to the idea of the conquest of disease. We have become accustomed to the idea of increased longevity. In Cambridge, Massachusetts, a firm called Orgogenesis is literally developing living human skin from synthetic materials. Now they are perfecting the molds in which they will form living replacement organs out of these synthetic materials. Just as you periodically replace the alternator or brake pads on your automobile, the prospect is that you can have your kidneys, lungs, or heart replaced by these laboratory-made replacement organs. It is an extraordinary future we see ahead in medical technology. And yet, here too, there is a dark side that seems certain to grow darker.

I refer to the perils of *new ills, escalating costs, and maldistribution of services*. We are chastened by the emergence and spread of AIDS, and by the realization that new viruses stay ahead of our treatment options with surprising and elusively destructive skill. We read statements by honest physicians that express their immense frustration at having to carry out expensive and taxing procedures that they normally would not prescribe in order to protect themselves against malpractice suits or to support the economics of new technologies in hospitals. We are seeing the cost of medical care going up exponentially, and we know that 31 million Americans have no insurance to cover it. This sad fact does not begin to take account of the billions of people worldwide who are effectively excluded from the quality of medical care that middle-class people in our society take for granted. We see ourselves on a terrible collision course: this extraordinary technology and capacity to heal coupled with a narrowing, increasingly exclusive ability to support it and pay for it. We have not begun to resolve the issues of the just use of heroic measures and the inordinate cost of prolonging lives whose quality has been radically reduced. New ills, exponential increases in costs, and inequality in the distribution of medical care haunt our future and are the dark side of the promises of continuing advancement.

My fourth set of promises in the new century center on the hope of *nuclear disarmament*. Since the breakthrough agreements reached between Presidents Reagan and Gorbachev in 1987, with evidence of the subsequent dismantling of missiles in Europe and North America, we have had reason for new hope that the two superpowers may have begun the arduous course toward a nuclear stand-down. President Gorbachev has acknowledged that the arms race is crippling our respective countries economically in the most serious ways. He has offered an alternative vision to our sustaining the impossible levels of investment in defense both countries currently pursue. In hope, we talked of a "peace dividend" that could be redirected toward providing rehabilitation, homes, and jobs for homeless persons, ecological mending here and in Eastern Europe, *genuine* aid to developing countries, and repair of our eroding infrastructure. Though threatened by costly Middle East intervention, such a recommitment of funds must be achieved.

Though we have high hopes for continuing superpower nuclear reductions, the danger side, the perils of the coming decades, still include the dangers of nuclear proliferation. This becomes plain when we recognize two alarming facts: First, most of the weapons being dismantled thus far are virtually obsolete. They are being replaced in our respective arsenals by newer and more frighteningly accurate weapons. Second, we stand in grave global danger from the proliferation of nuclear capacity among the more junior nuclear nations. Instabilities in Eastern Europe and the Middle East make the potential use of lethal weapons of biological and chemical warfare frightening possibilities.

A fifth set of promises of the twenty-first century I have called, simply and symbolically, *more American millionaires*. Governmental policies in the 1980s created the conditions for an unprecedented upturn in the number of millionaires in our society. Never mind that this status is being attained in inflation-decreased dollars, and that in order really to count now, it seems, one must be at least a billionaire. The stock market gave a strong warning in the fall of 1987 that our economy is finite and fragile, and that people and institutions can lose a lot of money on paper and in fact. I happened to be in the Lilly Endowment office in Indianapolis the Monday the stock market took its decisive dive. It was calculated that the $3.2 billion endowment of the foundation dropped in value by one billion dollars on that particular day. Despite our recognition of the finite nature of our system, large numbers of people have vastly prospered in this decade, and we can expect that many will continue to prosper. If those persons and corporate groups who succeed in forming and expanding their fortunes embrace the opportunity to use their resources for the common good, this can be a source of hope as the private sector contributes to healing and strengthening our society.

But we must face the perils of our situation, which have grown more dangerous as we enter this last decade. I name these perils *debtors, armorers, street people, and economic colonization*. There are two superlatives we citizens of the United States are having to incorporate into our identity that I fervently wish we could deny: we have come to be the world's greatest debtor nation, and simultaneously, we continue to be the world's largest merchant of arms. At the same time we may well have, among developed nations, the highest proportion of people in our population who are struggling to eke out food and shelter as homeless citizens in our streets. A fourth dimension of this grim side of American prosperity bears careful watching: corporate raiders have conspired to take over major companies, often depleting the capital and pension plans of solid corporations and jeopardizing their future with immense debt. At the same time—and partly as a consequence—our nation's real estate, financial institutions, and corporations are increasingly subject to purchase by Japanese, Canadian, West German, or British commercial interests. Japan now has the ten largest banks in the world. The value of stocks traded on the Tokyo stock exchange in 1989 exceeded the value of all those in the European markets combined, and also exceeded the total of those on the New York Stock Exchange. As U.S. firms move manufacturing and assembly line production to Third World nations in order to utilize cheaper labor they leave areas of severe economic depression in the Kenosha, Wisconsins, of this land. How can we expect foreign conglomerate owners of North American farms and businesses to be any more concerned about the economic viability of our towns, cities, or regions than our own multinational corporations have been? We are in danger of being economically recolonized. If these trends continue into the twenty-first century they constitute, indeed, a forbidding set of perils for this nation.

As a sixth cluster of promising possibilities for the next century I call to your attention what may be a *revival of religion and the pluralism of faiths*. I think we may be in the midst of something very like the first and second "great awakenings" in this nation, and indeed, around the globe. Before his death a dozen years ago Carlyle Marney would frequently say that religion and religious institutions may yet have another chance to make an impact upon our culture, not because we deserve it, but because the alternatives have defaulted. I believe that we are in the midst of a shift in cultural consciousness of major proportions. In face of the uncertainties and the threats of the emerging era people are turning to religion, mysticism, and spirituality in at least two directions. On the one hand, large groups are seeking to return to the established, authoritative grounding of traditional religious formulations and practices. Fundamentalists, biblicists, and those committed to the sacredness of institutional authority are seeking to find secure, if often regressive, anchors amid the winds of change and uncertainty. On the other hand, there seem to be growing numbers of folk who, having experienced the ambiguity and spiritual fragmentation of modern life, are recognizing in themselves a deep hunger for images, convictions, and communities of shared meaning that will hold. It was the Russian novelist Fyodor Dostoyevski who said that people require "miracle, mystery, and authority." In our time of cultural ferment and uncertainty it seems that people, on quite different levels, are being drawn again to miracle, mystery, and authority. I would only add to Dostoyevski's formula that people also long for community and for a cosmology—a coherent representation of ultimate reality that gives us place, hope, and a direction home. In our increase of armament, vigilance, and violence to try to eliminate the import and sale of drugs, we are not recognizing the spiritual hunger— the emptiness, anxiety, hopeless boredom, and deep rage—that fuels the market of precious human beings who become addicted to crack and other forms of lethal drugs. It seems clear that we are watching the demise of communism as an ideology and a form of government. As we continue through a transitional time culturally and politically, we may expect that the revival of religion and spirituality will not be just a fad. In its myriad of forms it may be a deepening and a redeeming source of renewal impulses in our society and in our world.

The dark side of this promise of religious revival and renewal is, of course, all too obvious. I call it *rigidity, exclusivism, and false consciousness*. In his 1981 book *The Public Church*, Martin Marty wrote:

> Many observers envision that the twenty-first century, far from being merely secular, may be hyperreligious. They go on to say that potent human organization may no longer follow the lines of nations but the outlines of religions until great tribes, well armed, will clash.[5]

In addition to the ayotollahs, the IRAs and radical Irish Protestants, and the Arabs and Israelis, I have in mind the tendency of many of the emerging new religions, or the renewed older ones, to lead people to a new kind of rigidity, a kind of exclusivism, and to provide reinforcement for new forms of false consciousness. These forms of religious false consciousness threaten to distract people from present conditions and responsibilities for the world with promises of rewards in heaven afterward. Or they provide, in their privatized systems of meaning, a kind of blessing for the economic and political status quo, allowing those who are privileged to justify their sense (or our sense) of deserving privilege in a world where others endure under quite different conditions.

Finally, in this listing of promises and perils of the twenty-first century, there is one set of perils that, in my view, assumes a larger significance than virtually any of the others yet mentioned. This is the peril focused in the radically endangered biosphere on which the future of the human species—as well as countless other species of flora and fauna—depends. We can name this peril, with Matthew Fox, *Our Mother Is Dying*. The following series of quotes are taken from Matthew Fox's recent book, *The Coming of the Cosmic Christ*.[6]

> Is our Mother Earth dying? Consider Bhopal; Chernobyl; Love Canal; Times Beach, Missouri; and . . . the Rhine River, where one thousand tons of chemicals, including eight tons of pure mercury, were spilled— the river where Hildegard of Bingen and Meister Eckhart, the two greatest creation mystics of Western Europe, lived and preached their message of compassion and interconnectivity with creation. (p. 13)

Consider these facts:

> Agricultural practices in North America today destroy topsoil at the rate of six billion tons per year. . . . It takes God and nature ten thousand years to produce one inch of topsoil. (p. 14)
>
> Each year forest land half the size of California vanishes. (p. 14)
>
> There are approximately ten million species of living things with whom we share this planet. These creatures range from fishes and porpoises to ash trees and rose bushes to coyotes and lions, to dogs, cats, and humans. . . . Currently, however, species are disappearing at the rate of one every twenty-five minutes. (pp. 14–15)
>
> And how about water? Holy, holy water. To the best of our knowledge, water is a unique creation of our planet. How are we treating this holy and essential gift—this original blessing without which there is no life? In the United States alone we dump eighty billion pounds of toxic waste into Mother Earth's lifeblood—her water—annually. (p. 16)
>
> At Love Canal, . . . where poisonous chemicals were dumped in the soil, there were eighteen pregnancies. Of these, only two resulted in normal children. Three resulted in still-born fetuses, four were

spontaneous abortions, nine had birth defects including incomplete skull closures, multiple rows of teeth, cleft palate, congenital heart defects, and genetic damage. (p. 16)

Is Mother Earth herself not the ultimate *anawim*, the most neglected of the suffering, voiceless ones today? (p. 17)

Were Fox writing today he would certainly add to these concerns what we have learned about spreading destruction of the ozone shields at both the poles and the grave signs of the greenhouse effect in the rising temperatures of our atmosphere and the seas rising with the melting of polar ice.

Your crystal ball might yield quite different pictures than mine has. Certainly, there are many other dimensions of promise and peril one could talk about—the aging of the American population and the further expansion of Third World populations, increasing the crowding of our world and leading to greater resource scarcity. We could speak of the probable increase in civil wars and terrorism and wars of liberation and of the growing gap between rich and poor, and of much else.

But now it is time to take a different tack. Using a brief overview of stages of faith as set forth in faith development theory and research, I propose to try to give more specificity and precision to my claim that we are experiencing a paradigm shift in levels of cultural consciousness.

STAGES OF FAITH

Faith development research and theory emerged in the late seventies and early eighties of this century. It was preceded by work on the development of moral reasoning by Lawrence Kohlberg and his associates. They in turn were dependent upon a tradition in philosophical psychology that began with Immanuel Kant and included centrally the cognitive developmental structuralism of Jean Piaget, the symbolic interactionism of George Herbert Mead, and the genetic epistemology of J. Mark Baldwin. In addition, faith development theory has depended upon the psychosocial theory of ego development offered by Erik H. Erikson. In its theological background it has relied upon the work of Paul Tillich, H. Richard Niebuhr, and the historian of religion Wilfred Cantwell Smith.

Faith development theory attempts to account for the operations of knowing, valuing, and committing that underlie a person's construal of self-other relations in the context of an explicitly or implicitly coherent image of an ultimate environment. Faith is understood dynamically as involving both the finding of and being found by meaning, both the construction and the reception of beliefs and commitments; and it is meant to include both explicitly religious expressions and enactments of faith, as well as those ways of finding and orienting oneself to coherence in an ultimate environment that are not religious.

In its empirical research and theory building, the faith development perspective has identified seven formal, structurally definable stages in the ways persons compose and maintain their life-orienting systems of meaning and valuing. Each stage represents the culmination of a revolution in the patterns of knowing and valuing by which a person finds or makes meaning. The emergence of these stages depends upon development across several structural aspects. These include cognition, social perspective taking, moral reasoning, personal authorization, widening social inclusiveness, cosmological coherence, and symbolic/aesthetic responsiveness.[7]

Development through the stages requires both time and physical maturation, though it is not inexorably tied to either. Biological maturation, time, and experience are *necessary* for the emergence of the sequence of stages, but not *sufficient*. A person can equilibrate or arrest in a stage or a transition between stages, either for long periods of time or permanently. The sponsorship of traditions, group membership, and the critical relations and experiences arising from interaction in life all affect the rate and extent of a person's development through the stages. Certain groups sponsor persons to particular stages but may also "seal" or "cap" their development to further stages. We believe that the stages are sequential and invariant. We do not have sufficient data to indicate the extent of their universality or cross-cultural validity. The following descriptions will serve as a brief overview of the structural developmental stages of faith:[8]

Primal faith (Infancy): A prelanguage disposition of trust forms in the mutuality of one's relationships with parents and others to offset the anxiety that results from separations that occur during infant development.

Intuitive-Projective faith (Early Childhood): Imagination, stimulated by stories, gestures, and symbols, and not yet controlled by logical thinking, combines with perception and feelings to create long-lasting images that represent both the protective and the threatening powers surrounding one's life.

Mythic-Literal faith (Childhood and beyond): The developing ability to think logically helps one order the world with categories of causality, space, and time; to enter into the perspectives of others; and to capture life meaning in stories.

Synthetic-Conventional faith (Adolescence and beyond): New cognitive abilities make mutual perspective-taking possible and require one to integrate diverse self-images into a coherent identity. A personal and largely unreflected synthesis of beliefs and values evolves to support identity and to unite one in emotional solidarity with others.

Individuative-Reflective faith (Young Adulthood and beyond): Critical reflection upon one's beliefs and values, utilizing third-person perspective-taking; understanding of the self and others as part of a social system; the internalization of authority and the assumption of responsibility for making explicit choices of ideology and life-style open the way for critically self-aware commitments in relationships and vocation.

Conjunctive faith (Early Mid-life and beyond): The embrace of polarities in one's life, an alertness to paradox, and the need for multiple interpretations of reality mark this stage. Symbol and story, metaphor and myth (from one's own traditions and others') are newly appreciated (second, or willed naíveté) as vehicles for expressing truth.

Universalizing faith (Mid-life and beyond): Beyond paradox and polarities, persons in this stage are grounded in a oneness with the power of being. Their visions and commitments free them for a passionate yet detached spending of the self in love, devoted to overcoming division, oppression, and violence, and an effective anticipatory response to an inbreaking commonwealth of love and justice.

THE PARADIGM SHIFT IN CULTURAL CONSCIOUSNESS

In a moving piece of fiction entitled *Night Thoughts of a Classical Physicist* Russell McCormmach tells the story of an aging German physicist, trained in the scientific order created by Newtonian physics, coming to the end of his life.[9] In the year 1918 Professor Victor Jakobs is sixty-nine, and World War I has just ended, shattering the economic and cultural foundations of a great era in his nation's history. Far more devastating, however, is the old scientist's recognition that his lifework has been in vain. The perfectly structured Newtonian worldview, in which he was trained and that has informed all his research, is being swept away by the theories of relativity and quantum mechanics. All the assumptions, all the research methods, and all the organizational principles for institutes of physics are undergoing dramatic change. The old man feels baffled and lost. He dimly perceives that this new science may radically alter and eventually endanger the fate of the earth. The night thoughts of Professor Jakobs provide a sensitive and affecting window into the feeling side of a scientist caught in the midst of a paradigm shift.

The term *paradigm shift* can be traced to the influential work of Thomas Kuhn in *The Structures of Scientific Revolutions.*[10] A paradigm is an example, model, or pattern. It derives from the Greek word for "example" (*deigma*), which is set up "alongside" (*para*) something to show what it is. A paradigm is a model on a small scale of a large, complex, difficult-to-grasp state of affairs.[11] A scientific or cultural paradigm consists of the shared frame of reference, the shared assumptions, the shared rules of research, inquiry, and validation that make possible the work of scientists in a particular era or the sharing of meanings in a culture. When a paradigm shift occurs, the whole frame of reference changes. Fundamental assumptions undergo transformation, with consequent alterations of all the rules and standards by which inquiry or conversation can occur. A new paradigm signals the emergence of a new worldview—new ways of seeing, interpreting, and making sense of the world and life.

We can trace four phases or movements in a major cultural shift of paradigms.[12] Such a shift begins with the increasing notice of anomalies—events and occurrences that do not easily fit the explanatory procedures of the existing paradigm. In passing I should point out that until anomalies begin to be noted, we are not usually aware that we are operating within a paradigm, as such. Rather, we take for granted the shared assumptions and frame of reference. We only begin to be aware of them as a paradigm when they are threatened and as alternate ways of seeing and making sense begin to bid for our attention. But that is to get ahead of the story. Anomalies begin to point to problems that our present understanding and shared frame of reference cannot adequately address.

The second step in a paradigm shift occurs in a crisis or a breakdown. This involves "tearing up and knocking down" the old paradigm—what Kuhn calls "paradigm destruction so a new paradigm can emerge. . . . Einstein's theory can be accepted only with the recognition that Newton's was wrong." In the sixteenth century Ptolemaic astronomy failed to solve the scientific problems being addressed to it, and thus it was time to give alternative approaches a chance.

In the third movement of a paradigm shift a transition period emerges in which Kuhn says one can expect "a large but never complete overlap between the problems that can be solved by the old and by the new paradigm. But there will also be a decisive difference in the modes of solution."[13] Factors that seemed trivial and of no account in the old paradigm may now be seen as having central significance.

The fourth movement in a paradigm shift is the consolidation and reintegration of science or culture in the light of the new, emerging paradigm. Generally this is a time marked also by strong resistance to the changes required. Paradigm shifts require more than conversions of the mind and heart: they require the shifting of priorities and resources in institutions; they bring political and economic changes; and, most extensively, they require changes in the worldviews that fund and make possible all our important communication and interaction.

The Enlightenment of the eighteenth century, beginning with an intellectual elite, brought about a paradigm shift in cultural consciousness that has funded the science, technology, and industrial development of the last two centuries. It has funded revolutions in our ways of dealing with politics, religion, philosophy, and the social sciences. Yet it has also given us weapons of mass destruction, the pollution of the earth and its atmosphere, and a widespread impoverishment of spirit and ethical sensitivity.

The question I pose in this concluding part of chapter 1 is whether we find ourselves now in the midst of a paradigm shift of cultural consciousness. Is this a watershed? Can a change of fundamental assumptions, frames of reference, and key metaphors and images guide us to recovery and new life in a global community?

The stages of faith development, presented briefly here, are ways of describing revolutions in consciousness—shifts in paradigms, if you will—that persons in our society seem regularly to experience in the process of moving from childhood to adulthood. However, evidence suggests that the majority of adults in our society arrest or equilibrate in either the Mythic-Literal or the Synthetic-Conventional stage. A smaller number construct the Individuative-Reflective style of consciousness, and an even smaller number evolve forms of consciousness described by the Conjunctive stage.

Here I want to make a bold hypothesis: I believe that we are experiencing in our time the emergence of a new cultural paradigm that has the power to address many of the anomalies of our present patterns of living. The "perils" side of our images of the future would constitute a beginning list of such anomalies. The new paradigm I would point to shares many of the structural features of the Conjunctive stage of faith consciousness, just as the paradigm of the Enlightenment shares many of the structures of the Individuative-Reflective stage of faith consciousness. As the conclusion of this chapter, therefore, I will briefly explore what the faith stages might provide by way of models for enabling us to consider the shape of a possible paradigm shift in cultural consciousness as we prepare to enter the twenty-first century.[14]

There is a parallel between the shift at the personal level from the Synthetic-Conventional to the Individuative-Reflective stage of faith and the cultural paradigm shift we associate with the Enlightenment of the eighteenth century. Let me explain:

The Enlightenment represented a movement in cultural evolution where inherited symbols, beliefs, and traditions were subjected to the scrutiny and evaluation of critical reasoning. Similarly, the development of the Individuative-Reflective stage of faith involves the critical examination and exercise of choice regarding a person or community's previous faith perspectives. In many respects this is a "demythologizing" stage. Creeds, symbols, stories, and myths from religious traditions are likely to be subjected to analysis and to [a] translation of their meanings to conceptual formulations. . . . Paul Tillich pointed out that a symbol that is recognized as a symbol no longer has the power of a symbol. The powerful participation of a symbol in that which it symbolizes, which makes it possible for the symbol to mediate relationship with its reality, is now broken. While the conceptual analysis and translation of the symbol makes its meanings explicit, we may fail to notice that in the process of communicating meanings the initiative has shifted from the symbol to the analyst of the symbol.[15]

The Enlightenment—beginning with an intellectual elite— affirmed the sovereignty of untrammeled reason. It confirmed the individual rights and dignity of each person. It turned the eye of critical reason upon traditions and myths. It challenged the authority of monarchies and attacked institutions of ecclesial power. Enlightenment thinkers completed the severence of physics and cosmology from theology and initiated the scientific study of psychology and sociology. In religion, thinkers of the Enlightenment turned the tools of analytic reason onto the record of biblical faith. Neither doctrinal traditions nor priestly hierarchies, nor the Bible itself, could withstand the relativizing impact of critical historical study. The Enlightenment produced a variety of social contract theories that provided legitimation for new governments. In economic philosophy it gave rise to what has been called "possessive individualism."[16]

Though there is much to be celebrated in the legacy of the Enlightenment, it is this paradigm, in the main, that has brought us to the point where we are poised, on the lip of the twenty-first century, precariously between the promises and perils we have sketched in this chapter.

If we are in the midst of a paradigm shift as regards the level of cultural consciousness, faith development theory suggests that we ought to look to the descriptions of—and examples of—the Conjunctive stage of faith in order to see something of its probable shape. Consider this fuller description of the structures of consciousness that characterize the Conjunctive stage of faith:

> The name for the Conjunctive stage of faith implies a rejoining or a union of that which previously has been separated. I take the name from Nicholas of Cusa (1401–1464) who wrote about what he called the *coincidentia oppositorum*, the "coincidence of opposites," in our apprehensions of truth. . . .
>
> In the transition to Conjunctive faith one begins to make peace with the tension arising from the fact that truth must be approached from a number of different directions and angles of vision. . . . Faith begins to come to terms with . . . apparent paradoxes: God is both immanent and transcendent; God is both an omnipotent and a self-limiting God; God is the sovereign of history while being the incarnate and crucified One. . . .
>
> The Conjunctive stage marks a movement beyond the demythologizing strategy of the Individuating stage. Where the latter followed the Enlightenment's tendency to reduce the symbolic and metaphoric to conceptual translations, this new stage reverses the flow of initiative. Acknowledging the . . . [richness] and density of symbols and myth, persons of the Conjunctive stage learn . . . to submit to their initiative and mediating power: Instead of "reading" and analyzing the symbols and metaphors, they learn to submit to the "reading" and illumination of their situations which these and other elements of tradition offer. In what Paul Ricoeur has called a "second" or "willed" naïveté, the Conjunctive stage manifests a readiness to enter into the rich dwellings of meanings which true symbols, liturgy and parable offer. Faith [re]-learns in this stage to be receptive, to balance initiative and control with waiting and seeking in order to be a part of the larger movement of spirit or being.[17]

Are there signs that we are, indeed, in the midst of a shift in a paradigm of cultural consciousness? Are we, in fact, involved in a culturewide transformation leading toward a new level of consciousness as we stand on the portals of the twenty-first century? If you remind yourself that in times of paradigm shift we can expect to see strong currents and tides flowing in retrogressive directions as well as toward the new, I think that the answer is yes. As evidence I would cite the growing numbers of post-Enlightenment approaches to hermeneutics and the philosophy of science, and at the popular level, the immense interest manifested in Bill Moyers's series of television interviews with Joseph Campbell, *The Power of Myth*.

Since the Second World War we have been formulating the groundlines of philosophical approaches that help to grasp and express the structural features of a revolution in Western consciousness—one that will likely prove to be as significant a watershed as the Enlightenment. Formulations of this new consciousness will have to incorporate the important contributions of the nineteenth century. These include a full-orbed doctrine of evolution and development (biological, cultural, ontological), the critique of ideology, and a full grasp of the role of overt as well as covert interests in shaping scientific and philosophical thought and behavior. The new paradigm will need to incorporate study of the social sources of religion, language, and the fundamental categories of thought. It must attend to and incorporate insights into how the cunning of psychological defenses and the repressed unconscious affect our knowing, valuing, and interpreting, as well as acting. These are some of the legacies of the nineteenth century to the emergent new paradigm of cultural consciousness.

But the new paradigm will also have to incorporate the great contributions of twentieth-century reflective experience: the awareness of the fundamental participation of everything in *process*; the relativity to each other, and to what they observe, of all perspectives on the universe and experience; the intrusion into and involvement of any investigator within phenomena being scientifically studied; the ecological interdependence of all systems, including systems of thought and consciousness. Thinkers such as Paul Ricoeur, Michael Polanyi, David Bohm, and Jürgen Habermas, and in theology, Jürgen Moltmann, David Tracy, Sallie McFague, John Cobb, Peter Hodgson, and, yes, that mystic theologian Matthew Fox, are pointing the way toward such formulations. In examining their work, and that of their co-workers and correspondents, we find characteristics that call for a "second naïveté" and the dialectical, multiperspective structures of knowing and valuing that descriptions of the Conjunctive stage of faith have tried to capture.

THE CHURCH AND THE TWENTY-FIRST CENTURY

This brings us, in closing, to the question of faith and the church in the twenty-first century. What is God calling us to be and to do in the era now unfolding? If we are in the midst of a shift of paradigms in cultural consciousness, what stance are we called to take toward this shift? Are we called to cling tenaciously to the forms of ecclesial life and practice that have evolved in the past two centuries, reworking, reasserting, trying to revive them? Are we called to a neoclassicism, a kind of return to a simpler, more sectarian view like that which Stanley Hauerwas and William H. Willimon propose in their book *Resident Aliens: Life in the Christian Colony?*[18] Or are we being called to build on both classical and modern experiences of church but go beyond them in faithfulness to the presence and creative working of God in the burgeoning, struggling promises and perils of the new century?

I have deep confidence that a creative, saving, and sustaining God is involved integrally in the process of our increasingly complex and richly dangerous project of interdependence on planet Earth. I believe that God is involved with us in the weaving of a new creation amid the rich promises and the terrifying perils of this unfolding new era. In order to discern God's presence and leading, however, and to learn to be attentive and responsive to it, we have to shape new paradigms of understanding and action. Working from the standpoint of one who is involved reflectively in trying to deal with these matters, this book tries to outline some dimensions of a new paradigm for responding to God's being and action in the Christian community, for the sake of helping to build a just and life-giving global community.

The next two chapters undertake the task of trying to see, through a new paradigm, the presence, character, and activity of God in the interdependent process of creation and human history. The first chapter works with biography and narrative, and the second with a more systematic elaboration.

NOTES

1. Peter Berger, Brigitte Berger, Hansfried Kellner, *The Homeless Mind: Modernization and Consciousness* (New York: Vintage Books, Random House, 1974).

2. Allan Bloom, *The Closing of the American Mind* (New York: Simon & Schuster, 1987).

3. William Butler Yeats, "The Second Coming," in Richard Ellman and Robert O'Clair, eds., *The Norton Anthology of Modern Poetry* (New York: W. W. Norton, 1973), p. 131.

4. Czeslaw Milosz, *The Witness of Poetry* (Cambridge, MA: Harvard Univ. Press, 1983), pp. 115–16.

5. Martin E. Marty, *The Public Church* (New York: Crossroad, 1981), p. 137.

6. Matthew Fox, *The Coming of the Cosmic Christ* (San Francisco: Harper & Row, 1988), from pp. 13–17.

7. Descriptions of these aspects under earlier names can be found in my *Life Maps* (Waco, TX: Word Books, 1985); *Stages of Faith* (San Francisco: Harper & Row, 1981); "Faith and the Structuring of Meaning," in Craig Dykstra and Sharon Parks, eds., *Faith Development and Fowler* (Birmingham, AL: Religious Education Press, 1986); and most comprehensively in R. M. Moseley, David Jarvis, and James W. Fowler, *The Manual for Faith Development Research* (Atlanta: Center for Faith Development, 1986).

8. A longer and fuller presentation and discussion of these stages will be given in chapter 4. Such accounts can also be found in my *Stages of Faith* (San Francisco: Harper & Row, 1981); *Becoming Adult, Becoming Christian* (San Francisco: Harper & Row, 1984); and *Faith Development and Pastoral Care* (Philadelphia: Fortess, 1987).

9. Russell McCormmach, *Night Thoughts of a Classical Physicist* (Cambridge, MA: Harvard Univ. Press, 1982).

10. Thomas Kuhn, *The Structures of Scientific Revolutions* (Chicago: Univ. of Chicago Press, 1962; enlarged ed., 1970).

11. I am indebted to Peter Hodgson, *Revisioning the Church: Ecclesial Freedom in the New Paradigm* (Philadelphia: Fortress Press, 1988) for this etymological data.

12. Fox, *Cosmic Christ*, pp. 80–81.

13. Kuhn, *Structures*, pp. 98, 76, 85.

14. For a longer version of the following discussion, see James W. Fowler, "The Enlightenment and Faith Development Theory" in *Journal of Empirical Theology*, University of Nijmegan, The Netherlands. Vol. I, 1988, No. 1, pp. 29–42.

15. Fowler, *Faith Development*, p. 70.

16. See C. B. MacPherson, *The Philosophy of Possessive Individualism* (New York: Oxford Univ. Press, 1962); see also Robert N. Bellah, et al., *Habits of the Heart* (Berkeley and Los Angeles: Univ. of California Press, 1985).

17. Fowler, *Faith Development*, pp. 72–73.

18. Stanley Hauerwas and William H. Willimon, *Resident Aliens: Life in the Christian Colony* (Nashville: Abingdon, 1989).

THEOLOGICAL OVERTURE

2. The Divine *Praxis* in Biography and Narrative

"Get up and make your way down to the potter's house, and there shall I tell you what I have to say." So I went down to the potter's house; and there he was, working at the wheel. But the vessel he was making came out wrong, as may happen with clay when a potter is at work. So he began again and shaped it into another vessel as he saw fit. Then the word of Yahweh came to me as follows, "House of Israel, can I not do to you what this potter does? . . . Like clay in the potter's hand, so you are in mine."

JEREMIAH 18:1–6, NJB

But when the Pharisees heard that he had silenced the Sadducees they got together and, to put him to the test, one of them put a further question, "Master, which is the greatest commandment of the Law?" Jesus said to him, "You must love the Lord your God with all your heart, with all your soul, and with all your mind. This is the greatest and the first commandment. The second resembles it: You must love your neighbor as yourself."

MATTHEW 22:34–39, NJB

In the midst of the American Civil War President Abraham Lincoln faced alone a terribly difficult situation. He found himself being held responsible for the early defeats of the Union army at Bull Run, Antietam, and other places. Cocky but inept generals and self-appointed civilian experts derided him as a wartime leader. Abolitionists pressed him to move more quickly to free the slaves at all cost. Meanwhile, many powerful interests, growing wealthy on the economic boom caused by full mobilization for war, jockeyed for position and influence at the expense of a whole-souled prosecution of the war effort. Meanwhile Lincoln, pilloried by caricatures and snide reflections on his abilities and qualifications, sought, without wavering or distraction, to bring about the restoration of the Union, which was his prime goal throughout the terrible war. Lincoln's skillful and inspired struggle to take the narrow visions, profiteering motives, jealous competitiveness, and sheer human cussedness of those he was trying to lead and orchestrate them into a workable team to bring about victory is a paramount example of the *praxis* of political leadership.

Part of the secret of Lincoln's *praxis* was his reliance upon his conviction and his imaging of the involvement of a righteous God in that great struggle. Lincoln believed in and counted upon—and sought to align his own efforts with—the *praxis* of a providential God. Moreover, he refused simplistic interpretations of the divine *praxis*. He saw that it was far too simple to assume that God was unambiguously on the side of one region in the country in that terrible war. Rather, he believed that this great fratricidal struggle was about the divine intention to rid this "almost chosen" nation of the curse of slavery.

> If we shall suppose that American slavery is one of those offenses which, in the providence of God, must needs come, but which, having continued through His appointed time, He now wills to remove, and that He gives to both the North and the South this terrible war as the woe due to those by whom the offense came, shall we discern therein any departure from those divine attributes which the believers in a living God always ascribe to Him? Fondly do we hope, fervently do we pray, that this mighty scourge of war may speedily pass away. Yet, if God wills that it continue until all the wealth piled up by the bondsman's two hundred and fifty years of unrequited toil shall be sunk, and until every drop of blood drawn with the lash shall be paid by another drawn with the sword, as was said three thousand years ago, so still must it be said "the judgements of the Lord are true and righteous altogether."[1]

The term *praxis* has roots in ancient Greece, where it referred to the kind of knowing good politicians needed for leadership. It refers to the knowing that one develops through reflective participation in action, knowing that is continually being shaped and reshaped by reflection and discernment in the midst of action. As a form of knowing, *praxis* can be contrasted with *theoria*, theoretical or speculative knowledge, and with *poeisis*, the knowing involved in the mastery of a craft. In *praxis* one draws upon a full range of knowledge and skill derived from reflective experience. In addition it requires grounding in the mythos and history of the city-state, and a hold on the vision and aspirations that guide its life. Note Lincoln's wide knowledge of and reliance upon the history, documents, and political, ethical, and spiritual vision that underlie this nation's founding. *Praxis* requires a practical knowledge of human nature and a mastery of the skills of persuasion and leadership. Here we remember Lincoln's humor and story-telling abilities, his discernment of the character of those with whom he worked and struggled, his fairness of mind and subordination of his own glory, and his ability in oratory and in close negotiations to persuade and lead persons beyond their narrow interests and stubborn selfishness. *Praxis* also involves the capacity to read and discern the shape of emerging challenges that threaten the well-being of the city-state and to mobilize the people to prepare to meet the approaching crisis. Lincoln's anticipation of the end of the war and of the great challenge of reconciliation and reunification led him (before his assassination) to put in place policies that made tangible his declaration that peacemaking should be approached "with malice toward none, and with charity for all."

Politics in the Greek city-states was regarded as the highest of activities and callings. Fittingly, my use of Lincoln as an example refers to one of the decisive periods of this nation's history, made sacred by the terrible sacrifices of life and blood it required. Therefore I intend no sacrilege in using this term to refer to the characteristic being and action of God. By speaking of the "divine *praxis*" I mean to focus the question of the characteristic patterns of God's involvement in and providential guidance of the processes of our evolving universe, including God's interaction with humankind.

In this chapter and the next we will pursue the patterns of divine *praxis* in two distinct but overlapping ways. In the present chapter I approach this question through biographical reflections and through narrative. Martin Luther King, Jr., and Thomas Merton both died in 1968. Neither died naturally; both died prematurely. Copious literatures now make the sweep and details of Dr. King's and Father Merton's lives available to us. In the first part of this chapter I reflect with you upon *how* King's and Merton's lives illuminate for us "God's ways" with humankind. In the second part of the chapter I take the risk of writing about one who was a beloved and deeply respected mentor to me, the Baptist minister and theologian Carlyle Marney (1916–1978). Not so widely known as King and Merton, Marney was an influence for racial justice in the cities of Austin, Texas, and Charlotte, North Carolina; he served ten years in each city from the late forties to the late sixties. In the last eleven years of his life he founded and led Interpreters' House, where, as his associate, I began the work that has led to the faith development research and theory. I write about Marney here both to suggest how, in my view, the divine *praxis* employed his personhood and to set forth some of the teachings Marney preached, wrote, and lived in his effort to characterize God's disposition toward and presence among humankind. In addition to his passion for racial justice, Marney was an early advocate of "creation spirituality" and a passionate advocate for ecological responsibility and mending of the Earth.

In the final part of this chapter I tell a story of how one person's response to an emergency, through her preparedness and fidelity to her vocation, seems to have played a surprising and significant role in the divine *praxis* in the realm of political-historical events.

PROPHETIC VOCATIONS:
MARTIN LUTHER KING, JR., AND THOMAS MERTON

Both Dr. Martin Luther King, Jr., and Father Thomas Merton have been rightly understood as prophetic voices and witnesses in this latter half of the twentieth century. Both were visible and influential representatives of public church. No North American has more forcefully taught, lived, and died for the principle of the love of neighbor—and for its social expression through justice—than Martin Luther King, Jr. No North American has more authentically witnessed to the transformation of life and consciousness through contemplative prayer than Thomas Merton.

I begin this chapter on divine *praxis* and a theology for public church with some reflections on the prophetic vocations of King and Merton. We will conduct our inquiry against the dual background of the two texts given at the beginning of the chapter: the great commandment, and the powerful image Jeremiah gives us of the shaping and redemptive judgment of the potter. I invite you to consider with me how the prophetic vocations of Merton and King are for us parables of God's commonwealth of love and justice— parables of the *praxis*, the being and action of God, in our history and in God's future. If this succeeds, it will lead us to illumination regarding our own vocations and the theological groundings of public church in a world grown no gentler since the deaths of King and Merton. It will lead us to try to bring to vision and word a sense of what God is doing in our time, that we might be in partnership rather than enmity with God's future.

Let me move us forward, then, by exploring with you three ways in which we can—and interpreters do—view the lives of King and Merton as parables of the divine *praxis*.

THEIR LIVES AS TEXTS: KING AND MERTON AS PIONEERS OF THE REIGN OF GOD

First the lens focuses on the unfolding life of King or Merton as a kind of "hero" of faith. From this angle our goal in studying them would be to illumine their passages in faith, the shape of their journeys, the dynamics of their becoming subjects before God. So viewed, they become exemplars for us: inspiring, courageous, gifted instances of what Erik Erikson has called *homo religiosus.*

Such approaches can have different purposes: Henri Nouwen's wonderful book on Merton, *Pray to Live*, gives us discerning access to a soul in motion. He helps us feel the depth of the young adult Merton's combination of brilliant, wounded cynicism and hunger for a grounding in the utterly dependable love of God. Nouwen traces the development of Merton's faith as it moves from the sweet, overconfident piety of the *Seven Storey Mountain* to the paradoxical grace of his Zen period and on into the quest for the universalizing unity of what Merton called the "final integration" in his last years. Here we have Merton as courageous pilgrim of faith, or as Sister Elena Malits's title puts it, *The Solitary Explorer: Thomas Merton's Transforming Journey.*[2]

Fred Downing's book on King, *To See the Promised Land*, gives us a solid psychobiographical study of his development in selfhood and faith.[3] In the same spirit of viewing King as *homo religiosus,* Downing takes pains to study the formation of King's faith in relation to the background of his family, his church, and the key persons and relations that helped to shape and awaken his vocation. Here we have a careful and inspiring depiction of movement in King's life through stages of growing maturity and authority, stages of growing inclusiveness and universality. Such a study is inspiring; it not only teaches us about the details and dynamics of King's growth in faith; it also illumines the path of ongoing transformation in faith that is a potential for all human beings.

For those of us interested in discerning the *praxis* of God, however, there is an obvious trap we can fall into with this kind of approach to Merton and King as "heroes" or "pioneers" of faith.

This trap, this pitfall, lies in the elevation of the subject to mythic dimensions. Subtly we begin to tailor the details of their stories to fit the needs of the faith ideals we hold and that we believe we find represented so powerfully in their lives and teachings. In making them *more* than human, we slyly render them *less* than human. At the same time, we elevate them to a plane where the examples of their utter seriousness about making themselves available to the reign of God, because they are religious "geniuses," no longer represent possibility or necessity for us. This kind of domestication through adulation allows us to evade invitation to our *own* vocations through the cheap grace of self-disqualification.

There are at least two ways of portraying figures like Merton and King as faith exemplars. In viewing them as heroes of faith we can interpret them in terms of the *romantic* myth of explorers and pioneers of faith—triumphant, even in death, because of their courage and the unselfishness of their spending and being spent. Or we can interpret them in terms of *tragic* myth. We can see them as the visionary, spirit-inspired messengers of transforming faith, cut off, or shunted aside, by the hard structures of a brutal and heartlessly fallen world.

In looking at Merton and King as "heroes" of faith, in succumbing to the spell of individualism or personalism in these matters, we can inspire thousands. We run the risk, however, of missing the principal point of their lives, which requires us to turn our eyes in quite another direction. I will return to this point further on. But first I invite you to look at a second way we can approach the vocations of these two prophetic figures as parables of the being and working of God.

THEIR LIVES IN CONTEXT: KING AND MERTON DEMYTHOLOGIZED

In Northrop Frye's great circle of types of Western literature the movement around the circle from the romantic and tragic genres of myths leads toward the genre of the *ironic*.[4] Romance pits innocent good against obvious evil in high adventure. Tragedy pits a noble but flawed hero against the intractable structures of a harshly realistic world. In the ironic approach, by contrast, heroes are shown to be all too human. As James Hopewell says in describing the ironic vision: "In ironic stories, reputedly worthy persons come to naught and what seem to be good plans go sour. Irony challenges heroic and purposive interpretations of the world. . . . Miracles do not happen; patterns lose their design; life is unjust, not justified by transcendent forces. . . . Instead of expecting such supernatural outcomes, one embraces one's brothers and sisters in camaraderie."[5]

Intended or not, great studies of both Merton and King, which have emerged only near the end of the two decades since their deaths, have had the effect of reinterpreting their lives in something of the ironic mode. I refer to the study by Michael Mott, *The Seven Mountains of Thomas Merton*, and to David Garrow's *Bearing the Cross*, which appeared in 1984 and 1986, respectively.[6] We are immensely in the debt of both these biographers. The research and synthesis underlying their magnificent studies are monumental. Neither biography will soon (if ever) be surpassed.

The student of King and Merton interested in their prophetic vocations, however, finds more in the studies of Mott and Garrow than he or she necessarily can use—maybe more than he or she even wants to know. These studies each found and used access to a wider range of personal and private documents than previous studies did. Both authors interviewed more widely than their predecessors the persons who knew and were associated closely in life with their subjects. Both writers have determined that the reading public is entitled to have access to their subjects' offstage and private lives—not just to the private domains of their professional and personal relationships, but also to the vicissitudes of their offstage hearts and wills. In the service of a kind of *cinema verité*, Garrow and Mott to a significant extent have broken down the barriers between the public and the private in the lives of King and Merton.

Intentionally or otherwise we participate as we read their books in a demythologization of the heroic in the stories of these two men. Through Mott's eyes we see Merton struggling with the illusion that his confrères might elect him abbot upon the retirement of Dom James and posting a foolishly adolescent letter to the community denying his willingness to serve. We see in great detail Merton's important but sad confusion about S, the lovely young nurse whose care for him in hospital reawakened and focused his suppressed and sublimated *eros* for the feminine. We participate in his fantasies that he might, through Buddhist contacts in Southeast Asia, play a negotiating role in reconciling the United States with Ho Chi Minh.

In King's life, in the last year and a half we see the ever more prophetic public persona speaking against the Vietnam War and brilliantly unmasking the connections between violence in that war and violence in our society and economy. At the same time, Garrow shows us an ever more exhausted King. He is hounded by the FBI and its pursuit of nasty secrets, baffled by the resistance to nonviolent methods in northern cities, and beset by dissension and competitive disunity in the ranks of the Southern Christian Leadership Conference. We see and identify with the King whose dream has turned to nightmare, and who fantasizes seriously about escaping the terrible burdens of his public role and moving to Geneva or Africa or taking a professorship or a church.

I only half mean it when I say that Mott and Garrow tell us more than we want to know about their subjects. The ironic mode puts us in unmistakable solidarity with our brothers Tom and Martin. How like *our* offstage fantasies and anxieties are those that beset these great figures. How vulnerable they were—in their great giftedness and committedness—to some of the same fears and anguishes, hopes and guilts, distractions and evasions to which we are subject.

The ironic mode, with its demythologizing power, is a necessary correction to our heroic romances and tragedies in the remembering and study of King and Merton. The breaking of our myths and the qualifying of our too-neat developmental schemas press us to ask the question about prophetic vocations and parables of the Kingdom in chastened, more cautious ways.

Is there a third alternative that neither negates nor ignores the converting of the heroic to the ironic? Is there a perspective from which to consider the vocations of Martin Luther King, Jr., and of Thomas Merton that may in deeper and more faithful ways help us to discern in them parables of a divine pattern of *praxis*—that is to say, parables of God judging and guiding—that *we* are also called to serve? Let us reflect on the possibility of a third way of interpreting and finding revelatory power in the memories and lives of our subjects.

TOWARD A THEOLOGICAL PERSPECTIVE:
KING, MERTON, AND GOD'S PRAXIS

Moving beyond the categories of Northrop Frye there is a genre of literature that promises to hold together the heroic and the ironic but to transport both onto another plane of interpretation, that offered by biblical theology. From this standpoint, to approach the revelatory luminousness of the lives of these two faithful servants properly, we need to see their stories as intertwined with a much larger and longer story already long in process. Both King and Merton understood this; they knew that whatever depth or meaning their life wagers manifested derived from their linkage and grounding in the purpose and working of God in and through the processes of creation and history.

King saw and said this in profound ways throughout his ministry. In an early formulation in *Stride Toward Freedom*, he asked the question, "Why did this event take place in Montgomery, Alabama, in 1955?" Then he answered:

Certainly, there is a partial explanation in the long history of injustice on the buses of Montgomery. The bus protest did not spring into being full grown as Athena sprang from the head of Zeus; it was the culmination of a slowly developing process. Mrs. Parks's arrest was the precipitating factor rather than the cause of the protest. The cause lay deep in the record of similar injustices. . . . There comes a time when people get tired of being trampled by oppression. . . . The story of Montgomery is the story of fifty thousand such Negroes who were willing to substitute tired feet for tired souls, and walk the streets of Montgomery until the walls of segregation were finally battered by the forces of justice. . . . But neither is this the whole explanation. . . . Nor can it be explained by the appearance of new leadership. The Montgomery story would have taken place if the leaders of the protest had never been born. . . .

There is something about the protest that is suprarational; it cannot be explained without a divine dimension. Some may call it a principle of concretion, with Alfred N. Whitehead; or a process of integration, with Henry N. Wieman; or Being-itself, with Paul Tillich; or a personal God. Whatever the name, some extra-human force labors to create a harmony out of the discord of the universe. There is a creative power that works to pull down mountains of evil and level hilltops of injustice. God still works through history His wonders to perform. It seems as though God had decided to use Montgomery as the proving ground for the struggle and triumph of freedom and justice in America.[7]

With the help of the excellent studies of Merton and King I have mentioned we can see the subtle but clear movements of a convergent providence in the shaping—we might properly say the election—of Martin Luther King, Jr., and of Thomas Merton to their vocations and in the waves of energy, imagination, and influence that flow from their lives. We see the persons who stood behind and beside them for generations back. We see the influence of teachers and mentors brought together with them at crucial moments for some element of preparation and development that would be decisive in an as yet unanticipated future. We see a quality of inspiration in their lives—often coming in the midst of fatigue, distraction, or despair—that cannot be accounted for solely by their creativity and abilities. Such factors as these begin to make visible to us how the divine *praxis* draws together long lines of convergent faithfulness in order to bring about redemptive transformation in the midst of peoples and of history. And they lead us to reflect how faithfulness in *our* vocations may contribute —far beyond any set of connections we can now see or imagine— to the movement and direction of the divine *praxis* in our time or the future.

From the standpoint of biblical theology King and Merton *are* symbols and signs and articulators of something far more primal and vast. In ways that neither the heroic nor the ironic modes can capture, they are story-formed and story-borne bearers of the Spirit of a creating, governing, and liberating God. In their struggling gracefulness we see the combination of an unmistakable individuality and a God-given newness in history. And this newness opens, as parables at their best always do, new pathways of being. In and through King and Merton, in quite distinct modalities, God opens ways where there is no way. In their vocations the divine *praxis* brings and manifests judgment, liberation, and redemption and brings forth new creation.

CARLYLE MARNEY: WITNESS AND MENTOR

The low-slung white Chrysler glided to a stop in front of our house. Seventeen, sitting on the front porch, I watched as the big man with the Texas hat turned toward me and boomed, "Where's your old man?" Already a little angry because he reminded me of another big Baptist preacher, Billy Graham, whom I had also seen that summer cruising through Lake Junaluska in a long, white car, I found this bass-voiced stranger's effrontery offensive. A high school senior and a little angry at *all* authority, I answered, "My *father* is at the barn."

This was my first taste of Marney's aggressive intimacy. He knew how to make contact, "to get under the feathers," as he put it. He had a way of assaulting you on first meeting, of making you a little mad and confused. Then he disclosed with eye and hand and, with an extraordinary investment of *particular* attention, that you matter, that you are some*body*.

Later that first summer Marney invited me to go with him, his red thoroughbred mare, Suzie Parker, and his quarter horse, Buck, for a long ride across Paul's Gap in the Smokies. As we pulled the trailer over Soco Gap and up past Heintooga, as we saddled the horses and rode through the matchless splendor of that big-poplared wilderness, we talked. As with no other to that point in my life, my heart, my head, my hopes found tongue. And I felt heard, known, understood. In ways that would be renewed at intervals across the next twenty-one years, I felt called out toward a significant manhood.

Marney opened an immense pathway for me when he invited me to come and be his associate at Interpreters' House. In that one year, the twenty-eighth of my life, I grew more, learned more, and began more that was new than in any other year of my adult life. Virtually all the issues I have worked on in my teaching and writing got focused in that year with Marney. I also worked harder, grieved more, and inflicted more stress on my marriage and my young family than in any other single year.

Marney was mentor and friend to hundreds of young men and women. If I tell about him now in these personal ways, it is not to claim that my view of Marney or my relationship with him is more special than those of others. Rather, I want to share personally some of the ways Marney became for me a mediator of enlarged theological awareness, an evoker of a deeper personhood, and a parable of the freedom, love, and authority of Jesus as the Christ.

MARNEY'S ROOTS AND SOURCES

Born in Harriman, East Tennesee, Leonard Carlyle Marney was descended from independent folk who settled there on land grants received for their service in the American Revolution. In the nineteenth century his forebears fought on the Union side in the Civil War and were part of an indigenous Southern opposition to slavery before the war. Theological dispute, he tells us, made Sunday afternoons lively for a little boy who tuned into the convictions and passions with which uncles, aunts, and parents discussed their Methodist, Baptist, Presbyterian, and Unitarian differences. The summer he turned nine marked Marney's first awakening to a set of intellectual issues to which he would attend for the rest of his life. Thirty miles away, over the mountain at Dayton, Tennessee, twenty-four-year-old John T. Scopes was on trial for teaching the theory of the "simian descent of man" as informed by Charles Darwin's theory of evolution. Marney followed the trial as best he could, getting accounts favorable to William Jennings Bryan and the fundamentalist cause from the *Knoxville Sentinel* and accounts favorable to Clarence Darrow and the defense from his grandad's *Cincinnati Post*.

Marney, writing in his adulthood about his memories of this time, expressed a resentment by then forty years old against the media's one-dimensional, prejudiced representation of his beloved East Tennessee during the trial. Let me quote part of his corrective:

It is true that on summer nights we could hear on soft breezes the shouting meetings of one of the sects in the red church building with no floor at the foot of our long hill, but I was reading one or another of the thousand books I borrowed in boyhood from the splendid Andrew Carnegie Library at the other base of the same hill. And likely we had already been to the Chautauqua Series for which our mother had saved ticket money from somewhere. We had heard Elihu Root on the tariff system, or some senator. . . . Or we had seen a Shakespearean touring company, or heard Bhomer Kriel's great band, or a symphony. Within an eight-block area in a little town of 3,500 souls not thirty minutes from Dayton, I can now recall graduates of Harvard College, . . . Yale University, the University of Tennessee, of Kentucky, of Alabama, Georgia Tech, the Cincinnati Conservatory, Cornell. A representative of Canadian culture at its best lived across the street and supervised twelve million acres of forest. (I rode with him as a boy, visited Sergeant York's parents, and wrote to Cornell to get a catalogue in forestry.) . . . My neighbor had retired from a distinguished Philadelphia pastorate to serve the Presbyterians (Northern) church. The professor of economics at the University of Tennessee was pastor of the Christian Church. There was a lot of Yankee commercial connections with timber, coal, iron; there was a Revolutionary War heritage; there were some devoted Roman Catholics, two splendid Jewish families; there was Boys' Week and Boy Scouts, photography, music, water sports, and all kinds of visiting pretty girls from Chattanooga. All in all, there was in East Tennessee a fantastic pluralism the reporters all missed.[8]

Another element in that pluralism in Harriman was the already mentioned family heritage of opposition to slavery: "Emotionally, I was Southern," Marney says. "The shock of my boyhood was to discover a picture of Grandmother's and say, 'Who is that?' She answered, 'That's your great Grandpa!' Then I asked, 'What's he doing in that kind of uniform?' She said, 'Well, he was a federal officer.' . . . I wasn't yet five years old when I heard my Grandpa talking about how blacks ought not to be treated. And my daddy was eighty-four and hallucinating in the hospital on his deathbed when he was saying, 'They're not treating those folks right.'" Marney concludes, "I had no choice but to be true to a heritage of which I'm proud, though it's not the typical Southern pattern."[9]

In his high school years, there was athletics and school music (Marney played the trombone); there was a church youth group and Ridgecrest. Summers he hammered out plows in the Oliver's plant where his father, Leonard Marney, was a blacksmith and designer. "I don't know," he said, "what made me go into the ministry. I had wanted to be a forester. But I discovered, I suppose, that my gifts with books and people were at least as good as my gifts with trees. I was floundering at nineteen and made a decision to move toward people. The Baptist part was more or less automatic because that was where I had been reared."[10]

At Carson Newman College Marney played three years of varsity football. He left school for a term because of failing grades in algebra. (Later he would say, in a critique of our culture's excessive faith in science, that there was no redemption in mathematics, as anyone who had taken algebra as much and often as he had knew for sure!) Apparently the hard railroad work he turned to, which required him to get up at four in the morning and started a working pattern he followed for a long time in his ministry, helped him clarify that he really *did* want that college degree. He graduated in 1938.

In 1940 Marney married Elizabeth Christopher. He brought his bride to join him at the Southern Baptist Theological Seminary in Louisville, Kentucky. For a time after their marriage he served a little church, soon to be closed, at Fort Knox in Kentucky. There he developed a ministry with officers and their wives and with thousands of the enlisted men on their way to the battlefields of World War II.

During Marney's years at Southern Seminary, his mind and heart caught fire. It was while he was working on his master of theology degree, if I have the story right, that one Syd Stealey, professor of patristics and church history, claimed a decisive mentorship. As Marney told the story (I have not found it in print), Stealey, along with other faculty members, heard Marney, as a student leader, "emcee" some banquet meeting at the school. Apparently he did an impressive job—articulate, witty, aggressive, outrageous. Stealey had been stirred by the performance. The next day, Marney said, as he walked through the seminary hall he felt the unmistakable jar of a foot laid with some force to his backside. Turning with surprise, he saw an intense little man with eyes flashing. He laid a hand on Marney's shoulder and bit out these words: "You were right impressive last night, Mr. Marney. You've got size; you've got poise and looks; you've got a voice and the gift of gab. You're going to go somewhere!" Startled, perhaps a little pleased, Marney started to respond, but Stealey snapped, "Well, let me tell you something, Mr. Marney. It's hell if you get up there in one of those high steeple pulpits and haven't got anything to say!" Stealey looked at him intently, then said, "Come see me." And he walked off. Marney did go see him. And before the year was out, he had read deeply and competently under Stealey's guidance into many of the original texts of the fathers of the Church in its first four centuries.

At about this time, Marney said, he formulated a three-part set of vows to which he aimed to remain faithful throughout his life and ministry. Writing about it in 1975, he said:

I have not, and I do not now, claim integrity for myself, but I have, so far, served faithfully an intention. I have intended to be part of the pilgrim people of God. I did, and I do, across my years since 23, claim to have served a set of vows:

—*I would never give to any adjective the rank of a noun.*[11]

For Marney, *Baptist, Methodist, Catholic,* and *Jew* are adjectives, not nouns. *Black* and *white, American* and *Christian* are adjectives, not nouns. For his beginning to one of the finest articles ever written on Christian community and homosexuality Marney began with the assertion that *homosexual* is an adjective, not a noun.[12]

—*I would follow any new light as soon as I knew it to be light.*

The life of faith, for Marney, is one of ongoing revolution; the New Testament Greek term he liked for this was *metanoia,* "repentance, return, fundamental change, ongoing conversion, in response to God's revelation." I would follow *any new light*—pilgrim person, open to the new.

But the second part of this vow to follow new light is equally important: "I would follow any new light *as soon as I knew it to be light!*" An astute, broad student of history, Marney knew how rare a genuinely new shaft of light is. He picked up a slang phrase in Korea that he used often when he saw an ignorant and pretentious claim being made for a supposed "new light": it's *samo samo,* he would say, and then tell you it was a third-century heresy that emerged again in the twelfth and showed up most recently in the nineteenth-century popular theology of so-and-so. *Samo samo.* He took seriously John Baillie's dictum that we already have more light than we have yet used; we have enough light to see and work. As Marney would put it, we should not expect new light until we have learned to be faithfully obedient to the light God has already given us in Jesus Christ.

—*I would respect and credit my sources, my teachers, my compadres, on a journey* . . .

My *sources,* my *teachers,* my *compadres* on a journey include, to be sure, the sources of his formal study—the *Scriptures,* the history of the Church's reflection on its *new*—the theology of each century; the struggle of the Church in each era to give its memory flesh and to live from its future promise in the present. His *sources* also include philosophers, social scientists, biologists, psychologists, moralists, and physicists. "I will credit my *sources.*" But by teachers Marney meant a lot more than the sources of his formal learning. He meant Mama and Daddy, and the culture that formed them; he meant the expressions of suffering and death he encountered and shared with others; he meant that relational presence of God in which the spirit slips up on us from the rear and blesses us with new light. And any person who spent much time with him at all realizes that part of what made him so special was his willingness to learn with and *from* us. Coming back from a trip with Elizabeth that carried them from Pittsburgh to Nova Scotia, Marney said,

> What a learning summer I have had! It began in Pittsburgh months ago with John Frye, a wiry little ex-marine Presbyterian pastor; and I was taught by a gorgeous Chilean psychiatrist woman, with the impossible name of Paulina McCullough—for a Chilean—and that lovely Episcopalian, William Stringfellow. I was taught by an eagle at Capstick Cove on Cape Breton, and a storekeeper at Aspey Bay, and a quadriplegic artist at the yacht races in Lunenberg, and a blacksmith, and a carrot grower, and a Frenchman writing more than a hundred years ago. These have all priested me and taught me.[13]

His teachers? They came from every Christian century. They came from the Talmud and the midrashic commentaries. They included historians, heads of state, social workers, scientists, philosophers—and theologians. Marney was passionately curious and had a willingness to be taught. He took his teachers for all they had to give, often calling out from them dimensions of significance of which they were unaware.

All this has to do with a theme that Marney shared with Martin Buber that has to do with the sacredness of *all* life: all life is sacramental. One attended to blacksmiths and carrot growers and quadriplegic artists, to children everywhere because *incarnation*—God dwelling among us everywhere—is the truth for those who have eyes to see.

> I believe with many distinguished predecessors, that the wholeness of life is sacramental. This view rests on the insight that the *purpose of our existence* as men and women *is to recognize Persons, to call out Persons fit for a Kingdom that may or may not come.* This, for me, is a Chris-

tian insight being acted upon everywhere—in bars and barber-shops, around campfires, in people's front rooms, and here and there in church.[14]

Marney knew with Mother Teresa of Calcutta that we are called to minister to the hopeless and dying, not out of some moral impera-tive, but because it is with them that we meet Jesus Christ.

"I would respect my *sources*, my *teachers*, my *compadres* on a journey." A word about *compadres* and the *journey:* One of the central shafts of light Marney saw generated from the Bible was our call to a full manhood and womanhood, which is redeemed and empowered by our participation in Jesus Christ. The Christian secret, Marney would say, is that in Jesus Christ *we see who we really are;* we see who we are *meant to be.* Our journey—an im-mense one, as a species with antecedents three to five million years old, and with an immediate species-history of five hundred thousand years—our immense journey is toward a humanhood embodied in the fidelity and wholeness of Jesus Christ. Our *com-padres?* Those in whom we see the Christ-mark, the secret calling, those who, knowing it or not, are apprehended by a divine love and vocation to be who God created us all to be. Marney could say with Terence, "Nothing human, therefore, is foreign to me." He truly saw in every person, and particularly in those whom the New Testament called the little ones—the oppressed, the poor, the sinners who know that they are sinners—the Christ vocation, the potential for full humanity. At the end of *The Carpenter's Son* he wrote:

> Some "theologians" [quotation marks meaning "so-called theolo-gians"] laugh at me for this, but you *do* become Christ. That emotional, erratic, impious Greek Russian Berdyayev is right. I become a Re-deemer, the only one some ever see. Is this not what breaks on Paul when he cries: "I am crucified with Christ, yet not I, for Christ liveth in me!"[15]

INCARNATIONAL REALISM:
MARNEY'S VIEW OF HUMANITY

Marney had both the highest and the lowest estimate of the human species I think I have ever encountered in one thinker. He knew human sinfulness; he knew the shape of gross evil, the murderous potential in all of us and the murderous actuality of many of us. Listen to how he talks about our kind:

> Man is the most dangerous and savage of the beasts: His bite is poisonous; his hand is a club; his foot is a weapon; knives, clubs, spears are projectiles to bear his hostility. Nothing in nature is so well equipped for hating or hurting. Confuse him and he may lash out at everything. Crowd him and he kills, robs, destroys, for his crime rate increases in proportion to his crowding. Deprive him and he retaliates. Impoverish him and he burns villas in the night. Enslave him and he revolts. Pamper him and he may poison you. Hire him and he may hate both you and the work. Love him too possessively and he is never weaned. Deny him too early and he never learns to love. Put him in cities and all his animal nature comes out with perversions of every good thing. For greed, acquisitiveness, violence were so long his tools for jungle survival, that it is only by the hardest [effort] that these can be laid aside as weapons of his continued survival.[16]

Marney saw, and rarely let us forget, that history shows us a record of almost uninterrupted warfare on our globe. The twentieth century, whose tenth decade we have just entered, was his century, too. The "war to end all wars," the Holocaust, and the bombing of Nagasaki and Hiroshima, death camps, tiger cages, defoliants, deformations, chemical warfare, intercontinental ballistic missiles, nerve gas, and neutron bombs—*samo samo*, just more technologically advanced, quantitatively expanding our capacity for exterminating each other and generations yet unborn. Marney saw all this. He knew that theology and Christian faith had to face and meet all this, or else they wouldn't help us much.

Some who heard him, or read him, found him too pessimistic. Their images of faith called for something more cheerful, more hopeful, more optimistic in their spokespersons. But Marney helped us see that any religion that enables us to evade the gross distortions and destructive potentials of our kind offers a pseudo-redemption and preaches a pseudo-Christ. When the New Testament claims that Christ ensures victory over sin, hell, and death, these had better not be understood merely metaphorically, merely figuratively. Evil is real; sin is a fact in our individual and our social lives; death haunts us and sooner or later consumes everything we hoped to gain. Hell is real in the slums of our cities, in the torturers' prison camps, in the hunger-weakened eyes of children too far gone to eat in Ethiopia. If the redemptive promise of a crucified Lord stops us on the hither side of this our *common* sin, death, and hell, then it is illusion and bad religion.

That's the realist side of Marney's vision of humanity.

But then there's a high side of Marney's understanding of our kind. In this he is just as paradoxical and just as scandalous as the gospel itself. In Adam all human beings die, in Jesus Christ all are raised up into wholeness, into completion. What advantage do we Christians have? Marney asked. Are we spared the suffering of the world? Are we ensured a pain-free, success-filled, long, rich life to a full old age? By no means. The Christian advantage is not an insurance policy, a protection contract, or a shield against all adversity. We are vulnerable. We will suffer; we are not exempt from the slings and arrows of capricious fate. The Christian advantage, then? It is that we know our true name, our true calling, our true vocation. In Jesus Christ, where true God takes form among us, there also do we see our proper form. There also, in Jesus the human being, do we see our potential, our true identity. As Marney puts it:

> The Gospel contradiction is Gospel incarnation. This is the only recon-ciling out we have. Incarnation. When God is God so much that it overleaps the Godhood, then man can become so much man that it overleaps the manhood. The effect is an overlap: God-man; the man-hood of God; the God-hood of man. They belong together! They, God and man always did belong together. . . . This is real *Imago Dei*. [This is real creation in the image of God.] And it means that given this view of the field, both our potential and our present actuality take in much more territory than we know. The least of us is much more powerful. The man (or woman) of us is much more Godly. The God of us is much more humanly. We have more room than we have used. We are closer to God than we thought.[17]

For Marney, these declarations were not just rhetoric. They were not pious sentiments offered like pablum for folk whom he ex-pected to go on living, obsessed by our own survival, security, and significance. These are revolutionary declarations pointing to a revolutionary truth: The truth about *me*, the truth about *you*, the truth about every human being made in the image of God is that we have a common calling, a common destiny. The truth about each of us—every single human being—is that we are made for a personhood like that of Jesus Christ. We are created for a person-hood that collectively, if grasped, would constitute a kingdom of God. Our proper calling is a personhood in which all our passions, all our wants, all our drives, find their fulfillment in God's right-eousness and God's peace. This is the real meaning of salvation in Jesus Christ; this is the real meaning of reconciliation with God.

MARNEY'S THIS-WORLDLY FAITH

Marney's incarnational realism called for a this-worldly faith. Despising docetic Christianity—any Christianity that denies Christ's real humanity—Marney pressed us to realize this revolu-tionary human potential in our common life. He saw that wher-ever we fail to take each person's future in Christ seriously, we begin to collude and collaborate with the patterns of life that resign us to inequality and to privilege for some and great burdens for others.

Marney had a way of putting questions: He asked his parish-ioners in Myers Park Church whether they were going to be Rebels or Tories—whether they were going to be sons and daugh-ters of this Christ revolution and pioneers of the kingdom of God, or whether they would settle into a genteel docetism, worshiping a Christ who blesses our myths and sanctifies our privilege. He published this description in *The Coming Faith:* "A Tory is a man who believes his own myths. His politics? Timeless. His eco-nomics? Just. His race? Pure. His religion? True. His sex? Superior. His region? Most favored. His family? Only."[18] How do we avoid being Tories? How do we avoid falling into the trap of those who live out the little ditty Marney (I think) once coined: "Come weal or come woe, Our status is *quo*"? How do we join the Christ revolution? For Marney it was through a proper under-standing of *church* and through a proper understanding of *vo-cation.*

Beginning with church the question is, Where and how do we put ourselves in position to be redemptively encountered by Jesus Christ? Where do folk like us, competent, coping, independent types, earning our own way—where do we confess our hungers, express our despair, expose our compromised integrity, and struggle with the question of who, in Jesus Christ, we are called now to be? The answer for most of us, I suspect, is mostly *nowhere*. Maybe with a husband or wife; maybe with a close friend; perhaps with a counselor, or if we're extremely blessed, with a spiritual director or pastor. But where am I bringing my images of myself to Jesus Christ for clarification and correction? If our answer is, "Mostly nowhere," then we are in need of church.

Let's come at this with Marney in a sermon he called "The Nerve to Submit." *Alta-ase leha kol pesel.* "You shall not make of yourself a carved substitute." You shall not make an image of yourself.

> We have made images of the self and believed our images enough to worship them. We have wrapped ourselves in layers of feathers—we have worshipped views of our selves and our surroundings—we have our views of our race, our religion, our economics, our sex, our class, our nation—all our treasures! And now, hear what I have learned these thirty years: There is no "redemption," and any claim to salvation is a farce, unless it penetrates sooner or later all these treasured feathers of our views of the self—and—this hurts! This hurts, because our feathers have grown to us. Yet this is the truth I shout from the housetops: *There is no growth that is Christian without the nerve to submit to the correcting of my images of the self.*
>
> I now see it clearly: The spinal cord of redemption is the nerve to submit all my images of the self to Christ and his people for correction. . . . The Book is clear, if you wish a text: "If *any* would come after me, let him deny himself" (MATT. 16:24, RSV).
>
> Let him deny himself what? There's no direct object here. . . . It's just "let him deny *himself!*" . . . Self is subject to be denied; there is no object.
>
> And where is this correcting to be done? . . . I am inviting you to release yourself from the dullness of a never ending Sunday school repetition of Zachaeus, Jesus, and the sycamore tree. I am talking Christian Education. . . . *The correction of our images of the self in Christ has to happen among my friends who care about Christ—my real church.* I wish to God I could just say "corrected by the church," but the modern church is the religious institutional encasement of our submission to the images of our society.[19]

I find two strong imperatives in Marney's vision of church. The first has to do with a quality of trust, required for any authentic submission of my images for correction—a trust, on the one hand, in the genuine regard others have for me and for the Christ potential in me. A trust, on the other hand, that some in the community know the script and know the Christ. Where there are those who hold me in regard—with whom I can afford to be who I am—and where there are those who know the script and are therefore helping me see the world and myself in God's eyes, *there* we can have church. The second imperative is that you and I, setting out to be this kind of church where we, and others, can submit ourselves to Christ for correction, must watch and pray and work to see that it is truly Christ to whom we ask others to submit, not just our graven images of Christ.

At base, Marney is saying, church is a community of relationships, covenanted to fidelity to Christ, where love and Christ are real enough that we can stand to let others help us find our Christian identity—and *vocation*. From the community, where we're getting straight about who we are called to be in Christ, we are urged into the world with our *vocation*. Vocation is a person's way of putting the self he or she is becoming in Christ to work in the service of the world's real needs.

GOD'S *PRAXIS* AND OUR VOCATIONS

Is God's providence still active in our world? Can we trace the subtlety and power of the Spirit of God in the affairs of nations? Let me share a story.

On September 1, 1983, Russian fighter jets shot down a Korean Boeing 747 jetliner bound for Seoul. Among the two-hundred-sixty-nine persons who died in its crash there were sixty-one Americans. Tensions leading to the brink of armed conflict arose between the two superpowers. For a dangerously long time after that incident communications between the Russian and U.S. governments were completely broken off. Vigorous American and United Nations condemnations backed the Soviets into a tight corner of moral isolation. In both Russia and the United States a mutual process of "demonization" of the other side bristled with mounting hatred and vitriolic rhetoric.

Mrs. Suzanne Massie, an American historian and specialist in Russian culture, arrived in Moscow at the end of September during the peak of the blackout of communications between the two nations. Though official communications and bureaucratic procedures were all in abeyance, Mrs. Massie held extensive unofficial conversations with scholars and representatives of the Soviet government.

Mrs. Massie's discussions were often heated. She described one particularly intense exchange with a highly placed soviet: "He looked at me with his eyes blazing and said, 'You don't know how close war is!' I was used to Soviet brands of bluffing," she continued, "but there was something about the urgent way he spoke, plus my knowledge of his high connections, which chilled me. I could not put it out of my mind."

Leaving Moscow briefly to attend a family celebration in Switzerland, Mrs. Massie found herself awakened in the middle of the night with an impelling sense that she must return home immediately. She had to convey to officials in the United States the seriousness and tension of the situation as she saw it from the Soviet side. She had to make clear how imperative it was that some kind of communication begin again with the Soviet Union as quickly as possible.

As her children were growing up she frequently had told them that anyone in the world with whom you might need to speak is only two introductions away. She decided to act on her own maxim. She flew back to the U.S. determined to find a way to communicate with President Reagan. After two attempts proved fruitless, she turned to several senators whom she knew. Senator William Cohen from Maine spent an afternoon with her. A member of the Armed Services Committee, he was roused by her description of the extremely tense atmosphere she had encountered and the need to renew some kind of dialogue. At the end of their talk he said, "You've got to speak to Bud McFarlane (Robert C. McFarlane, National Security Advisor to President Reagan). He called Mr. McFarlane and arranged a twenty-minute meeting.

Mrs. Massie prepared her presentation to the minute—a carefully calibrated, tightly argued case for the urgency of restoring dialogue. She explained that, in her view, based on her talks in Moscow, despite their hostile posture, there was a possibility of persuading the Soviets to reopen discussion on cultural exchange, which had begun before the shooting down of the Korean airline. When her twenty minutes were over she got up to leave. Mr. McFarlane remained seated. "What you have to say is so interesting. Would you come back again and talk longer?" She agreed and returned in a few days for a two-hour intensive discussion. "My proposal was audacious," she said. "Basically I suggested, 'Send me. I can talk to them. It is not so important *what* we speak about but it is crucial that we begin to talk again. The Soviets are like cats with hackles up. They are very defensive and nervous." Mr. McFarlane said, "Put it on paper; then come down again." She did.

Christmas, 1983: Communication from Mr. McFarlane's office: "We want you to go to the Soviet Union." Arranging diplomatic rank would have required Senate approval and bringing her mission to public visibility. And it would have required precious time. Both secrecy and urgency were crucial. So she prepared for the trip, ostensibly as a private citizen. After several meetings with presidential advisors she said to Mr. McFarlane, "The Russians are very personal people, and, no disrespect meant, but all the president's men don't add up to the president. Not for my credibility, but for his (the president's), I must look him in the eye. I don't need to take more than five minutes; I just need to be able to say honestly that I have looked him in the eye, that I have asked him a question, and that he has answered it."

On January 17, 1984 she came to the Oval Office for what she understood would be a five-minute meeting alone with the President. "I found to my absolute horror," she said, "that they were all there. Bush, Shultz, McFarlane, Baker, Mease, Deaver—the entire group; all men, all big, all taller than me by a long shot. Then to my total dismay the president did *not* say hello and goodbye, but said, 'Sit down.' " Mrs. Massie's five minutes turned out to be a forty-five-minute talk in which she had an opportunity to convey to the president the impact of her conversations with the Soviets and her sense of the urgency of the present moment in relations between the two nations. She also took the opportunity to communicate her sense of what the Russian people, as distinct from the government, felt about the United States.

A president who found white papers on arms negotiation tedious apparently found her accounts of conversations with soviet officials and ordinary people compelling. She made a strong impression on him. Without knowing it at the time, she had begun what was to become an important series of conversations with the president through which she helped him understand Russian attitudes and the relations between their history and their character.

She made her trip. Her mission was successful. Four years later, when the press finally pinned her down on her role in this crucial time in late January and early February, 1984, she explained it by saying simply, "I tried to get both sides to pick up the phone again. And that's what happened." Soviet leader Yuri Andropov had been seriously ill throughout the fall of 1983. On February 9, 1984 he died. She said, "I knew that my mission had succeeded at the time that Vice-President Bush went over for the funeral. The newspapers said, 'We had an unusually forthcoming speech from Mr. Chernenko.' I realized that connections had been reestablished. I felt a little bit like a ghost."

In all, Mrs. Massie would have eighteen talks with President Reagan. They also exchanged a number of letters and phone calls. She briefed him before each of his meetings with President Gorbachev, and it was she who taught Mr. Reagan the Russian proverb he began to use in that period, "Trust, but verify." Before the 1985 Geneva summit between the two leaders, where in the cottage they made the personal breakthroughs that lead to the subsequent meetings in Reykjavik and then in Washington, she had been called to the White House for a meeting with President Reagan. As she drove from Maine to Boston to catch the plane, she remembered a wooden egg she had found in Moscow and brought home to give to her son. Made by farmers from the Volga, the primitive but brightly colored egg had a picture of the Virgin Mary on it, with the statement in Russian, "Don't Blow Up the World." When Mrs. Massie had given the egg to her son, an Episcopalian minister, he had said, somewhat bitterly, "You should give that to President Reagan; he's the one who needs that message." When she reached Boston on her way to Washington she called him and said, "All right Bobby, give me the egg; I need it."

At the end of her conversation with the president she gave him the egg. She said, "Here's something I found in Moscow. For the Russians the egg is the symbol of new beginnings. Why don't you give it to Mr. Gorbachev? He'll know what it means." The president made no reply and she said nothing further. "You don't have to say everything," she told me. "God does His work as He wishes."

I asked Mrs. Massie what impelled her to take the initiatives that led to her meeting with the President, to her crucial role in the renewal of superpower communications, and to her advising the president. She replied, "I simply knew in a deep way that I had to get to the president, and that I was the one who had to do it."

To some it seems ironic that Mr. Reagan will go down in history as the American president who proved responsive to the new initiatives of the courageous and resourceful Russian leader who risked proposing a beginning of the stand-down of our nuclear arsenals. The confluence of initiatives and events that occurred in order to bring Mrs. Massie and the president together, to authorize her mission, and the influence of her teaching upon him, all bear the marks of the subtle power of divine providence quietly and effectively "making a way where there is no way."

Such a story, like the prophetic vocations of Dr. King and Father Louis, and like the faithful mentorship and witness of Carlyle Marney, provides a parable of the divine action and being. As parables do, it shows forth the contours and dynamics of the divine *praxis*. At the same time, as parables do, it makes apparent the way a person, while being faithful and resourceful in her or his vocation, can be made a crucial linkage in the surprising network of the Spirit's energy and will for the preservation, healing, and redemption of God's world.[20]

NOTES

1. Lincoln's Second Inaugural Address.
2. Henri Nouwen, *Pray to Live. Thomas Merton: Contemplative Critic* (Fides Publishers, 1972); Elena Malits, *The Solitary Explorer: Thomas Merton's Transforming Journey* (San Francisco: Harper & Row, 1980).
3. Frederick Downing, *To See the Promised Land* (Macon, GA: Mercer Univ. Press, 1986).
4. Northrop Frye, *The Anatomy of Criticism.* (Princeton, NJ: Princeton Univ. Press, 1957).
5. James F. Hopewell, *Congregation: Stories and Structures* (Philadelphia: Fortress Press, 1987), p. 61.
6. Michael Mott, *The Seven Mountains of Thomas Merton* (New York: Houghton Mifflin, 1984); David J. Garrow, *Bearing the Cross: Martin Luther King, Jr. and the Southern Christian Leadership Conference* (New York: Vintage Books, 1986).
7. Martin Luther King, Jr., *Stride Toward Freedom*, excerpted in James M. Washington, ed., *A Testament of Hope: The Essential Writings of Martin Luther King, Jr.* (San Francisco: Harper & Row, 1986), pp. 437–38.

8. Carlyle Marney, "Dayton's Long Hot Summer," in Jerry R. Tompkins, ed., *D-Days at Dayton: Reflections on the Scopes Trial* (Baton Rouge: Louisiana State Univ. Press, 1965), pp. 128–29.

9. "Preaching the Gospel, South of God," interview with Carlyle Marney, by Bill Finger, *The Christian Century*, Oct. 4, 1978, pp. 915–16.

10. Marney interview, *Christian Century*, p. 916.

11. Unpublished manuscripts of lectures written and delivered while Marney was Scholar in Residence at Virginia Military Institute, Lexington, Virginia, 1975.

12. Carlyle Marney, "Christian Community and the Homosexual," *Social Progress* 58 (1967):31–40.

13. From an audio tape, "How to Be a Human Being" (Nashville: Broadman Press, 1976).

14. Marney, VMI Lectures, no. 2, pp. 1–2.

15. Carlyle Marney, *The Carpenter's Son* (Nashville: Abingdon, 1967), p. 95.

16. Marney, VMI Lectures, no. 1, pp. 1–2.

17. Marney, *Carpenter's Son*, p. 77.

18. Carlyle Marney, *The Coming Faith* (Nashville: Abingdon, 1970), p. 76.

19. Carlyle Marney, "The Nerve to Submit," unpublished sermon, Interpreters' House, 1967.

20. My telling of Mrs. Massie's story is based upon an interview with her, and upon facts from other sources and is reported here with her permission.

3. God's *Praxis:* An Invitation of New Metaphors

And God created humans in the image . . . of God, male and female.
GENESIS 1:27, NJB

Not long ago in an Anchorage, Alaska, adult Sunday school class I, as visiting teacher and preacher for the day, began to present a version of my account, "God's Work and Our Vocations." As a preamble I referred to H. Richard Niebuhr's use of the metaphors of God as creator, God as governor, and God as liberator and redeemer. In the presentation I made the claim that all constructive theology employs metaphor to represent the divine-human relatedness. Further, I explained that "metaphor" comes from the Greek *meta*, meaning "beyond, behind, or across," combined with *pherein*, which means "to bear or carry." Metaphor, I said, is the employment of images drawn from familiar human experiences in fresh ways in order to "carry over" the hearer or reader to an imaging of realities that are not accessible to our everyday experience. I gave examples of metaphors such as "our God is a refiner's fire" and "the Lord is my shepherd." I then pointed out that I would be following the practice of the Bible by using multiple metaphors for depicting the divine-human relation. In order to avoid idolatry, I pointed out, the Bible draws on a wide variety of metaphors for helping us image God's way with nature and humankind. I also suggested, following Niebuhr, that the Bible's metaphors for God are always relational metaphors—God as God has been experienced in *relation* to creation and humankind—and never God as God might be known apart from the divine self-disclosure in relation to creation and history.

Then I began to launch into my familiar and confident discussion of God's creative, governing, and redemptive-liberating action and of our calling to partnership in these activities of God. Suddenly a man in the front row, sixtyish, ruddy-faced, stocky, in a pin-striped brown suit and red tie, interrupted me with evident agitation. "Wait a minute," he crackled, "what do you mean by suggesting that *Creator* is a *metaphor* for God? God *is* the Creator! And that's that!"

Trying to avoid getting hooked by the strong anger this man expressed, I explained that the imaging of God as creator likely arose from the human experiences of making tools, building shelter, weaving fabrics and stories, painting pictures, and participating in the mystery of bringing children to birth. "These familiar experiences," I said, "have become analogues we use to account for God's agency in bringing the universe into being. They have served, in creed and confession, to express our reverence for the awesome capacities that generated the universe, us and our kind, all the species of our fellow creatures, and the great gift of sun by day, and moon and myriad galaxies of stars by night. However," I said, "God's being and doing in giving birth to and nurturing all this can be only partially and incompletely—though suggestively—captured in analogies from our human experiences of creativity."

Obviously unpersuaded—and if anything more angered by my response—he asserted, "God *is* Creator." He followed with, "That *is* God's *proper name*. It is not a (he might have said *mere*) *metaphor!*" After another fruitless exchange, as one sometimes must, I simply said that it appeared that he and I would have to differ, and using the prerogative of visiting "authority," I closed the exchange and went on—though less confidently than before —with my teaching.

In two earlier books I made the effort to write about God's work and our vocations by focusing on this elaboration of the dynamic doctrine of the sovereignty of God. I learned to think that way while writing my doctoral dissertation on the theological ethics of H. Richard Niebuhr.[1] I am *still* deeply committed to the view of God's *praxis* and the vision of human responsiveness that I tried to understand and convey with that set of theological metaphors. As this chapter unfolds I shall take pains to be clear about the many elements from that way of speaking that continue to express my convictions about these matters. However, I have concluded that in my writing and speaking from now on I can no longer rely so centrally upon the metaphor of God as sovereign. There are several reasons for this judgment:

First, the symbol "sovereignty" derives from monarchal and imperial traditions. It carries connotations of God's *omnipotence, otherness, distance,* and *invulnerability.* In the history of the West it has also connoted patriarchy, maleness, and the exercise of reign through domination backed by the legitimate use of violent power. Hence, to characterize God as sovereign makes it difficult to refer to God's closeness to and compassion for creation. It makes it difficult to portray the ongoing risks and grief to which God would seem to be subject by virtue of having woven a texture of freedom into creation at every level and by nurturing the evolution of creatures who have developed and continually misuse some God-like capacities. "Sovereignty" can obscure recognition of the ways God participates in the suffering of nature and humans. And it makes for difficulty in speaking of God in gender-inclusive terms and imagery.

Second, in our nuclear age, when human beings have developed the capacity to end violently most life on this planet, the imagery of God's sovereignty, at least as exercised on earth, has to be significantly qualified. Though we humans certainly are not made "sovereign" by our terrible capacity for world destruction, any speaking of God that ignores this potential double death-dealing—the death to most living things and the death to planetary life itself—reveals a lack of touch with present realities.[2]

Third, in a similar way, when the biosphere of this precious planet suffers growingly disruptive abuse and is put at risk from human activities, theologies that lead with the affirmation of God's sovereignty and transcendence evoke little resonance with our experiences of the ecological threat to the very bases of all life. The accelerating impacts of climate-intrusive and biosphere-modifying technologies in this century and the last seem to be disrupting "nature's" capacity for self-healing and restoration of its life-sustaining balances. To a degree that many only dimly recognize, our images of God are subliminally tied up with our experiences of nature as transcendent, as other, and as the dependable bringer of daylight and nightfall and the cycle of the seasons. Our images of God derive in important ways from our experience of nature as bountiful supporter of all life, as author of unsurpassably intricate and varied aesthetic beauty, and as our self-restoring matrix. Sovereignty theology can be tone deaf to the deep anxiety that our intuitions of "the end of nature" evoke in us.[3]

Finally, it has been my experience that the metaphors of the sovereignty of God, worked out as God the creator, the governor, and the liberator-redeemer—at least as expressed from my mind, lips, and pen—have lost the leverage they once had to do what metaphors are supposed to do: namely, to shock us into new and enlarged sensibility and move us to deepened conviction through the novel use of familiar imagery to provide fresh access to the unfamiliar or the inaccessible. They simply no longer startle and gift the imagination of faith-hungry contemporaries. As Sallie McFague says, "Metaphors are imaginative leaps across a distance— the best metaphors always give both a shock and a shock of recognition." She goes on to say, "A metaphor that has lost its shock (its 'is not' quality) loses as well its recognition possibilities (its 'is' quality), for the metaphor is no longer 'heard': it is taken to be a definition, not a likely account."[4]

It is not just that the imagery associated with the sovereignty of God and its control of such metaphors as creator, governor, redeemer-liberator is merely neutral and no longer effective in some bland, archaic way. I have become convinced that its link- ages with patriarchy, monarchy, and historic patterns of male domination make this metaphorical system—no matter how hard I have tried to "clean it up" and render it inclusive—a barrier to faith for many women and a source of distortion for all of us. As I will try to show in subsequent pages, I believe the metaphors controlled by sovereignty continue to draw many toward images of the divine *praxis* in which God remains enthroned and remote. Humans are imagined as congenitally prideful and sinful. Christ is viewed as an atoning sacrifice for our inevitable, yet somehow chosen, guilt. And the human calling to service in partnership merely produces a perpetually bad conscience, or the numbness of its negation.

In what is admittedly a caricature, the theologian-poet Brian Wren has captured many of the negative dimensions that have tainted the sovereignty metaphorical system with his ugly acro- nym KINGAFAP (King, G-d, Almighty, Father, and Protector). I quote Wren at length so we can consider his unfolding of the KINGAFAP metaphoric system:

A Powerful King, seated on a high throne, receives homage and tribute from prostrate, beseeching subjects and praise from human and angelic choirs. The King rules by word of command and his decrees protect his subjects and stabilize the cosmic order. The King is all-powerful, awesome and terrifying, yet also merciful. As King, he is also Father, meaning that he is the origin of all things, humanity's lordly and merciful male parent, and the Father of his own Son. . . . The King is mighty, sometimes called All-mighty. His power is shown in making the world by a word of command, and by triumphing in battle over enemies. The "enemies" are supposed to be evil tendencies in each human, but human antagonists often claim that G-d is on their side in human wars. The King is also the supreme Judge, with power of life and death over his subjects, but it is believed that his last word is mercy and love.

The King has a son, the Crown Prince, who sits beside him. At his father's bidding, the Prince steps down from his throne and surrenders his royal power and privileges. He descends to earth and is born as a male human child. When he grows up he shows the King's love, cares for outcasts, announces the King's advent to the chosen people, is betrayed to the authorities and crucified. The crucifixion is often depicted as a battle with sin, death, and the devil. The Prince Royal lies dead, but is lifted up to life by his Kingly Father. There are two versions of what happens next. In [a few accounts] the Prince takes his human experience of humility and suffering forever into the being of G-d. This is a minority view, for in most texts the impression given is that the Prince *leaves behind* his suffering, humiliated, humble state, comes back to the throne, and waits till he can return to earth with supernatural power, fight and slay his enemies, and receive tribute and homage from everyone. He is often portrayed as a Judge who will come with awesome power at the end of the world.

Meanwhile, *the King and Prince (Father and Son) send their Spirit down to earth,* to help their followers and occasionally do good in the world as well.[5]

My own writing about God as sovereign creator, governor, and liberator-redeemer tried to avoid falling into the KINGAFAP pattern. I made serious attempts to account for the presence, involvement, and nonanthropomorphic character of God's modes of action and being in the processes of nature and history. Nonetheless, people persisted in hearing my language with ears and imaginations tuned by the KINGAFAP myth. Thus I have concluded that a different metaphorical approach is required for constructive theological imaging of the *praxis* of God for this era and the future. As a way of forwarding my own efforts at metaphorical reconstruction I propose in the next pages to enter into a dialogue with the work of the theologian Sallie McFague.

THE WORLD AS GOD'S BODY

Sallie McFague's constructive theological contribution in *Models of God: Theology for an Ecological, Nuclear Age* begins by recognizing the inevitably constructive and mataphoric character of theological language. She also makes clear that we require new metaphors if our faith is to enable us to make sense of our contemporary experience. At the end of the twentieth century we live most of the time and in most ways by outmoded, anachronistic metaphors. In our religious language we are naming ourselves, one another, our world, and our relatedness to God in terms from bygone times. Such anachronistic names, helpful in earlier times, are distorting and hurtful now. For example, we no longer live in a world under the guidance of a benevolent but absolute deity. Our world of systems and global interdependence can no longer be represented as being populated by independent individuals—with humans as the only beings who really count. Hierarchical arrangements of power are being eroded by revolutions in information and communication. We can no longer think adequately in terms of a special history of revelation existing on a different plane from a broader secular history and from the processes of nature. Biology and physics, chemistry and genetic sciences are presenting us with the possibility of modeling laws and principles that govern the processes of life and evolution in the universe from the smallest particles and energy fields we can detect to the patterns of galactic interaction. Consequently, we are called to holistic patterns of thinking and to metaphors that enable us to represent God's involvement and influences in unified ways in the world process in its many strands and complex unity.

To think holistically requires metaphors that capture the interdependence of all life, nonhuman as well as human. Holistic imaging requires that we take account of the interliving systems that maintain as well as constrain our lives. Relational, holistic thinking calls upon us to reconstruct cosmology—coherent images for the interrelatedness of all being from the microcosmic to the macrocosmic levels of the universe. In accordance with the most fundamental tenet of the evolutionary, ecological, and systems perspective we recognize that what an entity is most basically is determined in terms of its relationships. Behind this statement lie the insights of physicists in relativity theory and quantum physics and of biologists and psychologists in field and systems theory.

Process philosophers and theologians have sought to provide metaphors for the interrelatedness of all being and of God as immanent in the processes of reality primarily by using abstract and impersonal concepts. McFague's work is striking for its proposal that we develop a holistic approach to God as the grounding and unity of all being in relational, not abstract, concepts. She makes the case for imagining God with metaphors derived from the most intimate and personal relations of our human experience:

> In what metaphors and models should we conceive of God as Thou who is related to the world in a unified and interdependent way? To understand God as Thou, it seems to me, is basic for our relating to all reality in the mode of mutuality, respect, care, and responsibility. The qualities of personal relationship are needed in our time not only in the God-world relation but in the human-world relation as well. The problem, I believe, is not that personal metaphors and concepts have been used for God; it is not the personal aspect that has brought about the asymmetrical dualism. The problem lies, rather, in the particular metaphors and concepts chosen. The primary metaphors in the [biblical] tradition are hierarchical, imperialistic, and dualistic, stressing the distance between God and the world and the total reliance of the world on God. Thus the metaphors of God as king, ruler, lord, master, and governor, and the concepts that accompany them of God as absolute, complete, transcendent, and omnipotent permit no sense of mutuality, shared responsibility, reciprocity, and love (except in the sense of gratitude).[6]

In the effort to address the issues enumerated in this passage, McFague's *Models of God* tries to maintain continuity with and fidelity to the biblical and doctrinal sources of Christian faith, on the one hand, while marshaling images and metaphors that startle us and gift us with new responsiveness to God, on the other. Dennis Nineham has written that people find it hard to believe in God because they do not have available to them any lively imaginative picture of the way God and the world as they know it are related. What they need most is a story, a picture, a myth, that will capture their imagination, while meshing in with the rest of their sensibility in the way that messianic terms linked with the sensibility of first-century Jews, or Nicene symbolism with the sensibility of philosophically minded fourth-century Greeks.[7]

As part of keeping continuity with Christian tradition McFague is resolutely *Trinitarian* in her theological construction. Apparently she agrees with the poet and theologian Brian Wren that the Trinitarian pattern is "a unifying core of Christian tradition, based on the scriptural experience of God." Wren adds, "Trinitarian experience is unique to Christianity. Though formed within the KINGAFAP metaphor system, it broke through it, to see God not as a single, isolated being, the mon-arch, but as a complex, co-equal in relatedness. The Christian experience of God as Trinity is implicitly antipatriarchal and a rich resource."[8]

In her choice of metaphors and her way of setting the context for portraying the persons and dynamics of the Trinity, McFague breaks new ground. She proposes that we image the "world" as God's body.[9] Before we go further to explain what this might mean, let us pause for a moment and try to absorb the impact of imagining the world as God's body. How would viewing the world as God's body affect our thinking about cutting and burning all the trees off a rain forest tract of a thousand acres in order to create pasture for cattle? How would it change our readiness to blast vast craters in the earth in order to test nuclear devices? How would imaging the world as the body of God challenge or disturb our views of God as spiritual and transcendent? McFague seems to believe that such reimaging of the world would restore a sense of contact, tangibility, and participation in the reality of God. What does she mean by this idea?

Most times she writes as though "world," understood as God's body, is limited to "earth"—our biosphere and planet. At other times she hints that she might mean the universe, with its millions of galaxies and seemingly limitless expansion. This ambiguity resolves itself through her making clear that what is at stake in seeing world as the body of God is its suggestive impact on our sensibilities to God's presence in and throughout the universe. It would lead to our experiencing God as related to and the ground of being for all creatures of earth and nature.

McFague avoids any suggestion of reducing God or Christ to an identification with the "world," planet Earth, or even the "universe." The being and action of God is not *limited* to God's embodiedness in earth or universe. Rather, God "gives birth" to the world/universe through divine self-expression, and in doing so shapes an embodiedness and generates the presence of, and relation with, myriads of bodies—living and lively—who constitute God's body. In this sense we and all creation, with our bodies, become part of the body of God. Let me try to summarize several important results McFague sees of our trying an imaging of the world as God's body:

1. Though God is not reduced to the world, the metaphor of the world as God's body puts God "at risk." . . . God becomes dependent through being bodily, in a way that a totally invisible, distant God would never be. . . . The world as God's body may be poorly cared for, ravaged, and as we are becoming well aware, essentially destroyed, in spite of God's own loving attention to it, because of one creature, ourselves, who can choose or not choose to join with God in conscious care of the world. The notions of vulnerability, shared responsibility, and risk are inevitable.

2. The world as God's body . . . may be seen as a way to remythologize the inclusive, suffering love of the cross of Jesus of Nazareth. In both instances, God is at risk in human hands: just as once upon a time . . . humans killed their God in the body of a man, so now we once again have that power, but, in a mythology more appropriate to our time, we would kill our God in the body of the world. Could we actually do this? To believe in the resurrection means we could not. God is not in our power to destroy, but the incarnate God is the God at risk: We have been given central responsibility to care for God's body, our world.

3. God's knowledge, action, and love are markedly different in the metaphor of the world as God's body. God knows the world immediately just as we know our bodies immediately. God could be said to be in touch with all parts of the world through interior understanding. . . . God is internally related to all that is—the most radically relational Thou.

4. The action of God in the world is similarly interior and caring. If the entire universe, all that is and has been, is God's body, then God acts in and through the incredibly complex physical and historical-cultural evolutionary process that began eons ago. This does not mean that God is reduced to the evolutionary process, for God remains as the agent, the self, whose intentions are expressed in the universe. Nevertheless, the manner in which these intentions are expressed is internal and, by implication, providential—that is, reflective of a "caring" relationship.

5. The model of the world as God's body suggests that God loves bodies: in loving the world, God loves a body. . . . It is to say that bodies are worth loving, sexually and otherwise, that passionate love as well as attention to the needs of bodily existence is a part of fulfillment. It is to say further that the basic necessities of bodily existence— adequate food and shelter, for example—are central aspects of God's love for all bodily creatures and therefore should be central concerns of us, God's co-workers.[10]

In ways reminiscent of Marney—and of Teilhard de Chardin, who influenced both Marney and McFague—the metaphor of the world as God's body provides the basis for a rich and deep recovery of the sense of the world as sacramental. One gives regard to dogs, cats, and goldfish; one honors the Godness in each human being, from derelict to diva. One vibrates with the dancing electrons in granite. And one receives with gladness the divine caresses of yellow sunlight, the green miracle of photosynthesis, and the companionship of rain.

What this experiment with the world as God's body comes to, finally, is an awareness, both chilling and breathtaking, that we as worldly, bodily beings are in God's presence . . . a perception of the divine as visible, as present, palpably present in our world. But it is a kind of sacramentalism that is painfully conscious of the world's vulnerability, its preciousness, its uniqueness. (p. 77)

THE DANCE OF THE TRINITY

With McFague, I affirm the commitment to keep the Trinitarian structure of the Christian faith's understanding of God central in our efforts to bring the patterns of divine *praxis* to fresh metaphoric expression. How refreshing to learn that John of

Damascus, in the seventh century, used the Greek word *peri-choresis* (literally, "dance around") to characterize the dynamic ways the three divine Persons relate to one another. "Peri-choresis," writes Brian Wren, "means that the three Persons con-tinually exchange energy, being and power, so that each partakes of the other. It suggests a beautiful intertwining, unending dance, whose movement flows to and fro between the dancers. Trinitar-ian metaphors," Wren concludes, "should strive for that sense of dynamic, intertwining movement."[11] With a poet's sensibility informed by a recognition of the dangerous ways the term *person* has been reconstructed in modern societies toward images of atom-istic individualism, Wren urges that we take care to name God in terms drawn from the communal and relational meanings of personal existence. Drawing upon the formulations of Patricia Wilson-Kastner, Wren says that Trinitarian faith tries to express the conviction that God is "a unity of three centers of aware-ness and centeredness who are also perfectly open and inter-dependent . . . three centers of divine identity, self-aware and self-giving in love, self-possessed yet freely transcending the self in eternal trinitarian interconnectedness."[12] Wren adds, "The phrase 'centers of personhood' seems to me a useful way of sug-gesting this, because it includes the word *person*, but in a way that suggests we are not talking about 'persons' as we know them, and certainly not about individualists" (p. 203).

In ways that one may find initially shocking, McFague proposes that we reconstruct the three "centers of personhood" of the Trinity with the metaphors mother (parent), lover, and friend. This proposal provides the basis for her efforts to provide a fresh modeling of the *praxis* of God—God's modes and manners of being and acting in the processes of nature and history. In order to spell out this "oneness in threeness" so as to depict God's ways of relating to us and the world, she systematically considers each of these metaphors in terms of three questions:

1. What mode of divine love is suggested by this model?
2. What kind of divine activity is implied by this love?
3. What does this kind of love say about our existence in our world?

It may help to provide the schematic outline of her discussion of these three metaphors for God, each with its characteristic type of love, its distinctive exercise of action (power), and its form of ethic. In the chart that follows I have added a dimension to which McFague has not attended, namely, the underlying social root-metaphor implied in her use of the metaphors of God as mother, lover, and friend. By social root-metaphor I mean to indicate the model of community and of persons related to each other in community implied in her imaging of the Persons of the Trinitarian God in their "dance around." In the last part of this chapter I will draw on the implications of this last column for our use and evaluation of McFague's metaphorical reconstruction.

METAPHOR	TYPE OF LOVE	ACTION (POWER)	FORM OF ETHIC	ROOT-METAPHOR
Mother (Parent)	*Agape*	Creating	Justice, judging	Organism
Lover	*Eros*	Saving	Healing	Interpersonal relations
Friend	*Philia*	Sustaining	Companionship	Covenant faithfulness

Now I will try, in a few pages, to convey some of the richness of her developing of these three metaphors in their interdependence. In a final section I will go beyond McFague to suggest that she has, without noting it, included some very powerful shifts in the Christian characterization of God's way with creation and humankind—shifts that have strong implications for our forming of personal and public faith.

GOD THE MOTHER (PARENT)

We begin with McFague's effort to reimage the first Person of the Trinity, traditionally God the father. Though father is included in this reworking under the rubric parent, McFague wants to try to claim some elements of God that fatherhood, particularly as imaged in patriarchal societies, has had difficulty in expressing.[13]

Erik Erikson, in his many writings on stages of the life cycle, suggests in several places that fathers love us differently than mothers do. The love of fathers, he implies, is more distant, more dangerous, and emerges as especially significant in our early childhood differentiation from the maternal matrix—the initial embeddedness in the orbit of dominant relatedness with the mother. Father love is most important in completing a first differentiation into selfhood and in confirming the strengths and internal limits that guide autonomy and responsibility. Many persons today—forty years after Erikson's initial formulations were made —would dispute these characterizations, claiming that fathers can be important participants in the earliest lives of children and that mothers, too, can contribute to their individuation. My purpose in referring to Erikson, however, is to point up some of what startles us as McFague invites us to reconsider the first Person of the Trinity in terms of the metaphor mother, and secondarily, parent.

The shock of the maternal metaphor strikes us in elemental ways when we read McFague's further elaboration of why we must use *personal* metaphors in the depiction of God's patterns of loving and acting:

> Any imaginative picture attempting to unseat the triumphalist, royal model [for God] must be at least as attractive as it is. It must be an understanding of the God-world relationship that will move people to live by it and work for it; it must come from a place deep within human experience. It is no accident that much of the tradition's most powerful imagery does come from this place. It is imagery reflecting the beginning and continuation of life, imagery of sex, breath, food, blood, and water, as in the second birth, the breath of the Holy Spirit, bread and wine, the blood of the cross, the resurrection of the body, and the water of baptism. This language continues to be powerful because images arising from the most basic level of physical existence . . . are images of life and death.[14]

The royalist imagery for the God-world relation is taken largely from the arena of politics. Royalist metaphors, in league with patriarchal images of fatherhood, concern how we govern our lives. McFague suggests that a deeper question than that of governance focuses on how we live at all, and how well we live:

Metaphors of mothers, lovers, friends, and bodies come from this [deeper] level, as does the classic model of father understood as parent. If the imagery of mothers, lovers, friends, and bodies proved credible for picturing the God-world relation, it would certainly be attractive, for it is unmatched in power: it holds within it the power not of mere kings but of life and death. (p. 81)

As we move from controlling metaphors of God as sovereign to seeing God in terms of body and relationship we recast our accounting of God's love and its patterns of expression. We recast our images of the power of God, moving from dominance and hierarchy to more participatory, persuasive, and vulnerable expressions of power. We recast our understandings of sin and salvation and our imaging of God's patterns of provident sustaining and guiding of creation and humankind.

What sort of divine love is suggested by the metaphor of God as mother? God as mother implies a cosmic generosity, an *agape* love, that gives life to all being with no thought of return. What kind of divine activity is implied by this love? The divine activity of *creation* is central to our understanding of God as mother. God, as mother, gives birth to the world/universe in an ongoing physical event. The universe is bodied forth from God and is expressive of God's very being. The Mother-Creator rejoices in the rich diversity of created being and is interested in all its forms. The first word of God the mother affirms the goodness of creation: "It is good that you exist." But this must be followed immediately by the second: "The household or economy of the universe must be ordered and managed in a way so as to bring about the nurture and fulfillment of life" (pp. 102–3). The metaphor of God as mother has special power to characterize the pattern of an *inclusive* justice that attends to the most basic needs of all creatures. God as parent wants *all* to flourish.

McFague rather consistently uses "parent" as qualifier or alternative formulation to "mother" in the development of this use of the mother-creator metaphor. At points she includes "father" as well. To help us grasp what the creator-mother-parent metaphors need to convey she is careful to distinguish between "feminine" and "female" in attributing qualities to God. "Feminine" qualities are culturally and historically determined and bound, so that to refer to a feminine dimension of God endows God with the qualities that go with a particular society's images of the feminine. In our society such a move tends to stereotype God's feminine side in terms of the tender, nurturing, passive, and healing qualities of divine activity. God's creative, redeeming, peacemaking, and justice-administering activities are stereotypically represented as masculine. In extending such stereotypical cultural images of the feminine and the masculine to the Godhead we further crystallize and sanctify gender differences and the power differentials contained in these stereotypes. The characterizations of God as female—as mother—on the other hand, yield possibilities that neither the feminine nor the traditional patriarchal or kingship metaphors evoke. She is creator, but she is also judge. The metaphor of God as mother is not built on stereotypes of feminine softness, tenderness, sentimentality, and pity. Rather, this metaphor builds on the female strength and fierceness involved in gestation, birth, lactation, and defense of the young. "Those who produce life have a stake in it and will judge, often with anger, what prevents its fulfillment." McFague continues:

> In addressing the mother-God as both creator and judge—as both the giver of life and the judge who is angry when for any reason the fulfillment of the life given is thwarted—we find a clue to the nature of sin. . . . In the picture of God as mother, God is angry because what comes from her being and belongs to her lacks the food and other necessities to grow and flourish. The mother-God as creator is necessarily judge, at the very basic level of condemning as the primary (though not the only) sin the inequitable distribution of basic necessities for the continuation of life in its many forms. (pp. 113–14)

Initially I found it curious that McFague identified the type of love characteristic of God as mother/parent as *agape*. Influenced by Anders Nygren's book *Agape and Eros*, as was all my generation, I had thought of *agape* love in terms of disinterestedness and a kind of cosmic, platonic, unconditional positive regard. It connoted for me a kind of detached love for the other regardless of merit or desert. But McFague's proposal stands this conception of *agape* on its head. She sees God's love as an unconditional love based upon the fact that God has given birth to all being. God the mother/parent does not love *in spite of* merit or desert but out of a parental attachment that can be fierce indeed. It is equitably directed to all being but is not detached or disinterested.

What does this kind of *agape*, creator love say about our human existence in the world? First, to see God in terms of the impartial, agapic mother love of creation displaces any humanocentric claim to priority in God's affections. Humans must live with restraint and mutual respect with other creatures and assume special responsibility for the tending and mending of creation. Second, it says that we participate in the divine mother's creativity and *agape* by becoming parental persons ourselves—whether through the wondrous process of biological parenting or through becoming caretakers of the world. This view enables McFague to state the calling in human vocation correlated with the *agapic* love of God the parent, mother and father. "We should become mothers and fathers to our world, extending those natural instincts we all have, whether or not we have children of our bodies (or adopted children), to universal parenthood" (p. 119).[15] McFague says that human beings are the only "conscious" (I would say "reflectively conscious") parents. "We have the special responsibility to help administer the process: to join God the creator-mother in so arranging the cosmic household that the birth and growth of other species will take place in an ecologically balanced way, both for our own well-being and for the well-being of other species" (p. 120).

The vocational expressions of this parental partnership with creator-mother God are many:

All people, therefore, who engage in work, paid or unpaid, that helps to sustain the present and coming generations are universal parents. The agapic, just love that we have designated as parental, the love that gives without calculating the return, that wills the existence and fulfillment of other beings—this love is manifest in ways beyond counting. It is found in the teacher who gives extra time to the slow or gifted student, in the social worker whose clients are drug-addicted pregnant women, in the librarian who lovingly restores old books, in the specialist in world population control whose days are spent on planes and in board meetings, in the zoologist who patiently studies the behavior of the great apes in the wild, in the owner of the local supermarket who employs ex-juvenile delinquents, in the politician who supports more funds for public education, in the botanist who catalogues new strains of plants, in rock stars who give their talents to famine relief. All of these are examples of universal parenthood. (p. 121)

In closing her reflections on our partnership with creator-mother God, McFague speculates whether we can think of governments modeling themselves as universal parents. "Our positive role in creation is as preservers, those who pass life along and who care for all forms of life so they may prosper. Our role as preservers is a very high calling, our peculiar calling as human beings, the calling implied in the model of God as mother" (p. 122).

GOD THE LOVER (CHRIST)

From the realm of *agape* love, a love that gives birth to all being and indiscriminately attributes to it worth and right to *be*, we move to a love of personal address. This is *eros*, the love that expresses personal affirmation of the worth and value of the beloved, the love that draws the beloved to itself, seeking to bring about the beloved's wholeness and completion. This is the love of healing, the love that reconciles the alienated and separated. It is the love of forgiveness that reaches in rescue to the depths of the finite experiences of stain, worthlessness, willful rebellion, or oppressed, silent passivity. *Eros* "expresses better than any other kind of love the *valuableness* of the beloved. In a time such as ours, when the intrinsic value of our world must be stressed, eros as the love of the valuable is a necessary aspect of both divine and human love" (p. 130).

The concept of erotic love allows us to affirm that God loves the world and its creatures and that God longs for and needs the response, in love, of creation. God as lover has a particular desire for union or reunion with those creatures who uniquely have the gifts of reflective consciousness and finite freedom and the capacity to respond with love in personal ways. This erotic love, especially important for the creatures who bear the divine image, does not negate or push aside God's *agape* love, with its affirmation of *all* creatures and being. It does, however, express, in personal forms of address, God's longing for our response in love and for intimate relationship. This is the love expressed in incarnation. This is the love expressed in the grace of Christ that awakens us to our alienation and separation, our enmity and opposition to God. It lures us toward a reunion in which our worth to God is restored and confirmed, and we are released toward perfect freedom as the beloved of God.

The erotic love of God as lover affirms that the value of creation —and of creatures—is not destroyed by sin. God as lover—as in Christ—comes not to *condemn* the world but to save: to restore, heal, and reunite the world with God. This kind of love, says McFague,

> is . . . a crucial aspect in the change of consciousness needed in an ecological, nuclear era. One of the greatest barriers to developing the sensibility needed in our time is the traditional Christian, and especially Protestant, view of sin as corrupting, depraving, and making worthless both human beings and the rest of creation. It results in a low view of life, in general and in particular. . . . Life is not worthless, nor is it made worthy only through divine forgiveness; as such, it is valuable and precious, and we need to feel that value in the marrow of our bones if we are to have the will to work with the divine lover toward including all the beloved in the circle of valuing love. (p. 133)

A full appreciation of God as lover leads to the recognition that God, in some real sense, needs the response of the beloved. This view is to be contrasted with theistic images of God's detachment, self-containedness, and self-completion in the inner-Trinitarian life. It carries the implication of a dynamic relationship between God and humanity in which the finite responsiveness of the latter affects and leads to mutual changes and growth in the relations of lover and beloved. Theistic models for God, based upon ancient Greek philosophical assumptions, led to a preference for images of God as immutable, motionless, and without need. The models of God as mother-creator and as lover, however, portray a very different God—in fact, a biblical God. For

> neither the covenantal God of the Hebrew Scriptures who pleaded with Israel to be his faithful partner nor the compassionate God of Jesus of Nazareth who healed the sick and cast out demons is an unmoved mover or an absolute monarch. . . . Change, growth, and development are all positive attributes for contemporary human beings; they are also characteristics of an evolutionary view of our universe. Hence, on the principle that we image God according to what we find most desirable in ourselves and what we find constitutive of our world, there is reason to include change as a divine attribute. (p. 134)

The metaphor of God as creator-mother gives rise to a revived sacramentalism in which God is shown forth in the world through embodiment, the giving birth to that which expresses the essential being and generosity of God. With the metaphor of God the lover a second, and somewhat more selective, sacramentalism can be expressed. It suggests—as did Carlyle Marney's theology and our consideration of the lives of King and Merton—that human beings, evolved as the image of God, and who have the greatest potential for responding as beloved to lover, can reveal the God-world relationship in special ways. This insight sheds special light on the incarnation:

> Jesus' response as beloved to God as lover was so open and thorough that his life and death were revelatory of God's great love for the world. His illumination of that love as inclusive of the last and the least, as embracing and valuing the outcast, is paradigmatic of God the lover but is not unique. This means that Jesus is not ontologically different from other paradigmatic figures either in our tradition or in other religious traditions who manifest in word and deed the love of God for the world. He is special to us as our foundational figure: he is our historical choice as the premier paradigm of God's love. But all creation and all human beings have potential as the beloved of God to reflect or respond to their lover. That many, most human beings do not is in our model the definition of sin, the refusal to be the special part of creation, of God's body, that we are called to be—namely, those who among the beloved can respond to God as lover by working to reunite and heal the fragmented world. Those who do are called the disciples. (p. 136)

I fully affirm McFague's thesis that we are called to a humanity like that of Jesus the Christ, and that humans are meant to be "saviors of the world." I find compelling her identifying as sin our failure or choice not to reflect or respond to God as our lover. In her formulations in the passage I have just quoted, however, I believe she unnecessarily risks forfeiting her claims for continuity with the historic doctrines of the Trinity and of Christology. Though supporting her point that the human vocation is to a responsiveness to the divine lover like that of Jesus, I would underscore the dimension of divine initiative in the Christ event. I would point to the "convergent providence" that led not only to the event of Jesus' paradigm-forming responsiveness to the divine lover, but to his full embodiment of that love in finite form. And I believe she could affirm the singularity, uniqueness, and absoluteness of Christ without jeopardizing either the claim that all humans have a calling to unity with God the lover like that of Christ or the claim that others than Christians have been addressed by and responded to that calling.[16]

If the form of God as lover is *eros*, the divine activity—the power—of God the lover is exercised in *saving*. McFague consciously chooses not to express the lover's saving action in terms of "redemption." God the lover loves not "in spite" of humanity's (and creation's) "corruption," making the self-sacrifice of death on a cross to atone—to Godself—for human sin. Rather, the divine lover loves because of humanity's and creation's *worth*. Because of personal resistance, and because of the distortions of sin compounded in social institutions and historical-cultural patterns, restoration of right relatedness between humans and the beloved requires the active approach of God. The element of profound truth in atonement christologies arises from the fact that God's confrontation with entrenched resistance and evil is costly and requires that Lover and lovers be prepared to suffer and die. The death and bloodspilling are not sacrifices *to* God to propitiate divine wrath. Rather, they are sacrifices *for* God and for alienated humanity, disclosing a love that will not give up on the possibility of healing and reconciliation.

The healing work to which humans are called in partnership with God the lover is of a piece with this understanding of salvation. Healing must be addressed to both body and spirit. And healing is not limited to healing in the human community; it extends to mending of the ecological integrity of earth and biosphere. The healing engendered by God the lover implies human resistance to and overcoming of all that cripples and exploits human beings and nature. It also, in solidarity with God the lover, requires identification and solidarity with sufferers in their pain. "If the one thing needful is reunification of the shattered and divided world, there must be many saviors. Jesus of Nazareth, as paradigmatic of God as lover, reveals God's passionate, valuing love for the world" (pp. 146–50). In passages that will give flesh to our descriptions of Universalizing faith in the next chapter, McFague writes about persons who respond to God the lover by joining the divine *praxis* as saviors of the world. She points to "other paradigmatic figures who reveal in their own lives and often deaths the same passionate, valuing, inclusive love for the world that we see in the figure of Jesus." Her list includes John Woolman, Dietrich Bonhoeffer, Sojourner Truth, Dorothy Day, and Mohandas Gandhi, among others. She writes:

> There are several qualities that many of these people share, but two of the most outstanding are the *inclusive* and the *radical* character of their love for others. . . . These lives reveal once again the inclusive, non-hierarchical love of God, and they do so with the passion and intensity of those who find others, all others, valuable and worthy. None of these people, however, is a "saint": they are not miracle workers, and they did not reach their vision of inclusive love and their willingness to practice the healing ministry of this vision easily or quickly. . . . They are at one level very ordinary human beings battling their desire for money and comfort, afraid for their families, lonely in prison and frightened of death, discouraged by the slight gains they make against the forces of discrimination, fear, and prejudice that divide people. Nonetheless, they are, in our model of God as lover, illustrative of the many saviors of the world: their stories flesh out the paradigmatic story of Jesus of Nazareth. (pp. 150–52)

Such persons—joined by others of us still involved in *metanoia* toward a real indwelling of God the lover in our hearts and wills— will not save the world alone. Nonetheless, their lives, as reflections of the life and death of Jesus of Nazareth, are revelatory of God's love. "To have faith in the God whom the lives of Jesus and these others reveal is to believe that the universe is neither malevolent nor indifferent but is on the side of life and its fulfillment. . . . We do not work alone, but the work cannot be done without us (p. 152).

GOD THE FRIEND (SPIRIT)

We come now to consider the metaphoric reconstruction of the third Person of the Trinity offered by Sallie McFague's *Models of God*, God the friend (Spirit). By this time certain insights that the author does not discuss, and of which she may not be aware, begin to emerge. In relation to God as creator-mother, it begins to become apparent that the underlying root-metaphor for the divine human relation in that model is that of *organism*. It is as though human beings, as well as all other living creatures, are distinctive cells in the vast organism of God's "body." God's creativity gives birth to the bodying forth of God in the evolving, rich, complex evolutionary process, with its myriad kinds of being. God the mother's love for creation is inclusive and undifferentiated. Her affirmation of dynamic creation and all its interconnected, teeming life is a resounding, "Good, Good! It is good that you exist." This affirmation of all creation, however, taking in the universe as a whole, cannot allow for the differentiation and recognition of particular beings, or for God's relation with particular selves. It makes its contribution at the organismic level, and in doing so allows for the affirmation of God as the parent of all creation in ways that can include the richest explanations of astrophysicists and particle physicists and evolutionary biologists. In its great power the model of God as creator-mother does not, however, allow for a human relation of subjecthood, of responsible selfhood. It primarily illumines the experiential domain of the child in relation to the mother, receiving nurture and undifferentiated affirmation and being part of a larger ecology of being—a vast extended family—with whom one must share mother and the resources for the sustaining of life.

The realm or root-metaphor of McFague's representation of the second person, God the lover, is to be found on a different level. I suggest that here it is the experience of interpersonal relatedness that gives rise to the root-metaphor underlying the model of God the lover. In this domain McFague, without always being explicit about it, shifts more fully to the human level. She addresses the consequences of the human experiences of becoming selves in relation to others and to God, with all the hazards, wounds, and distortions to which the process of differentiation and development of identity are subject. Of particular importance, I believe, she carries out a subtle but important shifting of the discussion of human sin and divine redemption, which arise in the context of human differentiation from the divine "matrix." Traditional doctrines of original sin have addressed the consequences for humans in terms of *guilt*. McFague has shifted the discussion from the axis of *guilt* and divine forgiveness of human infractions to the axis of *shame* and the divine reaffirmation of worth.[17]

Developmentally, shame is the emotion associated with the child's first dramatic moves toward autonomy. When moves toward autonomy are greeted with too much freedom and no boundaries, the child can develop anxiety, a tendency to self-injury, and the feeling of not being *worth* anyone's investment of time and care. On the other hand, when moves toward autonomy are greeted with excessive expectations of perfection, control, and requirements regarding both goals and allowed feelings, the child is likely to develop a "false self," an overcompliant striving, tied into the motivations and constraints of the superego but cut off from the child's own centers of feeling, experiencing, or strong desiring. Such children are severed from their own sense of evaluation and self-chosen agency. Shame is the consequence of "war in the autonomous zone." Even under the best of parenting circumstances some significant measure of shame—the feeling of inadequacy, of being empty, of being "damaged goods," of being pervasively "bad" or "worthless," will result. In situations of abuse or excessively controlling parenting of the "double bind" sort—what Alice Miller calls "poisonous pedagogy"—severe distortions can result.

Much of what the Christian churches have identified as guilt can be better understood as shame. Guilt is an emotion that emerges developmentally after shame. Guilt presumes enough differentiation of the child's selfhood from the maternal and parental matrix to allow him or her to make a distinction between judgments of specific acts or infractions—for which one properly feels guilt—and indiscriminate evaluations of the worth, the goodness or badness, of the child in his or her very being. This latter feeling of global judgment and devaluation is the experience of shame. Shame, in this sense, is a central dynamic in most of the addictive behaviors and patterns of codependence that we see at epidemic levels in our society at present.

McFague addresses, in the manner of creation spiritualities across the centuries, the initial affirmation of the goodness of *all* being as part of God's gracious creation.[18] What I find distinctive about her development of the model of God the lover, however, is her reworking of "saving" and "healing" in terms of God the lover's radical, personally transforming affirmation, "You are valuable beyond all imagining!" She explicitly downplays forgiveness and redemption, the salvific acts most appropriate to the guilt arising from self-conscious willful choices to act unjustly against God or the neighbor in a way one knows to be wrong. Instead, she focuses on "saving" and "healing" through the affirmation in personal address that we "are loved by God with the greatest love we can imagine—the love that loves us not in spite of who we are but because of who we are." In a way that undercuts all the origins and dynamics of shame, God the lover communicates "that the beloved is not evil but is loving wrongly. . . . We are loved deeply and passionately by the power whose love pulses through the universe," and we want "to return the love, [want] to be one with the lover" (p. 144).

I suggest that the interpersonal model of God the lover, addressing and healing the bases of shame that arise out of our differentiation from the maternal (parental) matrix, correlates with the developmental period of transition from adolescence to young adulthood. In adolescence we first begin to incorporate the full human capacities for self-reflective consciousness and for seeing ourselves as others, including God, see us. Here the struggle is for identity, a sense of coherent unity among the different roles we play, and a first sense of integrity. In adolescence the struggle for a sense of assured worth must come to terms with the deep residues of shame that resulted from the early childhood move into differentiation, first consciousness, and selfhood. Experiences of affirmation and the confirmation of worth in adolescence open the way for the movement in young adulthood toward the kind of intimacy in which one can offer the self to others without shame and enter into the full nondefensive love of the other.[19]

With the model for the third person of God in McFague's Trinitarian theology—God the friend (Spirit), we see the emergence of a full-orbed reliance upon the root-metaphor of *covenant*. Covenant recognizes that we live by promise making and promise keeping. It recognizes that we are born into communities and cultures constructed around beliefs and values, and that to become fully participating members is to affirm and assent to those commitments.

The covenant metaphor, properly speaking, operates in the domain of adulthood. The form of love expressed in convenant friendship is *philia*. Unlike the love of parent or the love of lovers, the love associated with friendship is not a biological necessity. We can live and breed without friendship. According to C. S. Lewis, "Friendship is . . . the least *natural* of loves; the least instinctive, organic, biological, gregarious, and necessary."[20] There-fore, friendship alone, among human relationships, exists outside the bounds of duty, function, or office. At the center of friendship, its power and mystery, is the fact that of all our relationships it is the most free.

McFague identifies three paradoxes in the understanding of friendship as a relationship. I spell out these paradoxes here, in brief, because they—and indeed this entire discussion of God the friend—have special importance as background for the model of church presented in chapter 6. First, there is the paradox that in a free relationship, bonding occurs. "Once chosen, a bond is created that is one of the strongest bonds: the bond of trust." McFague, in ways that echo the teachings of Josiah Royce and H. Richard Niebuhr, goes on to point out that the bonding of friendship is deepened and ratified by a mutual commitment, between friends, to some absorbing interest they have in common.

> Such friendship is no longer just delight in another but is now delight together in something, some vision or project, that unites the friends. Thus, the Quakers, known as the Society of Friends, illustrate this motif in friendship of engagement in a work that is sustained by a common vision. Likewise, the covenant between Yahweh and Israel can be understood as a common vision or project to which each was committed and which join the partners, the friends, together. Or again, friendship between God and human beings in our time can be seen as focused on a common project: the salvation, the well-being of the earth. (p. 163)

McFague's second paradox associated with friendship states that in a relationship between two people that is based on commit-ment to a common vision an inclusive element is implied: commit-ment to a common vision is not exclusive and therefore not limited to two parties. Again, this paradox has critical significance for the vision of church offered later in this book. The friends who join together in mutual commitment to a common cause must have similar vision but not necessarily similar minds. Shared commit-ments can unite persons of diverse ages, backgrounds, abilities, and gifts. McFague points out, "One can, at least theoretically, be friends with anyone across the barriers of gender, race, class, nationality, age, creed. . . . Likemindedness is not the only kind of attraction; difference has its delights as well." And if all life, including nonhuman as well as human, is basically relational, then there are ways of being friends across species barriers, as well. "We can be friends with other forms of life in our world— and we can be friends with God" (pp. 163–64).

The third paradox associated with friendship says that in a relationship often celebrated in relation to children, adult characteristics are required. In her development of this paradox we see the working out, in explicit ways, of the implicit developmentalism I pointed up earlier in this section in my discussion of the root-metaphors underlying McFague's three models for God. I quote her at length:

> Children are obviously dependent upon parents, and even the beloved is dependent on being valued by the lover, but friends are mutually interdependent in a way characteristic of adults. Part of what we mean by becoming adult is being ready to take on responsibilities, being able to share in the work of the world rather than being sustained by others. . . . It is, above all, our willingness to grow up and take responsibility for the world that the model of friend underscores. . . . God the lover of the world gave us the vision that God finds the world valuable and desires its wounds healed and its creatures free; God as friend asks us, as adults, to become associates in that work. The right name for those involved in this ongoing sustaining, trustworthy, committed work for the world is neither parents not lovers, but friends. (p. 165)

The characteristic pattern of action of God the friend is *sustaining*. McFague looks for indications of the kind of world that God's sustaining envisions. She finds clues in the central role of shared meals in the biblical tradition, and especially in Jesus' ministry:

> Whether one thinks of Jesus's table fellowship, the feeding of the thousands, the parables of the prodigal son or the great supper, the last supper and the agape feasts of the early church, the recognition of the stranger on the road to Emmaus in the breaking of bread, Paul's insistence on inclusiveness at meals, or the heavenly banquet in the kingdom, the importance of shared meals can scarcely be overstated. The shared meal among friends suggests some clues to the kind of community we seek: it is a joyful community; it is an inclusive fellowship; it is concerned with basic needs. (p. 172)

Building from this metaphor of the shared meal, McFague draws out a number of implications for those who would be friends of God. For example, she points up the paradox that in this tradition of the shared meal for friends, the stranger is welcome. Present in both the Hebrew and the Greek roots of Western culture is a tradition of recognizing the interchangeability of the roles of host and stranger. In the biblical tradition and in the early Christian practices of hospitality one of the characteristics "is the unexpected presence of God in ordinary exchanges between human beings—and especially in exchanges with the stranger, the outcast, the outsider" (p. 173).

These clues from the Christian tradition open out into indications for the ethics deriving from friendship with God, namely, *companionship*. Such an orientation points toward extending the welcoming of the stranger to form a fellowship of friendship based on shared loyalty to a common vision uniting all who love God's world. Such a community will overcome the extreme xenophobia —that fear of the collective stranger—that leads to the maintenance of nuclear arsenals. It will lead to the "deprivatization of friendship": "What is usually seen as a personal relationship between two (or a few) is politicized and becomes a model for public policy" (pp. 176, 178). Finally, with this powerful model of God as friend to sustain them, Christians may go about their work of feeding, healing, and liberating the world. They find that prayer becomes both natural and necessary:

> We ask God, as one would a friend, to be present in the joy of our shared meals and in the sufferings of the strangers; to give us courage and stamina for the work we do together; to forgive us for lack of fidelity to the common vision and lack of trust in divine trustfulness. Finally, we ask God the friend to support, forgive, and comfort us as we struggle together to save our beleaguered planet, our beautiful earth, our blue and green marble in a universe of silent rock and fire. Just as betrayal is the sin of friendship in which one hands over the friend to the enemy, so intercessory prayer is the rite of friendship in which one hands over the friend to God. When we pray for our friend the earth, for whose future we fear, we hand it over not to the enemy but to the Friend who is freely, joyfully, and permanently bonded to this, our beloved world. The model of God as friend defies despair. (pp. 179–80)

SOME CHALLENGES FOR METAPHORIC,
CONSTRUCTIVE THEOLOGY

In this extended dialogue with Sallie McFague on the *praxis* of God we have explored some of the implications of trying to re-image the Trinitarian God in terms of the metaphors of God the mother/parent, God the lover (Christ), and God the friend (Spirit). McFague grounded her experiment with these metaphors in relation to an imaging of the world as God's body. Though her formulations are bold and at some points undoubtedly shocked or raised questions for many readers, I find that in the main she has sought to remain faithful, in creative ways, to the *regulae fidae*—the rules of Trinitarian faith—as established in creeds and doctrine. Her formulations have sought to account for the presence of God in and through the universe, and particularly in and through the processes of nature and history that provide our "home."

In concluding our dialogue with McFague we must ask, What is missing in this rich, promising effort at metaphorical reconstruction? What dimensions of the *praxis* of God are not so adequately included in this gender-inclusive sketching of a systematic Trinitarian theology? In what other ways must Christian theology try —biblically and philosophically—to imagine faithfully God's involvement with the processes of life in the universe? Of the many things one could address, I offer, as promissory notes, perspectives on three dimensions of the *praxis* of God that seem to me to be missing or obscured in McFague's project.

First, we must find a way to account for and incorporate the presence of God as a structure of lawfulness—a structure intending justice and right relatedness—in the processes of nature and history. Such a structuring can be detected in the lawfulness constituted by the forces that maintain symmetry and orbital integrity in our expanding universe. It can be detected in the laws governing the combining of elements in biochemical processes. Such structuring can be discerned in the operations of the complex coding guiding cell reproduction and determining the genetic integrity of organisms. Such structuring can be discerned in the fundamental conditions of trust and loyalty, mutual regard and ethical sensitivity necessary for human communities to flourish. Such a structuring that intends justice and right relatedness is implied when MacFague speaks about the wrath of God the mother at the violation of the being that issues from her creativity. But there are no "teeth" identified in her discussion of that wrath. There is no accounting for how we do not so much break the laws of God as we break ourselves upon them. There is no accounting for how corrupt regimes collapse as much from internal injustice and contradiction as from external opposition and correction. There is no accounting for the kind of judgment Lincoln saw falling upon both North and South in the protracted bloodletting of the Civil War. I am calling here for an exploration and imaging of a deep *logos*—a structuring of reason and lawfulness that intends justice and right relatedness—in creation and the evolutionary process that cannot be continually violated or flouted without self-injury and destruction. We need to characterize a structural manifestation of divine presence and intentionality in the universe, while honoring and preserving a texture of genuine freedom and randomness at every systems level.[21]

Second, in my judgment, McFague's doctrine of the Spirit as friend renders that dimension of God's *praxis* too passive and too much a function of a kind of multiplier effect on human goodwill. As I read her, there is no way to account for "the very stones crying out" at ecological injustice, the starvation of populations as a strategy of war, or the scandal of outrageous expenditures for the provision of nuclear weapons. God's Spirit must be recognized as "blowing where it listeth." It must be seen as subtle, as in the convergent providence we cited in the background of Martin Luther King and the civil rights movement. It must be seen as resourceful, as in the consequential will of God being worked out in the callings of Mikhail Gorbachev and F. W. DeKlerk. And the Spirit must be seen as creative, as in the roles of the Suzanne Massies of the world, whose creativity and faithfulness help to move processes of transformation forward. Contemporary scientists are leading the way in accounting for what the physicist David Bohm has called the "implicate order," the stratum of spirit underlying and funding phenomena at the level of everyday life and interaction, which he calls the "explicate order."[22] This level of metaphysical speculation by first-rate theoretical physicists is promising for constructing doctrines of the Spirit that disclose its power for shaping consciousness and awakening and directing conscience. Though we should not expect supernatural interventions and overt miraculous deliveries by the Spirit, there is a power of Spirit operative in our world that helps to quicken the forces of decency and goodness among us. Spirit is an elemental factor in the providential "maintenance of the world." This is also the Spirit that comes into play when people are at the end of their own resources for survival and do not otherwise have the courage or the energy to begin again. And there is a Spirit that marshals the resources of the universe to support great dreams and causes when people have banded together and pressed themselves to their limit in commitment, planning, and acting. "God did not part the Red Sea waters until the people of Israel were out in the water up to their earlobes."[23] Even when it seems that a holy one has been abandoned—"My God, My God, why has thou forsaken me?"—the Spirit can bring transformation of life through death. Innocent suffering *can be* redeemed.[24]

Finally, I find McFague's theological account of the divine *praxis* lacking at the point of seriously carrying forward the central thrust of Jesus' teaching and preaching centering in *basileia tou theou*, the kingdom of God, or as I call it, the divine commonwealth of love and justice. There is no symbol or metaphor in McFague that gathers up and represents the power and direction of the transformation God seeks to bring about. With this omission we also face the lack, in McFague's theology, of a basis for illumining and confronting our own and others' embeddedness in the structures of our present economic and political arrangements and the ideologies that legitimate them. There is no leverage for precipitating the crisis of choice; there is no metaphorical power to mediate the power of the Spirit that can lure persons toward the transformation of life. When we do not give adequate credence to the revelatory gestalt that comes to expression in Jesus as the Christ we either yield to a fated waiting on a largely passive God, or we claim inordinate responsibility for being the agents of transformation. McFague's theological beginnings need a strengthening at the point of eschatology and a visioning of the *praxis* of God toward the fulfillment of creation in an inclusive commonwealth of love and justice.

Metaphorical reconstruction of the divine *praxis*, I suggest then, cannot adequately honor what is essential and true in the conviction of the sovereignty of God until it incorporates the following: (1) an accounting for God as the structuring in nature and history that intends justice; (2) an imagining of God as the Spirit who, in many subtle and convergent ways, inspires the maintenance and transformation of the world; and (3) a representation of God as the power of a future commonwealth of love and justice, envisioned and enacted by Jesus of Nazareth, that already is breaking into and transforming nature and history, and that demands our choice and loyalty.

NOTES

1. James W. Fowler, *Becoming Adult, Becoming Christian* (San Francisco: Harper and Row, 1984); *Faith Development and Pastoral Care* (Philadelphia: Fortress Press, 1987). The dissertation was titled *The Development and Expression of the Doctrine of the Sovereignty of God in the Theology of H. Richard Niebuhr* (Ph.D. diss., Harvard University, 1971). In revised and expanded form that work was published under the title *To See the Kingdom: The Theological Vision of H. Richard Niebuhr* (Lanham, MD: Univ. Press of America, 1985; Nashville: Abingdon Press, 1974).

2. This point has been most graphically and powerfully made by Gordon D. Kaufman, in his *Theology for a Nuclear Age* (Philadelphia: Westminster Press, 1985).

3. For a moving and well-argued statement of these concerns see Bill McKibben, *The End of Nature* (New York: Random House, 1989).

4. Sallie McFague, *Models of God: Theology for an Ecological, Nuclear Age* (Philadelphia: Fortress Press, 1987), p. 35.

5. Brian Wren, *What Language Shall I Borrow? God-Talk in Worship: A Male Response to Feminist Theology* (New York: Crossroad, 1989), pp. 119–20.

6. McFague, *Models of God*, p. 19. See also Theodore W. Jennings, Jr., *Beyond Theism: A Grammar of God-Language* (New York: Oxford Univ. Press, 1985).

7. Dennis Nineham, "Epilogue," in John Hick, ed., *The Myth of God Incarnate* (Philadelphia: Westminster Press, 1977), pp. 201–2.

8. Wren, *What Language?*, p. 134.

9. In this proposal McFague anticipated the work of Matthew Fox's similar proposal. See Fox, *The Coming of the Cosmic Christ* (San Francisco: Harper & Row, 1988). I find McFague, however, to be more cautious, precise, systematic, and consistently Trinitarian in her work than Fox. She also more adequately addresses issues of sin and evil in her constructive theology than he does.

10. McFague, *Models of God*, pp. 72–74. These passages have been selectively edited from much longer formulations. I give them a form here that presents them almost as summary principles, whereas in McFague's account they are offered in more discursive and artistic prose.

11. Wren, *What Language?*, p. 202.

12. Ibid., p. 203, quoting Patricia Wilson-Kastner, *Faith, Feminism and the Christ* (Philadelphia: Fortress Press, 1983), pp. 125–26.

13. McFague, *Models of God*, p. 80.

14. The phrase "universal parenthood" is taken from Jonathan Schell, *The Fate of the Earth* (New York: Alfred A. Knopf, 1982).

15. McFague's Vanderbilt colleague Peter Hodgson has a way of formulating the point I am making here that avoids the reifications of maintaining that Jesus as the Christ was of the same "substance" with the Father, resulting in a problematic affirmation of Jesus' uniqueness. At the same time he affirms that the gestalt, or the form and pattern, of God came to unique, full, and revelatory historical expression in and around the life and mission of Jesus and became a powerful living presence in the world through the spirit-empowered witness of the church, formed as the "body"—the gestalt—of Christ. See Hodgson, *God in History: Shapes of Freedom* (Nashville: Abingdon Press, 1989), pp. 186–235.

16. My remarks in the next several paragraphs are especially indebted to Erik Erikson, who first alerted me to the important distinctions between shame and guilt; to Helen Merrill Lynd, who elaborated this distinction in rich literary and biographical examples; and to Alice Miller, whose discussion of the false self has been particularly illuminating for me.

17. For an explanation of "creation theologies" and a listing of figures he includes in that tradition, see Matthew Fox, *Original Blessing* (Santa Fe, NM: Bear and Company, 1983).

18. The question may be raised whether the pattern I have identified here is pertinent for males, but less so—or plain wrong—for females. The emphasis upon separation and differentiation in early childhood may be greater for males, if the positions of Nancy Chadorow and Carol Gilligan are to be taken as established. If so, however, the pertinence of God the lover as bringing recognition of one's individuality and uniqueness and affirmation of worth for females becomes even more significant than for males, in that the differentiation involved comes at a later and more conscious stage of development. Such separation is still, I would argue, an indispensible element in the full realization of intimacy.

19. Quoted in McFague, *Models of God*, p. 159.

20. For a preliminary effort at such a characterization of God as the structuring that intends justice and right relatedness in the processes of the world, see my *Faith Development and Pastoral Care* (Philadelphia: Fortress Press, 1987), pp. 42–44.

21. See Renee Weber, ed., *Dialogues with Scientists and Sages: The Search for Unity* (London: Routledge & Kegan Paul, 1986), esp. chaps. 2 and 4.

22. I was given this statement by my friend Robert Graham Kegan.

23. Though it does so incompletely, the basis for such a doctrine of the Spirit as I am calling for here is offered in Peter Hodgson, *God in History* (Nashville: Abingdon Press, 1989), esp. chaps. 4 and 5.

TWO STORIES OF FAITH

4. Stages in Faith Consciousness

From now onwards, then, we will not consider anyone by human standards: even if we once thought of Christ according to human standards, we will not think of him that way any longer. So for anyone who is in Christ, there is a new creation. The old order is gone, and a new being is there to see. It is all God's work. God reconciled us through Christ, reconciling the world to God's self. Not holding anyone's fault against them, but entrusting to us the message of reconciliation. So we are ambassadors for Christ. It is as though God were urging you through us, and in the name of Christ we appeal to you to be reconciled to God.

2 CORINTHIANS 5:16–20, NJB

We turn now from the effort to imagine the *praxis* of God in fresh ways to examining the patterns of human appropriation and responsiveness to God's self-disclosures in being and action. Here we return to a more detailed study of the stages of faith introduced in chapter 1. We will examine the dynamics of faith as a succession of ways of constructing and interpreting our experience of self, others, and world in the light of relatedness to God. In chapter 5 we will examine the particular way of interpreting and responding to God that takes shape in the life, teachings, death, and resurrection of Jesus of Nazareth. There we will be looking at the Christian story in a new key. Hence I have titled this section of the book, "Two Stories of Faith."

CONSTRUCTION AND CONVERSION: TWO PATTERNS OF GROWTH AND CHANGE IN FAITH

The apostle Paul teaches us that there are two major kinds of growth and change in faith. First there is a process of gradual maturation and reworking of our faith, as when we move from childhood to adolescence, and from adolescence to adulthood. Like cognitive, moral, or ego development, faith development occurs across the life cycle. We alter the ways we understand, interpret, and commit to the images, meanings, and ethical imperatives of faith. This first type of change in faith is represented in the familiar passage from 1 Corinthians 13 in which Paul sums up his reflections on love: "When I was a child, I spoke like a child, I thought like a child, I reasoned like a child; When I became an adult, I put an end to childish ways. For now we see in a mirror, dimly, but then we will see face to face" (11–12, NRSV). Jean Piaget in the writings of Paul!

We hear Paul elaborate on gradual development in faith through the movement from childhood to adulthood in Ephesians 4:11–16:

> Christ gave some as apostles, and some as prophets, and some as evangelists, and some as pastors and teachers, for the equipping of the saints for the work of service, to the building up of the body of Christ; until we all attain to the unity of the faith, and of the knowledge of the son of God, to mature adulthood, patterned on the model of the fullness of maturity, represented in Christ. As a result, we are no longer to be children, lured here and there by every wind of doctrine, by people's trickery and craftiness, but speaking the truth in love, we are to grow up in all aspects into him who is the head of the church, even Christ, for the building up of the church in love. (Tr. based on NAS [modified for gender inclusiveness])

Part of what I will be saying later is that maturity in faith involves reclaiming some childlike dimensions of faith—reclaiming some of the imagination, the wonder, the capacity to be moved by mystery and symbol of childhood. But here in Paul's writings we get a model of the kind of stability, balance, and maturity involved in the gradual growth in faith. He implies a movement from childish understandings to adult perspectives, from egocentrism and simplicity—a first simplicity—to a capacity for firmness, clarity, and commitment to one another in love. This is what characterizes adult faith, in Paul's view. In another place he suggests that this process of maturation in faith is like moving from being "milk eaters" to being those who can eat "solid food" (1 Cor. 3:2). We are called to grow up into being eaters of "solid food," in Paul's language. This is the gradual maturational process of growth in faith.

But second, Paul witnesses to a more dramatic and radical process of recentering in our lives, a process of conversion, a *metanoia*, leading to the transformation and intensification of faith. This second kind of change in faith is a process of transformation, an ongoing deepening and intensification of our commitment to Christ. This dynamic of growth forms in us the deep emotions, the deep virtues or strengths that make it possible for us to be disciples of Christ. This conversion process requires breaking our attachments to false centers of value. It requires giving up our efforts to be self-grounded persons. It calls for an attachment of our souls to God as source and center of life and as lover of our souls. Paul writes from this more radical and transformative understanding of the conversion dynamics of faith in Galatians:

> For you have heard of my former manner of life in Judaism. How I used to persecute the church of God beyond measure, and tried to destroy it. And I was advancing in Judaism beyond many of my contemporaries among my countrymen, being more extremely zealous for my ancestral traditions. But then God, who had set me apart, even from my mother's womb, and called me through his grace, was pleased to reveal God's son in me, that I might preach him among the gentiles. (1:13–16, NAS)

In Paul himself we see a dramatic process of conversion, moving from Judaism, in which he was deeply grounded and from which he was persecuting the followers of Christ, to a vital, total, reorienting of his life in commitment through personal encounter with the risen Christ. I invite you to read again the several accounts of this radical recentering that Paul gives in the Book of Acts. It's very interesting how he shapes his telling of the story to differing audiences to give them what they need to hear in order to identify with his experience. He captures this total experience of change and recentering of life in that passage from 2 Corinthians quoted at the outset of this chapter. "So for anyone who is in Christ, there is a new creation." From that passage and others like it you sense that the re-formation of persons in Christ is "from the bottom up." It is a new creation. The old has passed away; behold, the new keeps on coming:

> It was for freedom that Christ set us free, therefore, keep standing firm, and do not be subject again to the yoke of slavery. . . . Now the deeds of the flesh are evident: immorality, impurity, sensuality, idolatry, sorcery, enmities, strife, jealousy, outbursts of anger, disputes, dissentions, factions, envyings, drunkenness, addictions, carousing, and things like these. But the fruits of the spirit are love, joy, peace, patience, kindness, goodness, faithfulness, gentleness, self-control. (GALATIANS: 5:1, 19–23, NAS)

Congressman William Gray, the majority whip in Congress at this writing, was a classmate of mine at Drew Theological Seminary many years ago. He was the son of a distinguished preacher in north Philadelphia, the pastor of the Bright Hope Baptist Church, and Bill himself now is pastor of that church in addition to being a congressman. I visited that church one morning, and I never will forget his father's sermon. He built it around one of those vivid illustrations that stays with you across thirty years. William Gray II was preaching that morning about the change one experiences when Christ comes into our life. He told about a restaurant in downtown Philadelphia that seemed continually to fail, a miserable little hole in the wall. And then he said he had driven by this place the previous week and had seen a big new sign on the front emblazoned with a new name and a new owner. It was completely refurbished, and the sign said, Under New Management. And that was the theme of the sermon. We are under new management when we are in Christ. That's what Paul is getting at when he says the old has passed away; behold, the new has come—from the inside out, from the bottom up, we are under new management.

Now the dance of faith development in our lives, I am saying, is a dance that has these twin movements: of maturation and development, on the one hand, and of recentering and transformation in Christ, on the other. Faith involves a process of maturation and growth as we move from one season of our life to the next. If we do not rework our faith as we move through these seasonal changes we run the risk of our faith's becoming anachronistic, faith that's out of date in relation to the level at which we're functioning. But that process of maturation is not enough. Our lives' centering and grounding is vital. To what love, to what center of value, to what devotion is my heart given? Where do I rest my heart? What is the source of my hope and trust in life? What calling gives shape and passion to my spending and being spent? Here we are dealing with the question of conversion. All sorts of centers of value bid for our time and energy and attention. All sorts of seductive idols lure us to place our faith and rest our hearts and invest our trust in them. The ongoing process of centering and recentering, of deepening and making integral our commitments to partnership with God in Christ—these are the conversional dynamics of faith. In this chapter and the next we focus on this dialectical dance, the interplay, in Christian faith, of the developmental and the conversional dynamics of faith.

In the present chapter we will look especially at that first understanding of change and growth in faith: the developmental, maturational process of gradual growth and change as we move from one season of our life to another. In the next chapter, we will look at ongoing conversion in relation to the Christian story of the divine *praxis*.

FAITH IN MOTION: THREE VIGNETTES

ROGER

A young man named Roger is speaking.[1] He tells us about his teen years and a family in turmoil. His parents were divorced in a northern city, and the family moved to a southern state. Division tore apart the extended family, bringing anger and alienation. There seemed to be times of recovery: his mother remarried, and that lasted for a time. But then that marriage broke up as well. The family made more moves. His Catholic faith was under stress. He said God was not supposed to let things like this happen to good people. He felt that his young life was in crisis. His way of describing his feelings about God in this period is interesting. He said, "God became lofty, distant, unavailable. The ceiling blocked my prayers. Faith seemed like it was static. There was nothing personal in my relationship with God, yet I seemed hungry for it." And then he said, at seventeen something happened to change things for the better. "I was invited by a girlfriend to a new church. In this community they talked a lot about a personal relationship to God, and I began to realize that I was known by God and loved by God. I felt that God became a friend. I felt that life mattered; I formed new relationships in that community, and I felt I was beginning to walk with God."

This was Roger, describing the passages in faith from his troubled childhood to his late adolescence and young adulthood.

MARIE

To give you a window into Marie's story, I tell it from her vantage point at twenty-one years old. Marie starts by describing an experience in summer camp when she was thirteen. She says, "On the last night of camp there was a campfire, as there always is in youth camp. The dark night sky was beautiful; the sparks rose from the big campfire against the velvet sky; there was music. Different people told about what God meant to them and had done in their lives. We felt close to one another after an intensive week together. There came over me a feeling of unexplainable, universal love. I felt as though nothing human was alien to me. I thought at that time I could even love Hitler if he were there. Out of that experience of closeness to God, I developed a kind of peace and love that I carried with me for the next five years. I seemed to know just what to say to help my friends. They turned to me as a kind of confidante and adviser. It was as though God was in me, a part of me. But then, in the second year of college, I began to see the injustice in our world. I began to be aware of people starving in Bangladesh. I began to be aware of the brutality in Ethiopia. I began to be aware of homeless people in the streets, in the richest nation in the world. And for a year I dated a boy who was an atheist. I could see that he was a very ethical person, a good person, yet he did not believe in any God."

Then speaking about her own present faith, Marie says, "Now God is more remote for me. I no longer automatically know what God would have me say to people. I am committed to Christ and his way. His principles and teachings are the truth about how we should live. But now it's as though God expects me to be responsible. I'm studying psychology, so that I can understand people and their personalities and their needs, so that I can help them and help to make this world a better place. I'm involved in politics and nuclear disarmament and feeding the homeless and the hungry. For me, following Christ's way means doing these things."

CARL, JEAN, AND THEIR SONS

We are seated at table in a northern state with a husband and wife, Carl and Jean. Carl is a seemingly bluff and hearty man, a Texan by birth. He's in his mid- to late forties; his face is flushed; he seems tense and keyed up. His apparent buoyancy seems just a bit overdone.

As we get acquainted he tells us that he grew up in an evangelical Protestant denomination. He mentions the name of his pastor during high school, and we get a sense that he had been significantly involved in church while growing up. When he went off to college and then to the Marine Corps, he says he left the church behind. After he and Jean married and two sons came along, they joined a traditional mainline church, where they have been members for about eight years. Carl has been a highly successful entrepreneur and recently sold the pharmaceutical company he had developed for multiple millions of dollars. Carl is speaking:

"The last year has brought dramatic changes in our faith life. The Bible has just become very important for us. It has become the central thing in our lives. We have become a Bible-centered family." His father, Carl tells us, had been a very strict parent. "He did everything strictly by the book. But it is different with me," Carl said. "I have two fine sons, godly sons," he said. "They set me straight. They tell me when I'm wrong. They make me toe the line." (Carl's choosing this direction in his talk is initially puzzling.) "We are finding that our old church is just not Bible-centered enough. We go there for Sunday school and services and spend most of the day there on Sundays, and it's as though we work all day. Of course we hear a good sermon, but it just doesn't give me any uplift. It's more like another day at work." Then with enthusiasm, "But recently the Lord has put us in touch with some of the most dynamic Christians you could ever hope to meet. They are Bible-grounded, Christ-centered Christians. We are just growing in our faith in unbelievable ways. Actually it was Jean who began our move in this direction. Hon," (turning to his wife) "just break in here at any point and explain," he says, without any pause in his talk.

Carl continues, more excitedly: "When all this began I was in McDonald's one day and some lines from an old hymn I hadn't heard since my boyhood in church in Texas came back to me: 'Thou art the potter, I am the clay,' and I said to myself, That's the Lord telling me, 'I'm not through with you; I'm going to make something of you yet.' But it was Jean who got me into this new relationship with the Bible. Tell them, honey."

Jean, an attractive woman in her late thirties, has blue eyes and wears her highlighted brown hair in a pageboy. She is very trim—almost gaunt. Until now she has seemed to be withdrawn from the conversation, tight-lipped mouth and subdued eyes. Responding to Carl's urging, she indicates, without elaboration, that she has been involved in a women's Bible study group. She indicates that it has meant a lot to her and has awakened her to the Bible. She shows a little more animation when she declares that their old church and its pastor are all right—she expresses appreciation for his good sermons. "But," she says, "there is nothing solid there that you can really stand on."

Someone asked her, "Tell me about the Bible study group you have been attending." Jean takes center stage at this point. "It is a group of women. We gather each week to study the word of God. I believe the Bible *is* the word of God. We do not rely on commentaries or interpreters who put their intellects into the word and say, 'Well it says that, but it doesn't really mean that,' and then dilute the absolute word of God."

Upon further questioning, Jean becomes quite animated. She tells about reading the Book of Romans, taking eighteen months. "We read the whole book. Then we took it chapter by chapter, sentence by sentence, and line by line. We have tape-recorded lessons from a leader who guides each of these steps. She stresses the importance of believing that the Bible is the *inerrant* word of God. For example, Jonah and the whale." Jean asks us, "Do you believe that story is true? Do you believe it really happened just as the Bible says? I do. If I didn't, if I thought it was just a story someone made up, I would be giving up my faith that the Bible is God's word to us just as he intended it and that we can *stand* on that word without *any* doubt." Jean then pointed to the account of the feeding of the five thousand as reported in the synoptic Gospels. "I see this as a genuine miracle by Jesus. You can't explain it away as Jesus' getting people to distribute and share the lunches that they had prepared but were not willing to share. I believe that Jesus took those five loaves and two fishes and, by praying over them, produced all the food and more that it took to feed that multitude of people. Jesus really can and does bring miracles in our lives. I believe that; I stand on that as my absolute foundation."

At this point Carl breaks in, turning the conversation back to their sons: "Their mother is really helping them grow up as godly men—godly boys," he said. "They straighten me out. Let me tell you: my ten-year-old was having trouble with a bully in his class who was picking on him. I just told him," (expressed with surprising anger) 'If he does that again" (muttered oath) "you just knock his block off and fix his clock!' But then the eight-year-old says, 'But Daddy, Jesus wouldn't want him to do that!' "

Jean, eyes shining, breaks into the pause. "My father was an army officer. We moved a lot. I just went to church where my friends did. As a young adult I went to the Catholic church. But I just never got a foundation. Now for the first time in my life I really feel that my life is based on the word of God. It is the absolute guide for our lives, and I just want to share this truth with everyone!"

FAITH AS CONSTRUCTION AND COMMITMENT

How shall we make sense of these three vignettes? How shall we understand Roger's move at seventeen toward a relation with a God very like the one that Marie has given up at twenty-one? What shall we make of the interaction between Carl and Jean and their sons? What will become of them as they look for and align themselves with a community of faith more compatible with Jean's commitment to the Bible as the inerrant word of God? Can Carl adapt to Jean's insistence on the Bible as the absolute guide for their lives? Can he continue to accept the "straightening out" that his "godly sons" administer to him? Will Carl find a vocation, now that he has sold his company, that will satisfy his deep need to have God "make something out of him yet"? As we work our way through a description of stages of faith we will refer back to our encounters with Roger, Marie, and Carl and Jean.

Let us begin by considering faith as a dynamic and universal human experience. Faith understood generically as a human universal includes but is not limited to or identical with religion. One can have faith that is not religious faith. Common examples include communism, materialism, or what some fundamentalists call "secular humanism." A religion, as a cumulative tradition, is made up of the expressions of the faith of people in the past. It can include scriptures and theology, ethical teachings and prayers, architecture and music, art and patterns of teaching and preaching. Religion, in this sense, gives forms and patterns for the shaping of the faith of present and future persons. Religions are the cumulative traditions that we inherit in all their varieties of forms. Religious faith is the personal appropriation of relationship to God by means of a religious tradition.[2]

Just as we can distinguish faith from religion, it is also important to clarify the relation between faith and *belief*. Belief is one of the important ways of expressing and communicating faith. But belief and faith are not the same thing, particularly today. Since the Enlightenment of the eighteenth century many people have come to understand belief as intellectual assent to propositions of dubious verifiability. Or as Archie Bunker once put it, spicing up a quote from Mark Twain, "Faith is believing what any damn fool knows ain't so."[3]

Faith is deeper than belief. We hope our beliefs are congruent with and expressive of our faith. But faith is deeper and involves unconscious motivations as well as those that we can make conscious in our belief and in our action.

In speaking of faith as a generic feature of human lives—as a universal quality of human meaning-making—I make the assumption that God has prepotentiated us for faith. That is, as human beings we have evolved with the capacity and the need for faith from the beginning. Whether or not we are explicitly nurtured in faith in religious or Christian ways, we are engaged in forming relations of trust and loyalty to others. We shape commitments to causes and centers of value. We form allegiances to and alliances with images and realities of power. And we form and shape our lives in relation to master stories. In these ways we join with others in finding and making of meaning. Let us look at these three dimensions of living faith in more detail.

First, faith is a dynamic pattern of personal trust in and loyalty to a center or *centers of value*. What do I mean by this term? We rest our hearts, we focus our life in persons, causes, ideals, or institutions that have great worth to us. We attach our affections to those persons, institutions, causes, or things that promise to give worth and meaning to our lives. A center of value in your life or mine is something that calls forth our love and devotion and therefore exerts ordering power on the rest of our lives and our attachments. Family can be one such profound center of value in our lives. Success and career can be important centers of value. The nation or an ideology can be of life-centering importance. Money, power, influence, and sexuality can all be idolatrous centers of value in our lives. For some persons and groups religious institutions constitute dominant centers of value. All these and many more can be centers of value. And of course God is meant to be the supreme center of value in our lives.

Second, faith is trust in and loyalty to *images and realities of power*. You and I are finite creatures who live in a dangerous world. We and those whom we love are vulnerable to arbitrary power and destruction. How in such a world do we align ourselves so as to feel sustained in life and in death? "The Lord is my Shepherd; I shall not want." That is a statement about alignment with power and the placing of reliance. You could also say, "My stock portfolio is my shepherd; I shall not want." Or we could say as a nation, "The Star Wars missile defense system is our shepherd; we shall not want." Ernest Becker said that in the face of death we all try to build what he called *causa sui* projects, projects of self-vindication, projects that help us have the sense that we will continue on even after we die.[4] It will live after I'm gone. With what centers or images of power do we align ourselves in order to feel secure in life? This is an important faith question.

Third, faith is trust in and loyalty to a *shared master story* or *core story*. In the 1960s Eric Berne offered his neo-Freudian theory of personality growth and change called transactional analysis. One of its key ideas is the notion that each of us in early childhood forms a "script"—a kind of unconscious story that takes form in us before we are five years of age. This script, like a fate, in a sense, shapes and guides unconsciously the choices and decisions that we make as we move along in our lives. A master story is a little like that. It often begins unconsciously, and gradually we make it more conscious and explicit as something to which we are committed. An acquaintance of mine studied prisoners in a federal prison some years ago; he found that of those who had tattoos, 60 percent had tattooed into their skin some variant of the phrase "Born to lose" as a kind of master story.

Unlike the unconscious scripts of Berne and the fated label on the felons, however, a faith master story is meant to give direction, courage, and hope to our lives. It should provide life-guiding images of the goodness—and the Godness—for which we are made. A faith master story shapes our consciousness regarding the character of the ultimate power and reality with which we have to do, and how we should shape our lives with our neighbors in light of that relation.

Faith is covenantal in structure. We are not alone or solitary in our faith. Faith involves trust in and loyalty to other persons. But that trust and loyalty with others is confirmed and deepened by our shared trust and loyalties to centers of value, images of power, and stories that transcend us as individuals and bind us together with others. This is what we mean by *covenant*. Covenant is trust and loyalty, commitment between persons and within groups, that is ratified and deepened by our shared trust in and loyalty to something, someone—Reality, God, or some set of values that transcends us. Faith always has this triadic, covenantal structure.

STAGES OF FAITH CONSCIOUSNESS

As I explained in chapter 1, for nearly eighteen years I and my associates in Boston and Atlanta have been asking people to talk with us in depth about their centers of value, their images of power, and the guiding stories of their lives. We have been asking people to tell us something of their lives and pilgrimages, their journeys, giving us access to how they have formed and are forming their particular ways of making meaning. Out of that work we have analyzed transcripts of over five hundred interviews. These interviews average about two hours each. In the course of an interview the respondent and interviewer, often strangers to each other, experience an unusual kind of intimacy and depth of sharing.

When transcribed the interviews average twenty to thirty single-spaced typed pages. From our analyses of these texts we have identified and continue to refine seven stagelike positions in the process of growth and transformation in faith. Here, in longer and fuller descriptions than provided in chapter 1, we will look at the evolving patterns of constructive knowing that have come to be called stages of faith.

PRIMAL FAITH

We all start as infants, and a lot that is important for our lives of faith occurs *in utero* and in the very first months of our lives. We describe the form of faith that begins in infancy as Primal faith. This first stage is a prelanguage disposition (a total emotional orientation of trust offsetting mistrust) that takes form in the mutuality of one's relationships with parents and others. This rudimentary faith enables us to overcome or offset the anxiety resulting from the separations that occur during infant development. Piaget has helped us understand infant development as a succession of cognitive and emotional separations toward individuation from those who provide initial care. Earliest faith is what enables us to undergo these separations without undue anxiety or fear of the loss of self. Primal faith forms before there is language. It forms in the basic rituals of care and interchange and mutuality. And, although it does not determine the course of our later faith, it lays the foundation on which later faith will build or that will have to be rebuilt in later faith. One can readily see how important families are in the nurturing and incubation of this first Primal stage of faith.[5]

INTUITIVE-PROJECTIVE FAITH

The next stage of faith emerges in early childhood with the acquisition of language. Here imagination, stimulated by stories, gestures, and symbols and not yet controlled by logical thinking, combines with perception and feelings to create long-lasting faith images. These images represent both the protective and the threatening powers surrounding one's life. This stage corresponds with the awakening of moral emotions and standards in the second year of life. It corresponds as well with the awareness of taboos and the sacred and with the struggle for a balance of autonomy and will with shame and constriction in the child's forming self. Representations of God take conscious form in this period and draw, for good or ill, on children's experiences of their parents or other adults to whom they are emotionally attached in the first years of life.[6] Such representations express the emotional orientation of children toward their world and the leeway, dependability, and support—or their opposites—that it offers them. If we are able to remember this period of our lives, we have some sense of how important it is, both positively and negatively, in the formation of our lifelong orientations in faith. When conversion experiences occur at later stages in one's life, the images formed in this stage have to be reworked in some important ways.

Some of the dynamics of this stage can be highlighted in a crisis case involving Julie, a four-year-old whose mother had been recently killed in an automobile accident.[7] The following is part of a longer conversation between the minister of her church—where her mother had sung in the choir—and Julie. The minister visited Julie and her father regularly after the accident. He and Julie would often sit on the floor in the family room and build things with small wooden blocks while they talked.

JULIE: Why did God take away my mommy to heaven?

MINISTER: That's a hard one to answer, Julie. When your mommy was hurt so badly in the car accident she was in a lot of pain. Maybe God did not want her to hurt so much, so he took her to be with him in heaven.

JULIE: But why did God make that man run into my mommy's car?

MINISTER: I guess I don't think that God made that happen, Julie. Sometimes things happen that God doesn't do. I think he probably felt very sad when your mommy was hurt.

JULIE: When Tabby died [the family cat] Mommy said that God took her to heaven. Didn't he take Mommy away too? I want her back. Why doesn't God bring her back?

In her Intuitive-Projective pattern of faith Julie does not distinguish between fact and fantasy. God took away Tabby; God took away Mommy; God could bring her back; God caused the other driver to run into her mother. Her imagination is not yet bound by reason in sorting out why things happen, yet her young mind stretches outward to find some sort of meaning. For Julie her mother both mediated cultural and religious understandings of God to her and *was* her God, in terms of emotional attachment. As yet, Julie's God representation is a fragile construction that rests on the support of significant others who embody, if only partially, the characteristics of God that she is beginning to form. Will Julie's emotional and cognitive relationship with God die along with her mother? Or will God become a kind of maternal figure who represents the possibility of a continued relationship with her dead mother? That she is willing to use religious language, even at age four, is a strong indication that she will struggle to make sense of her mother's death in terms of how she understands God.

MYTHIC-LITERAL FAITH

The emergence of the Mythic-Literal stage of faith comes in the elementary-school years and beyond. Here concrete operational thinking—the developing ability to think logically—emerges to help us order the world with categories of causality, space, time, and number. We now can sort out the real from the make-believe, the actual from fantasy. We can enter into the perspectives of others, and we become capable of capturing life and meanings in narrative and stories.

Some of the dynamics of the Mythic-Literal stage of faith—and its limits—become visible when we look at the struggles of twelve-year-old Charlie, a boy from a religious family. Charlie had asked his parents some questions about God but then had backed off, refusing to discuss the matter further with them. As he moved toward the confirmation class in his church, his youth minister scheduled an interview with Charlie as part of his usual way of coming to know the confirmands and their religious backgrounds. The parents mentioned their concern about Charlie's earlier questions and withdrawal to the youth minister, who listened with special care to what Charlie shared about God.

During the interview it did become clear that Charlie was experiencing a crisis of sorts. His Mythic-Literal understanding of God's activity in the world was breaking down in the face of a newly emerging recognition of the seeming incompatibility between the findings of science and his own religious beliefs. Here is a part of the interview dialogue:

MINISTER: Suppose a person came from another planet and did not know anything about God. What would you tell that person?

CHARLIE: I'd tell them that he was the creator and everything. He created the universe and all that. And I'd probably show them the Bible.

MINISTER: Do you think that everyone believes those sorts of things?

CHARLIE: No, not everybody believes that God created the world. Sometimes I wonder if I even believe it. We've been studying evolution in school, and I can't understand how what we're studying there and what my Sunday school teachers say to me about Adam and Eve can really be true.

MINISTER: Do you worry about that?

CHARLIE: Sometimes. I'm afraid if I don't believe then the Spirit of the Lord won't be with me anymore.[8]

At various points in the interview, Charlie gave indications of a predominantly Mythic-Literal faith stance. For example, after he spontaneously brought up the topic of heaven and was asked to describe it, he responded by saying, "I think it's way, way out in space . . . circling all the galaxies and all that." Likewise, hell was described as being "in the middle of the earth, and they say it's just fire." But now his Mythic-Literal faith was crumbling, and with some deep emotional consequences. Earlier in the interview Charlie expressed his fear that the "Spirit of the Lord" would no longer be with him. This proved to be a recurrent theme in the interview. When asked what sorts of things made him feel bad, Charlie replied, "When I've disappointed God. When I do things or say things or think things that I shouldn't." The interview continued:

MINISTER: What happens when we really disappoint him?

CHARLIE: He takes his Spirit out of you.

MINISTER: Has that ever happened to you?

CHARLIE: Yeah.

MINISTER: When does it happen?

CHARLIE: Different times. There's this song that we're singing in choir. It's a beautiful song. It's weird. It makes me sort of, my eyes start watering and all . . . I feel really empty. It's called "Here Am I, Send Me," and it's just like asking God to send me into his hands or something.

MINISTER: I wonder why that makes you feel empty?

CHARLIE: It makes me feel like he's left me . . . like I'm not as close to God as I used to be. I don't know if he's going to send me. I don't know what I think about him anymore.

Charlie is experiencing the beginning of a shift in the way he structures and relates to his centers of value and meaning. In his own way, Charlie is experiencing the void. We can see parallels between Charlie's experiences and those of Roger, who in this same period of his life experienced the breakup of his family and remembered that God "became lofty, distant, unavailable." What may not be so apparent at first glance is the way the structuring qualities of the Mythic-Literal stage also underlay Jean's deep attachment to the Bible as the inerrant word of God, and as the absolute foundation on which she can stand. In her total commitment to a literal dependence upon the Bible she has found the foundation her life never had before. This foundation fulfills both emotional and cognitive needs. The continuation of her marriage to Carl, in many ways, seems to depend upon his willingness to join her in this commitment to a Bible-centered family life and to the rearing of godly sons. What will happen when their boys begin to have to deal with the issues Charlie and Roger faced? And how will Carl, so hungry for vocation and seemingly so devoted to her, adhere to the emotional and cognitive fixity of her leadership in the family's life of faith?

SYNTHETIC-CONVENTIONAL FAITH

The next stage characteristically begins to take form in early adolescence. The emergence of formal operational thinking opens the way for reliance upon abstract ideas and concepts for making sense of one's world. The person can now reflect upon past experiences and search them for meaning and pattern. At the same time, concerns about one's personal future—one's identity, one's work, career, or vocation—and one's personal relationships become important. These new cognitive abilities make possible mutual interpersonal perspective taking. Here in friendship or the first intimacy of "puppy love" young persons begin to be aware of the mirroring of self provided by the responses of the persons whose feelings about them matter. "I see you seeing me: I see the me I think you see." As we begin to have the burden and the possibility of seeing ourselves as others see us, we face in conscious ways the struggle for identity. We begin to struggle with the task of integrating into a unity the multiple experiences of self brought by our being mirrored in relation to the range of different persons who are important in our lives. At the same time we begin to construct an awareness of our *interiority* and that of others. We are newly and deeply interested in "personality." New steps toward interpersonal intimacy and relationship are taken.

These newly personal relations with significant others correlate with a hunger for a personal relation to God in which we feel ourselves to be known and loved in deep and comprehensive ways. Roger's story reflects this when at seventeen he found a church community that invited him to this kind of personal relation to God and he began to experience the "friendship" of God. Marie's account of her early adolescent relation with God seems even more profound. Apparently her experience of God at the campfire—and in other contexts in her adolescence—led to a sense of a deep integration of God into her personality, so that for years afterward she "seemed to know just what to say to help [her] friends." It was, she said, "as though God was in me, a part of me."

Parallel with the task of integrating a set of images of the self into a sense of identity, the person forming Synthetic-Conventional faith must form a set of beliefs, values, and commitments that provide orientation and courage for living. This shaping of a worldview and its values proceeds as adolescents encounter persons and contexts that offer stories, ideals, belief systems, rituals, disciplines, and role models that can capture and fund their imaginations and hunger for adult truth. A culture is in deep jeopardy when it no longer can provide encounters for young people with persons and communities who can satisfy the need for role models committed to lives of truth. Synthetic-Conventional faith, in such a culture, risks becoming a tacit amalgamation of values, commended subliminally by the advertising industry, and coupled with an unthinking allegiance to the empty dogma that all values are individual choices and therefore relative. Every adolescent deserves a viable and vital Synthetic-Conventional ethos for the formation of faith.

INDIVIDUATIVE-REFLECTIVE FAITH

In this next stage two important movements have to occur. On the one hand, to move into the Individuative-Reflective stage, we have to question, examine, and reclaim the values and beliefs that we have formed to that point in our lives. They become explicit commitments rather than tacit commitments. "Tacit" here means unconsidered, unexamined, uncritically approved. "Explicit" means consciously chosen and critically supported commitments.

This making explicit our commitments usually involves a "demythologizing" movement. In a way that parallels the Enlightenment of the eighteenth century, we engage in critical analysis and reflection upon the symbols, rituals, myths, and beliefs that mediate and express our traditions of faith. Through such analysis we interrogate their meanings and try to translate them into conceptual formulations. In doing so, we gain clarity about our faith; we gain precision in our understanding and its articulation. At the same time, however, we lose our availability to some of the power of symbol, myth, and ritual to mediate our relatedness to the holy.

This critical and reflective examination of faith heritage does not mean that one must give up being an Episcopalian Christian, or an Orthodox Jew, or a Sunni Muslim. But it does mean that now one maintains that commitment and identity by choice and explicit assent rather than by unconscious formation and tacit commitment. In John Westerhoff's adaptation of faith development theory he names this dynamic of the Individuative stage "owned faith."

In the other move that this stage requires, persons have to claim what I call an "executive ego." In the previous stage, the Synthetic-Conventional, one could say that a person's identity is largely shaped by her or his roles and relationships. In that stage, "I am my roles and relationships." My "I" is defined by the composite of the roles I play and relations in which I derive and maintain my identity. In moving to the Individuative-Reflective stage, one has to face and answer such questions as, Who am I when I'm not defined by being my parents' son or daughter? Who am I when I'm not defined by being so-and-so's spouse? Who am I when I'm not defined by the work I do? Who is the "I" that *has* those roles and relations but is not fully expressed by any one of them?

The actors in classical Greek drama wore big wooden masks. One actor, employing several masks, would play multiple parts in a given play. The mask or "face" was called a *prosopon*, which translated into Latin became *persona*. So when today we speak about the *dramatis personae* in a play, these are the "masks," the "faces," the characters in the play. By the time we are adolescents, we have a number of different characters we play in the drama of our lives. The task of the Individuative stage is to put in place an "executive ego"—the "I" who manages and "has" all these roles and relations yet is not fully expressed in any one of them. It means taking charge of one's own life in a new way. It means claiming a new quality of reflective autonomy and responsibility. This doesn't necessarily mean "individualism," though in this society the task is often interpreted in individualistic ways. It does mean the critical exercise of responsibility and choice as regards the communities one will belong to. In making such choices one also excludes other options, so there is a kind of dichotomizing, either-or quality to the commitments of this stage.

Marie's account of what she is experiencing at twenty-one gives us a window into the transition into the Individuative-Reflective stage. Testifying that God now seems more remote to her, she speaks from a perspective in which the world has lost much of its enchantment. She states her allegiance to Christ and his way in terms of the principles and teachings that lead her to political responsibility and preparation for vocational living in which she can "help them and make this world a better place." Her forming clarity about identity, beliefs, commitments, and vocation seem to have required that she experience a kind of "exile" from the intimate relationship with God that sustained her with such assurance during her teen years.

My sense is that Carl, in his forties and just having sold the enterprise that absorbed most of his time, attention, and aspiration in the first half of his adulthood, is also poised to deal with the questions—and the call to vocation—that are intrinsic to the Individuative-Reflective stage. Though he has been an "executive," it seems likely that he has not yet deeply faced the question of who he is apart from the roles of breadwinner, entrepreneur, husband, churchman, father, ex-Marine—all understood in fairly conventional ways. Carl seems to be floundering for identity now that his chief executive role is gone. Perhaps he feels that Jean's absorption in her Bible study and close rearing of their boys leaves little room for their relationship, as well. For these reasons he is vulnerable to deep pulls as Jean recruits him so powerfully to join her in the "Bible-centered" family life she aspires to on the strength of the directive teaching she gets from the tapes and her women's group. His anger and frustration, largely concealed from himself, suggest that deeper urgings for integrity and the lure to present himself to God in vocation may make it hard for him to "submit" for long to his wife's type of church.[9]

CONJUNCTIVE FAITH

At mid-life or beyond we frequently see the emergence of the stage we call Conjunctive faith. This stage involves the embrace and integration of opposites or polarities in one's life. What does this abstract language mean? It means realizing in one's late thirties, forties, or beyond that one is both young and old, and that youth and age are held together in the same life. It means recognizing that we are both masculine and feminine, with all the meanings those characterizations have in our particular culture. It may mean reintegrating our masculine and feminine modalities. It means coming to terms with the fact that we are both constructive people and, inadvertently, destructive people. Paul captured this in Romans 7 when he said, "For I do not do the good I want, but the evil I do not want is what I do. . . . Who will rescue me from this body of death?" (19, 24, NRSV).

There are religious dimensions to the reintegration of polarities in our lives in Conjunctive faith. Here symbol and story, metaphor and myth, both from our own traditions and from others, seem to be newly appreciated, in what Paul Ricoeur has called a second or willed naïveté. Having looked critically at traditions and translated their meanings into conceptual understandings, one experiences a hunger for a deeper relationship to the reality that symbols mediate. In that deeper relation we learn again to let the symbols have the initiative with us.

The *Spiritual Exercises* of Saint Ignatius have been for me the most important single source of learning how to resubmit to the reality mediated by Christian symbols and story. In my thirties, through the ministry of Jesuit students of mine at Harvard

Divinity School, I was brought into relation with Father Robert Dougherty, S.J., then of the Center for Religious Development in Cambridge. Father Dougherty was an experienced spiritual director in the Ignatian tradition. He was also an insightful student of Carl Jung. Through gentle coaching he helped me to realize that contemplative prayer involves our reversing the usual flow of our encounter with scripture. I had been trained in seminary to approach scripture in historical-critical ways and, as Martin Luther said, to "crack open the text like a nut." Through Ignatian contemplative prayer I began to learn in fresh and powerful ways how to enter the text and to let it crack *me* open like a nut, to read me, and to nurture me. I began to learn to do that, spending about an hour a day with a passage of scripture, reading it with my senses and with my emotions, and then finally with my head.

The breakthrough text for me in that extended retreat was the passage in Mark 6:30–44 that tells about the feeding of the five thousand. Father Dougherty had me live with that text and enter into its narrative. This I did rather unwillingly at first, because that was one of those difficult pericopes I had neglected in my period of theological study because of its lack of historical probability. In theological school we were involved in demythologizing; we did not want to be caught up in first-century mythical worldviews. I entered the text reluctantly, envisioning myself as a kind of anthropologist on the edge of the crowd. As Jesus began to teach, I took notes on what was happening and how the crowd responded.

As the week of praying that text went on, however, I was gradually drawn toward the front of the crowd. Father Dougherty had suggested that toward the end of the week—and the end of the day with Jesus and the crowd—I might try to get in touch with my own deep hunger. "What is the hunger you have," he said, "and what is it you need from Christ, that you can't get anywhere else? What nurturance do you need?" As the shadows lengthened that day, seated on the grass, smelling the people around me, and listening to Jesus talk, I felt myself becoming more and more hungry. I began to be conscious of a deep void, a deep emptiness, a deep hunger. Bob, in his wonderful way of putting it, had earlier told me, "Your desolation is as important as your consolation; your times of depression or of emptiness or of hunger are as important as your times of fullness and ecstasy. Move into that pain." Following that guidance, I moved into the void of my deep emptiness and interrogated it. Absorbed in it, I probed to discern what I was hungry for, to name the shape of my emptiness.

Then I began to get in touch with the realization that I was hungry for a priest. I thought about those who had priested me in my live; I had been blessed with good priests. None of them now, however, could provide what I needed. What did I need? I needed someone who knew God better than I could know God, and who knew me better than I could know myself, and who could bring those two together. And it broke in me with a power that I'll never forget, "That's who Jesus Christ is. The mediator who knows God better than I know God, and who knows me better than I know myself, and who can bring these two together—the great high priest."

In this stage it becomes important to let biblical narrative draw us into it and let it read our lives, reforming and shaping them, rather than our reading and forming the meanings of the text. This marks a second naïveté as a means of entering into narratives, rituals, and symbols.

UNIVERSALIZING FAITH

Beyond paradox and polarities, persons in the Universalizing stage are grounded in a oneness with the power of being or God. Their visions and commitments seem to free them for a passionate yet detached spending of the self in love. Such persons are devoted to overcoming division, oppression, and violence, and live in effective anticipatory response to an inbreaking commonwealth of love and justice, the reality of an inbreaking kingdom of God.

As I understand it, the Universalizing stage of faith is a kind of completion of a process of decentering from self that begins in childhood with the Mythic-Literal stage with its advent of simple perspective taking, where the child begins to see things from others' points of view. Gradually across the stages, that taking of the perspectives of others widens to the point where persons best described by the Universalizing stage have completed that process of decentering from self. You could say they have identified with or they have come to participate in the perspective of God. They begin to see and value *through* God rather than from the self. This does not mean that the self is not valued: the self is included in God's loving and valuing of all creation. But the self is no longer the center from which one's valuing is done; it's done from an identification with God.

In the fourth grade I moved to a new town. The school year had begun a month earlier, and a wonderful teacher, Jeanne Andrews, assigned Tommy McBrayer to be my guide and sponsor as I joined her class. Tommy was a black-haired, brown-eyed, heavyset, pleasant fellow, and we got along swimmingly for the first month or so. I don't remember what happened, but we gradually came to be enemies. I came to hate Tommy McBrayer as genially as any fourth-grader could hate another. In that culture, a small town in North Carolina, when you hated somebody that much sooner or later one of you picked a fight. This led to a physical settlement of the issue.

You don't go into that sort of altercation without preparation—unless you are made too mad and simply can't avoid it. So I used to wake up in the early morning thinking maybe *this* was the day when Tommy and I would fight. I would try to get myself steeled up for the impending conflict. It happens that we never did have that fight.

One morning as I awoke, thinking this might be the day, and getting myself up for the potential encounter, it struck me—I don't know where it came from—that Tommy McBrayer had two parents who loved him in the same way that my parents loved me. This was an entirely new thought for me. It didn't immediately make me *love* Tommy. But it did do something to my hatred of him. Without especially meaning to, I had taken the perspective of Tommy's parents toward him. In doing so I was drawn out of my own angry and injured perspective and could see some of his vulnerabilities and goodness through imagining his parents' love for him.

My story is a very simple and childish one. You can imagine my gladness that our fight never occurred when, two months later, Tommy came down with the dread disease polio. This was before the Salk vaccine. For eight months he lived in an iron lung. This story is a small parable of a much greater decentration from self—a genuine participation in the being and love of God—that leads to a transvaluation of a person's valuing and to a universalization of her or his capacity for care, love, and justice. McFague referred to this quality of love when she wrote about the "saviors of the world" and referred to Gandhi, John Woolman, Sojourner Truth, and Dorothy Day. The persons whom we identify as representing this stage demonstrate that quality of universalizing and inclusive commitment to love and justice in a sustained way. They are, in my language, "pioneers of the kingdom of God." In our chapter on King, Merton, and Marney, we were consorting with such folk. They were persons who lived as though God's commonwealth of love and justice were already reality among us. They created zones of liberation for the rest of us, and we experience them as both liberating and threatening. Many of these persons do not die natural deaths. Their lives make us recognize the terrible structures of opposition to God's commonwealth of love and justice we are a part of and with which we compromise. We and the communities to which we belong do not want to face our collective and personal alienation and enmity toward God. At the same time, however, in their presence we also sense powerfully the quality of humanness and Godness to which we are called.

NOTES

1. All the names given in this section are fictitious, and the details of the persons' life situations have been changed to prevent identification.
2. These formulations are indebted to Wilfred Cantwell Smith, *The Meaning and End of Religion* (New York: Macmillan, 1963), chaps. 6, 7. Also see Fowler, *Stages of Faith* (New York: Harper & Row, 1981), pp. x–36.
3. Archie Bunker, as quoted by one of my students. Mark Twain, *Mark Twain's Notebook*, ed. Albert Bigelow Paine (New York: Harper Brothers, 1935), p. 237: "There are those who scoff at the schoolboy who said: 'Faith is believing what you know ain't so.' "
4. Ernest Becker, *The Denial of Death* (New York: Free Press, 1973).
5. For an extensive and in-depth exploration of the dynamics of Primal faith see James W. Fowler, "Strength for the Journey: Early Childhood Development in Selfhood and Faith," in Doris Blazer, ed., *Faith Development in Early Childhood* (Kansas City: Sheed & Ward, 1989), pp. 1–36.
6. See Ana-Maria Rizzuto, *The Birth of the Living God* (Chicago: Univ. of Chicago Press, 1981).
7. This vignette is drawn from Richard R. Osmer and James W. Fowler, "Childhood and Adolescence: A Faith Development Perspective," in Robert J. Wicks, Richard D. Parsons, and Donald Capps, eds., *Clinical Handbook of Pastoral Counselling* (New York: Paulist Press, 1985), pp. 201–5.
8. Like Julie's story, Charlie's interview can be found in ibid., pp. 198–201.

9. Vocation, as understood here, means the response we make with our total selves to God's call to partnership. It involves our work, our relationships, our private and public roles, and our use of our leisure. It is crucial to think of individuation in relation to vocation and with what our lives are *for*. We will go more deeply into this matter in the next chapter. Also, see Fowler, *Becoming Adult, Becoming Christian*, chaps. 4 and 5; and Fowler, *Faith Development and Pastoral Care*, chaps. 2 and 3.

5. The Christian Story in a New Key

Only faith can guarantee the blessings that we hope for, or prove the existence of realities that are unseen. It is for their faith that our ancestors are acknowledged.

It is by faith that we understand that the ages were created by a word from God, so that from the invisible the visible world came to be. . . .

It was by faith that Abraham obeyed the call to *set out* for a country that was the inheritance given to him and his descendents, and he set out without knowing where he was going. . . . It was equally by faith that Sarah, in spite of being past the age, was made able to conceive, because she believed that the one who made the promise was faithful. . . .

It was by faith that Moses . . . refused to be known as the son of Pharaoh's daughter and chose to be ill-treated in company with God's people. . . . It was by faith that he kept the *Passover* and sprinkled the blood . . . and that they crossed the Red Sea as easily as dry land. . . . It was through faith that the walls of Jericho fell down. . . . It was by faith that Rahab the prostitute welcomed the spies and so was not killed with the unbelievers.

What more shall I say? There is not time for me to give an account of Gideon, Barak, Samson, Jephthah, or of David, Samuel and the prophets. . . . These all won acknowledgment through their faith, but they did not receive what was promised. . . .

With so many witnesses in a great cloud all around us, we too, then, should throw off everything that weighs us down and the sin that clings so closely, and with perseverance keep running the race which lies ahead of us. Let us keep our eyes on Jesus, who leads us in our faith and brings it to perfection: for the sake of the joy which lay ahead of him, he endured the cross, disregarding the shame of it, and has taken his seat at the right of God's throne.

SELECTED PASSAGES FROM HEBREWS 11 AND 12, NJB

I, the prisoner in the Lord, urge you therefore to lead a life worthy of the vocation to which you were called.

EPHESIANS 4:1

The previous chapter began with some reflections on two dynamics of change and growth in faith as depicted in the letters of the apostle Paul. Then the body of the chapter focused on the first of these—on faith as a process of gradual construction and reconstruction, correlated with the processes of cognitive, moral, and ego development. We described and illustrated in some detail the stages of faith that provide names and benchmarks for understanding the course of faith development.

Now it is time to attend to the second of those dynamics of faith—the process of conversion and reintegration of life in relation to substantive centers of value, images of power, and the master story of a determinate tradition of religious faith. As has been the case throughout, my effort will be to set forth this faith dynamic in relation to Christian faith, especially as we have begun with McFague, and others, to explore fresh metaphors for a constructive theology to serve in this our nuclear, ecological, religiously pluralistic, and gender-equal age. With the special help of the poetry of Brian Wren, this chapter invites you to engage in a retelling of the main lines of the Christian story and vision. To begin that engagement, however, we need to weave into this account one of the central bands of color to be incorporated into the tapestry of this book, namely, the theme of vocation.

VOCATION, SACRIFICE, AND BLISS

A fine doctoral dissertation bringing together faith development theory and the hermeneutical philosophy of Paul Ricoeur has just been finished at Emory by a German scholar, Heinz Streib.[1] Through his dissertation Heinz taught me something about my own thinking that leads to this refocusing of the topic of vocation as we begin this chapter on the Christian story. He pointed out that I have chosen to use the term *faith* for the generic and inclusively human approach to meaning making—the theme that we explored in the previous chapter. This, he acknowledges, disturbs may Christian thinkers—theologians and believers alike—who would reserve the use of the term *faith* for describing an explicit and transforming commitment to God in Christ. But then Streib suggests what I believe to be an accurate insight: when I have sought to speak about the life lived in response to God's healing and transforming grace, when I want to speak about life "in Christ" and in active loyalty to God, he points out that I speak of *vocation*. A careful reading of my two most recent books bears out what he suggests.[2]

In this chapter we look at the substance, the content, of Christian faith and its narrative structure. This is an important turn, because we looked at faith in a more generic and inclusive way in the previous chapter. As a bridge to the narrative structure and content of Christian faith, I first share with you some additional thoughts about vocation.

The apostle Paul writes in Ephesians 4:1 "I, the prisoner in the Lord, urge you therefore to lead a life *worthy* of the *vocation* to which you were *called* (NJB). The context of this verse in the letter to the church at Ephesus is plainly concern about congregational *unity*. Here Paul's great metaphor of the church as the "body of Christ" is being appealed to as the purpose and basis for unity in the Church. But it is the premise lying behind the writer's appeal that most interests me as we undertake to clarify the substance of Christian faith and the way it shapes the constructions of our lives. That premise is this: Each of us has been called to a *vocation*, and we are to lead a life *worthy* of the vocation to which we were called.

What is the vocation to which we have been called? How are we to walk the walk of our lives so as to be worthy of our vocations? In order to answer these questions we have to clear away some common misunderstandings in the recent common usage of the term *vocation*. The Greek New Testament term for vocation is the noun *klesis*, taken from the verb, *kaleo*, which means, literally, "to call," and with the noun, "calling." In Latin these terms were translated with the noun *vocatio*, from the verb, *vocare*. From New Testament times to the Reformation the concept of vocation evolved in the direction of seeing each person as ontologically addressed by God and called to a relation of partnership with God. Meister Eckhart, Johannes Tauler, and most especially, Martin Luther made decisive breakthroughs toward the teaching that persons in all places and stations, through service to God and the neighbor, can be in vocational partnership with God.[3] In ways that our conversation with Sallie McFague in chapter 3 made clear, the divine Mother-Parent, Lover, and Friend calls us to partnership and frees us to utilize our gifts and energies joyfully in the service of our neighbors—both our human neighbors and our nonhuman companions in creation.

Since the early part of the twentieth century, however, we have increasingly come to use the term *vocation* in a more secular, flat, and narrow way. We have spoken of vocation as though it were synonymous with occupation or job—the work one does for a living, shorn of any sense of its being part of a calling, and shorn of any sense of its being devoted to partnership with God in joint care for creation. So we speak in narrow and specific ways about "vocational guidance" in our schools, describing activities by which young people are assisted in choosing careers. We speak of "vocational rehabilitation" in social agencies designed to assist disabled people to return to gainful employment. There are much more profound ways to speak of "vocational guidance" and the recovery of vocation.

Vocation is bigger than job or occupation or career. Vocation refers to the centering commitments and vision that shape what our lives are really about. Vocation, rightly understood, gives coherence and larger purpose to our lives. It gives one's life integrity, zest, courage, and meaning. Vocation links us with the purposes of God—or with what functions in our lives as God. Vocation is the fulfillment of the identity process. If pressed far enough, all questions of identity become questions of vocation. We move from the question, Who am I? to Whose am I? Or we move from the question, Who am I in relation to these significant others, who mirror me back to myself? To the question, Who am I in relation to that one who is Creator-Mother, healing Lover, and divine Friend, nurturing, restoring, and working justice in the universe, even God? Sooner or later, questions of identity become questions of vocation.

To be in vocation is to find a purpose for one's life that is part of the purposes of God. Vocation is the response one makes with one's total life to the call of God to partnership. As such, vocation involves our lives in *relation*—our friendships, our family memberships, our love relationships, our marriages. It involves our lives in *public*—our roles as citizens and as members of voluntary societies and our actions for justice and care for the common good. Vocation includes our ways of regularly finding re-creation—the use of our leisure and times for renewal and restoration. It includes our participation in religious community—our lives of worship, study, prayer, praise, and service. Finally, it includes the work we do—voluntary or paid—in childhood or retirement, as well as during the prime years of our adulthood. In vocation all these aspects of our lives find orchestration and coherence as we grow in the devotion of hearts in responsiveness to God. Vocation, as set forth here, involves a *process* of commitment, an ongoing discerning of one's gifts and giftedness in community, and of finding the means and settings in which those gifts—in all the dimensions of our living—can be placed at the disposal of the One who calls us into being and partnership. In this perspective, partnership with God constitutes the core of our evolving identity—the construction of our lives. We are called to an availability and to shaping a way of being that responds and is responsible to some part of God's purposes in the world.

As I reflect upon this matter of vocation in my and our lives in light of the theology and metaphorical constructions of chapter 3, I find that it involves four great paradoxes:

First, I find it paradoxical to the point of amazement that the cosmic God, creator of a universe so magnificent in extent as to boggle the mind, that such a Creator *knows us each one* and calls us into relationship and partnership. Psalm 139 puts this well:

You created my inmost self, knit me together in my mother's womb.
For so many marvels I thank you;
A wonder am I, and all your works are wonders. . . .
You knew me through and through,
My being held no secrets from you,
When I was being formed in secret
Textured in the depths of the earth. . . .

13–15, NJB

Here we encounter the paradox of the infinite and the finite: the high and the low. Here we are invited to see our lives, whatever the context of our service and living, as full of potential significance due to our callings to be part of the *praxis* of God. In our faithfulness and commitment we can be employed in the larger pattern of God's being and action toward the redeeming and fulfillment of creation. Psalm 8 captures the wonder of this first paradox: "I look up at your heavens, shaped by your fingers, at the moon and the stars you set firm—who are we human beings that you spare a thought for us? Or the children of Adam that you care for us?" (3–4, NJB).

A second paradox of vocation lodges in the beginning of the text from Ephesians placed at the opening of this chapter: "I, the prisoner in the Lord . . ." Because of the history of the apostle

Paul's frequent imprisonments we might tend to take this self-characterization literally, limiting it to his actual times in jail. But those actual imprisonments stand as tangible consequences of a much deeper relation involving captivity in Paul's life. That relation had a prehistory in the young Saul's role as a Pharisee in persecuting and trying to root out the adherents of a new sect centered on Jesus of Nazareth as the Messiah. That relation took a decisive turn on the road to Damascus. The risen Christ *captured* Saul on that day, *and in that captivity Paul found perfect freedom* (Acts 9).

The human heart is shaped for captivity. We are made for commitment and loyalty. Our captivities—our *captivations*—are what give us purpose and drive, meaning and motivation. We strive and struggle in pursuing the service of *what we value most*. In being captured by Christ Paul was freed from bondage to lesser gods. Vocation is our call to an allegiance—a captivity and captivation, if you will—that frees us for our deepest service and our most creative investment of ourselves. Here we are in touch with the paradox of a captivity—a *captivation*—that leads to freedom.

The third paradox will come to much sharper focus for us in the next chapter. For now it can be stated this way: it is through learning to *stand* each other in church that we are fitted for partnership with God in our vocations. The awakening to vocation, the forming, shaping, and integration of an identity that includes our relatedness and responsiveness to God, can never be an individual achievement. The church—particularly in its congregational form—constitutes an ecology of gifts and giftedness. Mary Cosby, one of the ministers of the Church of the Savior in Washington, D.C., points to the identification and calling forth of the gifts of the members of that community as one of the primary tasks of its ministers. In church, when it *is* church, we are among friends who know and shape their lives within the Christian story. In interacting and struggling with them in focusing discernment together on what God calls us to be and do, we awaken, begin to form, and launch out in the risks of vocation. In church—when it *is* church—we find support, strengthening, and accountability in our pilgrimages in vocation. Paradoxically, we become true *individuals* in relation to God and the neighbor, through community.

The fourth paradox may be paradoxical only in light of the

excesses of the Christian tradition's captivity to the doctrine of original sin. This affirmation seems most paradoxical when we learn and internalize in our depths that, by virtue of our conception and by biological transmission through the corrupted genes inherited from our fallen foreparents, we are inevitably "totally depraved" and that "there is no health in us." The air this book invites one to breathe is shaped more by a creation spirituality. That perspective acknowledges sin as the refusal/inability to place our giftedness at the disposal of God in a genuine partnership. It sees sin as the result of the anxiety born out of our peculiar human combination of self-conscious transcendence and freedom, coupled with our finitude and awareness of death. It sees sin as the defensive or capitulative inability—or un*will*ingness—to find purposes for our lives that are part of the purposes of God.

Though a creation spirituality makes the following point less dramatically paradoxical, in the light of Christian teachings about self-denial and their moralistic distortions it still has paradoxical shock: *what God wants for us and from us has something central to do with what we most deeply and truly want for ourselves.*

Understanding vocation in this way, you will recognize why I found it fascinating recently to review the wonderful taped interviews between Bill Moyers and the student of myths Joseph Campbell. I especially found it moving to see the tape of their fourth interview, "Sacrifice and Bliss." There Campbell, in his own universalizing way, is talking about vocation, and how what God wants for us and from us is connected to what we most deeply and truly want for ourselves.

In this fourth interview, you may remember, Moyers asked, "How do we know what will give one bliss, and how do we determine how to devote one's life?" Then to make it more personal, Moyers asked Campbell how *he* found his special calling. Campbell answered that he discovered as a young man three great terms in the Sanskrit language, which he calls the language of spirituality *par excellence*. The first term is *sat*, which means "Being," ultimate Being, and our participation in it. And then there's *chit*, which means "consciousness," awareness. And then there is the term *ananda*, which means "bliss or rapture." Campbell said, "I thought as a young man, I don't know whether my consciousness is proper consciousness or not; I don't know whether what I know of my being is my proper being or not; but I *do* know where my rapture is, where my bliss lies, so let me hang on to rapture, and that will bring me to both my consciousness and my being." Campbell, then in his eighties and facing death from throat cancer, said with a twinkle in his eye, "I think it worked."

Moyers than asked Campbell how one finds one's bliss. Campbell answered, in effect, that we find our bliss by following our own deepest intuitions, longings, and leadings. I was thirty-two and already a minister and teacher before I was led to ask about my heart's longings and hungers. As I mentioned in the previous chapter, in contemplative prayer with the story of the feeding the multitude my Ignatian spiritual director led me toward being deeply in touch with the empty places inside me and with my life's hungers. Until then no spiritual guide had ever helped me see that God might lead me through my being in touch with what I most deeply want, that for which I most truly yearn.

Campbell answered Moyers's question of how to find one's bliss by referring to Sinclair Lewis's novel *Babbitt*. He pointed to the last line of the novel, where Babbitt says, "I have never done the thing that I wanted to do in all my life." Campbell commented, "That is a man who never followed his bliss." Then he told a story: Before he was married he had already begun his teaching career at Sarah Lawrence. Having no companion to share the pleasures of preparing and serving food, Campbell ate out virtually every night. One Thursday night Campbell was in his favorite Greek restaurant, where he saw a mother and a father and their twelve-year-old son sitting at a table. He couldn't help overhearing the conversation. He heard the father say, "Drink your tomato juice." The boy said, "I don't want to drink the tomato juice." The father said louder, "Drink your tomato juice!" And the mother says, "Don't make him do what he doesn't want to do!" And the father says, "He can't go through life doing what he wants to do—if he does only what he wants to do, he'll be dead! Look at me—I've never done a thing I wanted to do in all my life!" And Campbell said, "And I thought, My God, there's Babbitt incarnate!"

Then Moyers followed up by asking, "What happens when you follow your bliss?" And Campbell said, "You come to bliss." He continued, "In the Middle Ages, a favorite image that occurs in many, many contexts is the wheel of fortune. There's the hub of the wheel, and there's the revolving rim of the wheel. For example, if you're attached to the rim of the wheel of fortune, you will either be above, going down, or on the bottom, coming up. And you'll never know where you'll be on that revolving wheel of fortune. But," he said, "if you're at the hub (and in the picture used to illustrate this, the hub comes out of the heart of the person) if you're at the hub of the wheel, you're in the same place all the time."

Then Campbell, who must have had an extraordinary relationship with his wife, immediately illustrated his point by talking about marriage. He said, "That's the sense of the marriage vow. I take you in health or sickness; in wealth or poverty; going up or going down. I take you as my center and you are my bliss—not the wealth that you might bring me, not the social prestige, but *you*. That is following your bliss." Then he told how when he taught in a boys' prep school, he used to talk to the boys who were trying to make up their minds about what their careers were going to be. A boy would come up to him and ask, "Do you think I can do this?" "Do you think I can do that?" "Do you think I can be a writer?" And Campbell would say "Oh, I don't know—can you endure ten years of disappointment, with no one responding to you? Or are you thinking that you're going to write a best-seller at the first crack? If you have the guts to stay with the thing you really want, no matter what happens, well, go ahead."

But then Dad would come along and say, "No, you ought to study law, because there's more money in that, you know." "Now, that," said Campbell, "is the rim of the wheel, not the hub, not following your bliss. Are you going to think of fortune, or are you going to think of your bliss?"[4]

Understood deeply enough, I think Joseph Campbell's advice to follow one's bliss incorporates a sense of social responsibility and service. It is of a piece with Augustine's counsel, "Love God and do what you will." The preacher, novelist, and essayist Frederick Buechner, put the same idea in more biblical and Christian terms. I quote from Buechner's *Wishful Thinking: A Theological ABC:*

> There are all different kinds of voices calling you to do all different kinds of work, and the problem is to find out which is the voice of God, rather than that of society, say, or the superego, or self-interest. By and large, a good rule for finding this out is the following: the kind of work

God usually calls you to is the kind of work (a) that you need most to do, and (b) that the world needs most to have done. If you really get a kick out of your work, you've presumably met requirement (a), but if your work is writing deodorant commercials, the chances are, you've missed requirement (b). On the other hand, if your work is being a doctor in a leper colony, you've probably met requirement (b), but if most of the time you're bored and depressed by your work, the chances are you've not only bypassed (a), but probably aren't helping your patients much, either. Neither the hair shirt nor the soft berth will do. The place God calls you to is the place where your deep gladness and the world's deep hunger meet.[5]

Vocation: Finding a purpose in Christ that aligns your life with the purposes of God. For Christians, this involves conversion to the work of God as disclosed in Jesus Christ. We turn now to the substance of life with Christ as depicted in the Christian story and vision.

NARRATIVE AND THE QUEST FOR MEANING

In the previous chapter as part of our discussion of the elements of faith I proposed that faith involves trust in and loyalty to a "master story." Narrative constitutes one of the first and most durable strategies human beings employ for the creation and shaping of experience. This may seem like curious language: the creation and shaping of experience. Though it could be said in more complex and sophisticated ways, this is the point I want to make: from birth (and really before birth, *in utero*) we are recipients of sensory stimuli from the environments that surround and impinge upon us. Very early in life capacities for focusing vision and attention, hearing, touch, and taste emerge in the infant's interaction with the environment. The capacity for "object permanence" (holding in mind the mental representation of objects no longer visually available) heralds the way for the ordering of sensations into patterns. Circular reactions in which babies repeat actions they enjoy for the sake of the reactions they evoke, establish beginning constructions of cause-effect relations. The "possession" of experience, however, the moments when one can begin to be said to "have" experiences, seems to be related to the revolutionary period—around one year of age and beyond, when the infant begins to use words and language to represent objects, persons, and events. The use of pronouns representing the self—*me, I, my, mine*—indicates the emergence of a beginning experience of "self." At ages two and three, when curious children ask hundreds of questions about where things came from and why they were made, the answers given by parents, other adults, and older siblings usually take the form of narrative. When, at the ages of four and five they awaken to death and to the questions of powers and realms beyond the everyday, they fantasize archetypal creatures and scenes; they savor myths, biblical sagas, fables, and fairy tales. Later, as children become capable of mentally reversing processes they observe and therefore understanding cause and effect relations, and as they begin to exercise simple perspective taking, they become proficient at making narratives of their own experiences. They capture, conserve, and communicate their experiences through stories. Stories come to provide linkages with their families and communities, thereby becoming crucial to a sense of identity. Narrative, therefore, serves as the most primal and memorable means we have for ordering and communicating the experiences that shape our personal and collective lives. Our senses of identity and identification, our horizons of personal and collective meanings, and the convictional bases of our faith arise in the telling of our religious and cultural stories and myths and in their enactment in rituals.

The stage theory of faith development shared in the previous chapter is itself a narrative, a kind of "everyperson's" story of faith in pilgrimage. It is told in formal language, focusing on the unfolding and evolution of the operations of knowing, valuing, and committing underlying faith. Nonetheless, in its account of stages and transitions between stages it constitutes a form of story—a story of struggle and transcendence, of suffering, disruption, and loss of meaning, and of sometimes painful reconstruction.

As I indicated toward the end of chapter 3, the Trinitarian metaphors for God's *praxis* offered in our dialogue with Sallie McFague exhibit a certain developmental relation to each other. The move from the organic root metaphors of God the mother-creator to the interpersonal root metaphors of God the lover-Christ suggests a powerful experience, personally and culturally, of the development from an undifferentiated relation to the maternal matrix toward the painful experiences of autonomy. Then the shift from the interpersonal root metaphor of God the lover to that of God the friend represents, in my reading, a shift from the root metaphor of the interpersonal and subjective to that of covenant. To see McFague's work this way recognizes her discernment of a narrative movement in the relationship between God and creation—a movement, at least, in the forms of consciousness by which persons make sense of the divine-creation relation and of the ethical correlates to which that vision invites us.

Now it is time to turn to the question of narrative and faith in a more familiar and accessible way. Given the importance of narrative among our modes of making and committing ourselves to meanings, the question of the narrative structure—the story pattern—of the Christian faith becomes an important issue. As we address the question of the outlines of the Christian story and vision, we are asking substantive questions about the *contents* of Christian faith and about the horizons of meaning, virtue, and passion the story implies.

As I give a brief account here of the major chapters of the Christian story and vision, I will attempt to build upon the strengths of the theological work of Sallie McFague we discussed earlier. At the same time, however, I will draw upon one of the most exciting bodies of hymnody and poetry to claim our attention in the last half of this century. As far as I know, Brian Wren is the first person since Charles Wesley who believes that the Church can be reformed through its poetry and hymnody. A minister in the United Reformed Church (UK), Wren has engaged in ministries of peace and justice. Combining his interests and expertise in education with his poetic and theological knowledge, he employs imagery, produced in part in workshops with laypersons, to compose hymns of striking depth and power. Working in knowledgeable intercourse with scripture and the history of Christian thought, Wren in recent years has also engaged the work of Sallie McFague that we examined earlier. His recent book, *What Language Shall I Borrow?*, weaves together in a unique way the strands of a discourse on theological method for our time and a treasury of poetic expressions of a theology for the nineties and the twenty-first century. Like an adroit teaching chef, Wren alternates in his book between theological discussions of the intent of traditional doctrinal formulations and the criteria for shaping contemporary metaphors, and the presentation of poems and hymn texts that work with such metaphorical reconstructions. I here weave together the narrative flow of the Christian story with metaphors and images from a selection of Wren's most recent poems.

THE CHRISTIAN STORY IN POETRY AND PROSE

IN THE BEGINNING, GOD . . .

Where does our Christian story begin? In my judgment, it begins where the first chapter of John's Gospel starts, "In the beginning was the Word." We can't get behind that beginning point. As a nine-year-old, I asked my Methodist minister father, confident that no one else had ever thought of this question, "Dad, if God created the universe, then" (smugly) "who created God?" I expected my father to agonize and be perplexed and finally say, "Huh, good question." But he didn't. He leaned back and looked at me with a half smile and then said, "In the beginning was the Word, and the Word was with God, and the Word was God. The Word was in the beginning with God; all things came into being through Him, and apart from the Word, nothing came into being that has come into being" (John 1:1–3, NAS). And I said, "Is that all?" I thought it was a kind of cop-out; a nine-year-old didn't respond to that as though it was profound. But as I've lived across the years (forty of them since then) that answer has grown in profundity for me, and I sense that we cannot get behind "in the beginning, God."

Let me share with you Brian Wren's way of talking about that God, a Trinitarian God, from the very beginning:

> How Wonderful the Three in One
>
> How wonderful, the three in one
> whose energies of dancing light
> are undivided, pure, and good,
> communing love in shared delight.
>
> Before the flow of dawn and dark
> Creation's Lover dreamed of earth
> and with a caring, deep and wise,
> all things conceived and brought to birth.

> The Lover's own Belov'd, in time,
> between a cradle and a cross,
> at home in flesh, gave love and life
> to heal our brokenness and loss.
>
> Their Equal Friend all life sustains
> with greening power and loving care,
> and calls us, born again by grace,
> in Love's communing life to share.
>
> How wonderful the Living God:
> Divine Beloved, Empow'ring Friend,
> Eternal Lover, Three-in-One,
> our hope's beginning, way and end.[6]

This Trinitarian imagery, clearly resonant with McFague's meta-phorical reconstructions, conveys a sense of the dynamic, rela-tional inner life of God before the creation of the universe—the *perichoresis* or "dance around" referred to in chapter 3. At the same time it expresses the experiential references of the ongoing human sense of relatedness to the divine creator and sustainer and the lover who heals and makes things right.

As we contemplate the lively intertrinitarian life of God, this mystery of the divine oneness with its three centers of energy, awareness, and centeredness, before there was universe, before there was creation, let me share another Wren poem.

> Bring Many Names
>
> Bring many names, beautiful and good;
> celebrate, in parable and story,
>   holiness in glory,
>   living, loving God.
> Hail and Hosanna!
> bring many names!
>
> Strong mother God, working night and day,
> planning all the wonders of creation,
>   setting each equation,
>   genius at play:
> Hail and Hosanna,
> strong mother God!
>
> Warm, father God, hugging every child,
> feeling all the strains of human living,

caring and forgiving,
till we're reconciled:
Hail and Hosanna,
warm father God!

Old, aching God, grey with endless care,
calmly piercing evil's new disguises,
    glad of good surprises,
    wiser than despair:
Hail and Hosanna,
old aching God!

Young, growing God, eager, on the move,
seeing all, and fretting at our blindness,
    crying out for justice,
    giving all you have:
Hail and Hosanna,
young, growing God!

Great, living God, never fully known,
joyful darkness far beyond our seeing,
    closer yet than breathing,
    everlasting home:
Hail and Hosanna,
great living God![7]

We are becoming used to thinking in terms of the potentials and planfulness built into creation from its very beginnings. But this poem of Wren's invites us to ponder the potentials in the Godhead—or Godhood—prior to the creation of universe. Perhaps the infinite desire giving rise to creation was in part rooted in the expansion of relatedness within God's life that creation promised. This expansion of relatedness promised vastly multiplied and deeply enriched interplay with centers of awareness and spirit, energy and creativity, within but also capable of resistance to the divine being: in the beginning, God.

CREATION

The second chapter of the Christian story has to be creation. In an affirmation of the sole initiative and nonduality of ultimate reality, we are told in the Christian tradition that creation is *ex nihilo*, out of and from nothing. How exciting to read the accounts of contemporary physicists who say that this is exactly right: *ex nihilo*, out of and from *nothing*. Not only was there not some sort of primal stuff that God reached down and grasped and formed into the beginnings of the universe, but there was no space either. Space and matter, as well as time, came with creation. God conceives, and what the physicists call the big bang happens. An infinitely dense nucleus, containing in potentia all the elements and all the forces that will constitute and maintain the balance and symmetry of the universe, releases a primal bursting fireball of creativity. Scientists like Stephen Hawking are trying to move back to the very instant of creation as a way of trying to understand the nature and relation of the four forces that hold the universe in balance and in symmetry. Originally undivided, these forces began to separate in the first milliseconds of creation. Mathematicians have provided theoretical reconstructions back to 10 to the minus 34 of a second of creation. Who can comprehend that? Not I.

Creatio ex nihilo. Our universe is thirteen billion light years in extent and still expanding. There are billions of galaxies. We are not certain whether we share this universe with other forms of life. But what an extraordinary thing, that in such an extensive, expansive universe, there is earth, with its biosphere, its water, its thousands of millions of living species of plants and animals and human beings. Creation and nature, what an incredible cosmic story!

And then there is the astonishing fact that as part of that creation, there should be beings made *imago dei*, beings evolving into the image of God. For the enrichment of divine experience, for the increasing of God's interest and relatedness, for the releasing and expansion of an infinite love yearning to be drawn out and actualized, for God's "good pleasure," a patient, triune God broods over and nurtures the processes by which finite centers of awareness, spirit, and reflectiveness could come into being. In need of eyes to behold the wonders of creation from finite perspectives, in need of ears to hear the sounds of growing plants and crashing thunder, in need of tongues to taste the green glory of plants and skin to feel sunshine and rain, the creative Spirit orchestrated the emergence of our brother and sister animals. In need of finite minds to reflect, dream, invent, inquire, aspire, and name the world, God placed creation on earth at risk by nurturing the emergence of human beings—as partners and counterplayers, as rebels and friends. Such wonders lead us to ask, with Wren:

Are You the Friendly God?

Are you the friendly God, shimmering, swirling, formless,
nameless, and ominous, Spirit of brooding might,
presence beyond our senses, all-embracing night,
the hovering wings of warm and loving darkness?
    If hope will listen, love will show and tell,
    and all shall be well, all manner of things be well.

Are you the gambler-God, spinning the wheel of creation,
giving it randomness, willing to be surprised,
taking a million chances, hopeful, agonized,
greeting our stumbling faith with celebration?
    If hope will listen, love will show and tell,
    and all shall be well, all manner of things be well.

Are you the faithful God, watching and patiently weaving,
quilting our histories, patching our sins with grace,
dancing ahead of evil, kissing Satan's face,
till all of our ends are wrapped in love's beginning?
    If hope will listen, love will show and tell,
    and all shall be well, all manner of things be well.[8]

Creation: The second chapter of the Christian story and vision.

FALL

The third chapter in this story would have to be "Fall." Variously we call it sin, estrangement, alienation, gap, or enmity with God (Pannenberg). I have come to believe that we need some serious revisions of our understanding and expression of the fall. Augustine won too clear a victory over Pelagius in establishing the doctrine of original sin. The power of his argument for a biological transmission of the corruption alleged to have resulted from our foreparents' disobedience has suppressed that long tradition that Matthew Fox and others are retrieving, the tradition of creation spirituality.[9] With its intent to highlight the grace and initiative of God, and its establishing as indispensable the Church's sole mediation of that grace, the Augustinian teaching has claimed its hegemony in both Catholic and Protestant forms. It has functioned as a blunt instrument that indicts humankind as having an unavoidably corrupt nature. In classic double-bind communication, it declares that there is no way for us to avoid being corrupted by sin, yet we are responsible for our tendency toward disobedience, our pride, and our inordinate desire to possess and control the world.

I have come to believe that the double-bind character of this doctrine has made it a major contributor to the Church's consistent evocation of a sense of shame and bad conscience in its adherents. In face of this excess I have begun to call for a distinction between fallenness and *be*fallenness in accounting for human distortion and alienation from our essential goodness. We are seeing a lot of befallenness in our time. Little children have parents who are too distracted or too unloved themselves to love as they ought to love, and the child experiences befallenness, a lack of trust, a heightened anxiety. A child is born to substance-addicted parents and suffers physical, emotional, and spiritual distortions resulting from abuse, neglect, and genetic damage. This is befallenness. Fallenness is when we have some choice about the matter. Because of our anxiety, our creativity, our capacity for self-transcendence, and our freedom, we *will* exhibit fallenness; we will prove to be anxious, defensive, and distorted in our obsession with trying to ground and secure ourselves. But this is not the first thing to say about us. Nor, in Christ, is it the last thing to say about us. Befallenness is not equally distributed in the world. Life chances are not equally distributed in the world. Part of what gives God profound grief and sorrow is the befallenness of God's creatures.

The fall represents our experiences of estrangement from our own essential being, our estrangement from each other, our estrangement from God, our estrangement from our vocations. Though sin is a reality in our lives, I think we have to affirm that when God created earth and humankind and said, "It is good," God *meant* it is good, including us. So the first word about us is not "bad—damaged goods, stained irreparably," but "good, good!" Wren affirms this in a remarkable poem that celebrates the goodness of finite, enfleshed, human life.

Good Is the Flesh

Good is the flesh that the Word has become,
   good is the birthing, the milk in the breast,
   good is the feeding, caressing, and rest,
   good is the body for knowing the world,
Good is the flesh that the Word has become.

Good is the body for knowing the world,
   sensing the sunlight, the tug of the ground,
   feeling, perceiving, within and around,
   good is the body from cradle to grave,
Good is the flesh that the Word has become.

Good is the body, from cradle to grave,
   growing and aging, arousing, impaired,
   happy in clothing, or lovingly bared,
   good is the pleasure of God in our flesh,
Good is the flesh that the Word has become.

Good is the pleasure of God in our flesh,
   longing in all, as in Jesus, to dwell,
   glad of embracing and tasting and smell,
   good is the body for good and for God,
Good is the flesh that the Word has become.[10]

In passing I note, the implied significance *for God* of God's experiencing, through participation in human embodiedness, the joys and sufferings that go with being in flesh. In the popular movie *Cocoon* immortal creatures from another planet placed some of their comrades, who had been put into long-term comatose states inside cocoonlike shells, into specially nurturing swimming pools on earth for safekeeping. When elderly earthlings found the pools and experienced rejuvenation through bathing in their specially treated waters, the life-preserving additive became used up and some of the somnolent aliens died in their cocoons. For the immortals this was the first experience of grief through the death of loved ones. Their tears—new and strange to them—were suggestive of the new tears of God made possible and necessary through God's participation in finitude and flesh in the lives of all animate beings.[11] Wren's poetry suggests God's love and gladness at sharing in the entire range of embodied experience through participation in finite life. It also suggests God's pain and grief—

and wrath—at the violations of flesh brought about through the terrible distortions caused by fallenness and befallenness: the fall.

LIBERATION, COVENANT, AND EXILE

Seen biblically, it is that participating grief and pain of God in the experiences of human sinfulness and the distortions of nature and creation that gives rise to divine strategies of judgment, saving love, restoration, and reconciliation. Here we come to the chapter we can call "Liberation and Covenant." Again and again the biblical record tells us of how God releases God's people from slavery, reforms them as a people of Torah—of Way, Path, Law— and carries them through the wilderness into new beginnings. My old Jewish friend Sam Buchlander used to say, "Yahweh took the slaves out of Egypt overnight, but it took forty years in the wilderness to get Egypt out of the former slaves." Here we have liberation and forming of a new people, a nation of covenant faithfulness, a nation of prophets and priests.

But then we see that alarming pattern of alternating faithfulness to covenant and Torah, and then rebellion and whoring after alien gods. A prophet would be sent to call the people back to covenant, and righteousness and uprightness would be reinstituted. But then the pattern would repeat: falling away, leading eventually to the terrible bondage of a new enslavement and exile:

> By the rivers of Babylon
> we sat and wept
> at the memory of Zion.
> On the poplars there
> we hung up our harps.
>
> For there our gaolers had asked us
> to sing them a song,
> our captors to make merry,
> "Sing us one of the songs of Zion."
>
> How could we sing a song of Yahweh
> on alien soil?
> If I forget you, Jerusalem,
> may my right hand wither!
>
> (Psalm 137:1–5, NJB)

INCARNATION

That pattern of liberation and new captivity keeps being repeated until, in a kind of divine impatience, leading to a singular act of divine creativity, we come to the chapter that we call "Incarnation." This chapter sets the stage for a big story, a story that includes the birth of Jesus, his life, his teachings, and his preaching about the inbreaking of a commonwealth of love and justice. The promise of this story's beginning Brian Wren captures in a remarkable poem of identification.

Birthsong

Her baby, newly breathing,
    with wailing needful cry,
by Mary kissed and cradled,
    is lulled in lullaby.
Long months of hope and waiting,
    the thrill and fear of birth,
are crowned with exultation,
    and God is on the earth.

The eyes that gaze at Mary
    have yet to name or trace
the world of shape and color,
    or recognize a face;
yet Holiness Eternal
    is perfectly expressed
in hands that clutch unthinking,
    and lips that tug the breast.

The milk of life is flowing
    as Mary guides and feeds
her wordless Word, embodied
    in infant joys and needs.
Enormous, formless strivings,
    and yearnings deep and wide,
becradled in communion,
    are fed and satisfied.

How mother-like the wisdom
    that carried and gave birth
to all things, seen and unseen,
    and nurtured infant earth:

> unstinting, unprotected,
>> prepared for nail and thorn,
> constricted into maleness,
>> and of a woman born.[12]

As the story continues, it portrays the encounters with those who found Jesus' teaching and embodying the promises of a new era a threatening message, as well as those who found it exhilarating. In this chapter we are drawn inexorably into the Beloved's collision with the structures of congealed enmity in empire and in temple toward God's new creation. This systemic resistance and hostility is shown forth in the cross with its double revelation. There we see the exposure, on the one hand, of the extent of our resistance, the terrible reality of our enmity toward God, as the holy one suffers, torn and stretched upon the cross. On the other hand, the cross shows forth the extent to which God the lover will go (and does go) to liberate us from our bondage and to heal and reconcile us to God and our true callings. Both the heart-split of the cross and the new world opened by this death and resurrection find voice in "Magnificat."

> Daughter Mary, saying yes
> to the angels' visitation,
>> no disgrace shall cloud your face.
> Thrill us with your expectation:
>> As in heaven, so on earth,
>>> God will work salvation
>> as the child you bring to birth
>> checks the wealthy, feeds the poor,
>>> ends all domination.

> Mother Mary, crying no
> at your son's disruptive vision,
>> he must roam away from home,
> breaking family cohesion:
>> Planting heaven here on earth,
>>> God's new invitation,
>> brings the outcasts to rebirth,
>> lifts the humble, shifts the proud,
>>> ending domination.

> Sister Mary, pierced and torn,
> as the child your arms protected,

> Chokes and dies before your eyes,
> trust again the unexpected:
>   Love has broken free on earth!
>   Tiers of domination
>   tumble as the spirit's mirth,
>   weaving friendship, sparking hope,
>   sings of new creation.[13]

My meditations with Wren occur, as I write, at the point of entry into what Christians call Holy Week, the week leading up to the cosmic wrenching of Jesus' death on the cross. Those whose lives have been formed in the wake of his life and teachings, his suffering death and resurrection, have special memory images of the Thursday evening before Good Friday. This is the night of the Last Supper, when Jesus, in an act of love, solidarity, and servant-leadership, performed the servant's role of washing the feet of his followers. Wren puts us there and puts into words the cosmic meaning of these events:

> Great God, in Christ you call our name
> and then receive us as your own,
> not through some merit, right or claim,
> but by your gracious love alone.
>   We strain to glimpse your mercy seat
>   and find you kneeling at our feet.
>
> Then take the towel and break the bread,
> and humble us, and call us friends.
> Suffer and serve till all are fed
> and show how grandly love intends
>   To work till all creation sings,
>   to fill all worlds, to crown all things.
>
> Great God, in Christ you set us free
> your life to live, your joy to share.
> Give us your spirit's liberty
> to turn from guilt and dull despair
>   and offer all that faith can do
>   while love is making all things new.[14]

The chapter called "Incarnation" is the center of the story, the hinge of history. The paradoxical disclosure in the boondocks of an ancient empire, in a carpenter-prophet, of God's face to humanity—a pivotal, powerful chapter.

CHURCH

With death and resurrection of Jesus the Christ, we come to a sixth chapter, the chapter we call "Church." My favorite account of Pentecost is not the one in Acts 2, where the spirit of the risen Christ became manifest in the burning flames above the heads of the apostles and the gospel began to be preached in diverse tongues. As impressive and as powerful as that is, it is preceded in time and in priority by the account in John 20:19–23. There the assembled followers of Jesus are described as being together on the Sunday after his death, trying to deal with the experience of his loss and the loss of the movement. Perhaps they are meeting in the same space where the last meal with Jesus occurred. Suddenly they are surprised by the presence of the risen Christ. He enters the room. John's Gospel tells about it in this way:

> Jesus came and stood among them. He said to them, "Peace be with you," and after saying this he showed them his hands and his side. The disciples were filled with joy at seeing the Lord, and he said to them again, "Peace be with you. As the Father sent me, so I am sending you." (NJB)

After saying this, he breathed on them, and said:

> "Receive the Holy Spirit. If you forgive anyone's sins, they are forgiven; if you retain anyone's sins, they are retained." (NJB)

In my mind's eye I see something that recalls the washing of feet: he moved around the circle, and there was an exchange of energy with each person in the room. That is what the breathing means, the power and energy of God coming from the risen Christ into that set of our forebears who became the Church. And he said to them, "Receive the Holy Spirit. If you forgive anyone's sins, they are forgiven; if you retain anyone's sins, they are retained." Were I to do an exegesis of this passage, I would suggest that it means that we, as those who have been forgiven and reconciled by God in Christ, are called and empowered to hear the confession of others and help them be reconciled. We are not given some sort of authorization that sets us apart to require that others repent. Rather, we are called to be present as reconciling persons in the world. And if we fail to offer that reconciliation by bodying forth the love of God, the reconciling may not get done. That is what is meant by "they will be retained." If one does not throw up and disgorge what one needs to have heard and forgiven, it is retained and is toxic. In that passage we are called to minister to the world's need to throw up and to be relieved of its toxicity.

This event constitutes the real birth of Church: Christ's breathing Holy Spirit into the body of Christ. Here the Church—and we—take upon ourselves the mission and the ministry of reconciliation, liberation, and healing that Jesus brought forth into the world in and through the incarnation.

A last Brian Wren poem seems to me to catch something of our situation as Church in the present time and of our calling as public church as we will examine it in the next chapter.

> Great Lover, Calling Us to Share
> Great Lover, calling us to share
> your joy in all created things,
> from atom-dar :e to eagle's wings,
> we come and go to praise and care.
>
> Though sure of resurrection-grace,
> we ache for all of earth's troubled lands
> and hold the planet in our hands,
> a fragile, unprotected place.
>
> Your questing spirit longs to gain
> no simple fishing ground for souls,
> but as life's story onward rolls,
> a world more joyful and humane.
>
> As midwives who assist at birth,
> we give our uttermost, yet grieve
> lest folly, greed, or hate should leave
> a spoiled, aborted, barren earth.
>
> Self-giving Lover, since you dare
> to join us in our history,
> embracing all our destiny,
> we'll come and go with praise and care.[15]

This is the mission of the Church: to tend and mend the world, to witness to and enact transforming love and rectifying justice, and to come and go with praise and care.

COMMONWEALTH OF LOVE AND JUSTICE

The seventh, the final, chapter of the Christian classic in its narrative structure is that already in-breaking but not yet realized "Commonwealth of Love and Justice," or as we've called it for centuries, "The Kingdom of God." The Christian conviction about the in-breaking, already-but-not-yet commonwealth of love and justice transforms our sense of time. With Jesus' message we begin to understand that God's creation and dream for the world point us toward the fulfillment that a provident God intends for creation. Here God is the Power of the Future. Each moment in the moving present, and each of the cumulative moments that constitute the past, come and have come to us as gifts from the Power of the Future. Each new moment is pregnant with possibilities for the growth in richness of experience and in splendidly varied unity in which all being will enjoy fulfillment. And the diversity that makes up that unity is part of its greater beauty and contributes to an expanded and universally inclusive *perichoresis*, the universal and cosmic "dance around" of reconciled and fully realized creation.

This view gives us a new understanding of the past and gives us freedom and responsibility in the present. Present and past keep coming to us from God's future. Worship, and in particular the Eucharist, constitutes precisely that time when, again and again, we enter into God's time. Here we are grafted into God's people, and empowered and reconciled for openness and expectation toward the commonwealth of love and justice that is breaking in upon our present, giving us both freedom and responsibility.

In these pages we have rehearsed, with gifts of the poetry of Brian Wren, a version of the narrative structure of the Christian classic—the Christian story and vision as it opens out into a cosmic view of the universe's becoming. We have marshaled its images as it proclaims the central, saving identification of God with us in the Beloved. We have lifted up the horizons and meanings it offers as it orients us toward our callings in partnership with God.

We have looked at the structures and contents of faith as response to God's *praxis*. Now we turn toward the question, What kind of Church is God calling us toward in the paradigm shift that leads us toward the twenty-first century?

NOTES

1. Heinz Streib, *Hermeneutics of Metaphor, Symbol, and Narrative in Faith Development Theory* (Ph.D. diss., Department of Theology and Personality, Division of Religion, Emory University, 1989).
2. James W. Fowler, *Becoming Adult, Becoming Christian* (San Francisco: Harper & Row, 1984); and *Faith Development and Pastoral Care* (Philadelphia: Fortress Press, 1987).
3. See my brief overview of the evolving understanding of vocation in my *Faith Development and Pastoral Care*, chap. 2.
4. The quotes and narrative in these paragraphs on Campbell can be found in print in Joseph Campbell, with Bill Moyers, *The Power of Myth* (New York: Doubleday, 1988), pp. 117–18.
5. Frederick Buechner, *Wishful Thinking: A Theological ABC* (New York: Harper & Row, 1973), p. 95.
6. Brian Wren, *Bring Many Names* (Carol Stream, IL: Hope Publishing Co., 1989), p. 22.
7. Wren, *Bring Many Names*, p. 9.
8. Wren, *Bring Many Names*, p. 5.
9. For an important tracing of the struggle between the Augustinian and Irenaean traditions regarding the depth and primordiality of sin, see John Hick, *Evil and the God of Love* (New York: Harper & Row, 1977). For an overview of creation spirituality, see Matthew Fox, *Original Blessing* (Santa Fe, NM: Bear and Company, 1983).
10. Wren, *Bring Many Names*, p. 16.
11. I am indebted for this idea to Ron Flowers, who preached a sermon in Glenn Memorial United Methodist Church that included these thoughts soon after *Cocoon* was released.
12. Brian Wren, *What Language Shall I Borrow* (New York: Crossroad, 1989), p. 191.
13. Wren, *Bring Many Names*, p. 11.
14. Wren, *What Language Shall I Borrow*, p. 181.
15. Wren, *Bring Many Names*, p. 17.

ECCLESIA

6. Public Church: Vision and Actuality

> There are many different gifts, but it is always the same spirit; there are many different ways of serving, but it is always the same Lord. There are many different forms of activity, but in everybody it is the same God who is at work in them all. The particular manifestation of the Spirit granted to each one is to be used for the general good. To one is given from the Spirit the gift of utterance expressing wisdom; to another the gift of utterance expressing knowledge, in accordance with the same Spirit; to another, faith, from the same Spirit; and to another, the gift of healing, through this one Spirit; to another, the working of miracles; to another, prophecy; to another, the power of distinguishing spirits; to one the gift of different tongues and to another, the interpretation of tongues. But at work in all these is one and the same Spirit, distributing them at will to each individual.
>
> 1 CORINTHIANS 12:4–11, NJB

I came of age theologically in the 1960s. Secularization and the celebration of the secular were themes that buoyed us in that decade, as we sought to express Christian discipleship in sit-ins and marches, in voting rights bills and antiwar hearings, and through writings that celebrated a "worldly theology" for a "world come of age." There was a time when so many clergy had left their parishes to go to work for government-funded community organization efforts that we jokingly referred to the OEO as the "Office of Ecclesiastical Opportunity." During that decade theological school and then graduate studies found me in church but out of the pulpit. And though I frequently found myself defending the Church against its despisers, I certainly had no burning sense that the local church congregation represented the front edge of ministry. Across the years of my teaching ministry I have gained a steadily growing sense of the fundamental importance of congregational life and ministry.

During the last two years my colleague Tom Frank and I have led a small group of researchers in studying three congregations selected because—by reputation, and through previous study— they were recognized as having many of the characteristics we associate with *public church*. In this chapter I give a preliminary description of those characteristics. In the course of coming to know these three church communities my estimation of the crucial significance of what is at stake in congregational life—both for congregation members and for our larger society—has undergone another deepening.

These recent experiences and my work with Tom Frank on a full-length book about our findings provide part of the backdrop for this chapter.[1] My excitement about the congregations we have studied also gives what I have written in the opening part of this chapter a somewhat *rhapsodic* character. We might, in fact, title this first part of the chapter "A Rhapsody to the Congregation." As I played with that title, I looked up the word *rhapsody*, thinking of it as roughly equivalent to *love song*. The dictionary definition says, *Rhapsody*—"A spoken or written work of an ecstatic sort, depending less on logical structure than emotional appeal" (Webster's Encyclopedic Dictionary of the English Language). To begin our reflections, then, I offer you a rhapsody to the congregation. After that we will come to public church.

A RHAPSODY TO THE CONGREGATION

Congregations are strange, wonderful, and unique communities. In our research on public congregations we have seen three such communities:

"Cornerstone"—An urban African-American congregation where offerings of a nickel a week early in this century helped to build and complete a magnificent stone edifice; where special offerings, sacrificially given, founded and nurtured a college; and where the community gathered the determination to confront and end unchallenged police brutality long before the "civil rights" era.

"Saint Stephen's"—A midtown congregation where church women paid the minister's salary and kept the Christian education ministries going during the hard times of the depression by opening a restaurant; and where one woman's bringing sandwiches in the trunk of her car to feed lunch to street men grew into a ministry of feeding, health care, education, and employment assistance involving eighteen hundred homeless persons.

"Covenant"—A near suburban congregation where ministries to Iranian students in Atlanta were launched during the height of the hostage crisis hostilities and where a ministry with Cuban prisoners in the federal prison has been sustained for ten years; where the membership, shrunk by attrition in face of a racially changing neighborhood, covenanted to stay and witness, and buried a twenty-ton stone at an awkward angle in their front lawn to remind themselves, and all who pass by, that they are in ministry to this city and are here to stay.

Congregations are strange, wonderful, and unique communities. Think about some of the dimensions of their uniqueness: Where else in our age-stage segregated era do you have communities where three or four generations interact across age and stage barriers—with children sponsoring grand- and great-grandparent-aged adults and elders sponsoring children? What other communities are constituted as *ecologies of care* and *ecologies of vocation*, where people call forth and confirm each other's gifts and giftedness for the service of God, and support and hold each other accountable in the use of those gifts? Where else will you encounter the generativity and generosity that characterize congregational life at its best—a generosity that has gratitude to God as its motive and approaches investment in others as an opportunity to return something of what one has been graciously given by others? In what other community do people work at seeing each other whole, offsetting the societal reduction of the person to customer, client, patient, student, boss or employee, or sucker in the marketplace?

What other community works at forming deep emotions of goodness in persons—emotions of the love of God and love of neighbor—and tries to shape the virtues requisite for discipleship? In what other community do persons offer outpourings of presence and support, at least in tangible symbols of food and assistance, when there is death, tragedy, severe illness, or relational rupture?

A three-and-a-half-year-old girl whom I know recently told her mother, in the midst of a contest of wills, "I only have *one* boss, and that's God. I don't have to do what you say." But then, a night or two later, either out of anxiety caused by this defiance or just the standard anxiety that comes at about this age when children become aware of death and the possible loss of those on whom they feel absolutely dependent, she woke up terrified in the middle of the night. She was afraid, she told her mother, that her parents might die and leave her all alone. Taking the anxieties seriously, her mother asked her if that should happen what she would do: "I think I'd call the people at the church," she said. She had already learned something of the church as community of care.

Of course I know there is a down side to congregational life: I know that congregations can be petty, stodgy, complacent, and mediocre; I know we can be prideful, petrified, arrogant, and ignorant. I know that in many congregations we operate on the basis of a bland "covenant to niceness," which means, in effect, we come to church trying to look like the person we wish to God we were, rather than disclosing to each other the struggling, needy, ambiguous, bored, and soul-crippled parts of ourselves. I know that many clergy in my denomination and others have developed a franchise mentality that, like tenure in the university, can make security, modest institutional gains, and lock-step career advancement the main goal of ministry, while avoiding the risks, conflict, and spiritual challenge that keep us open to the deep movements and guidance of the Spirit. Looked at from this angle, no one has put it more forcefully than Carlyle Marney, who claimed he was quoting Augustine: "The Church is like Noah's ark: the stench in side is almost unbearable. But," he added, "the alternative is unthinkable." In many of our parishes and congregations our young people are mirroring this down side of congregational life to us. They are voting with their feet. They find among us no joy, no adventure, no risky call to discipline or discipleship—no *bliss*, to use Joseph Campbell's phrase.

But there is a lot of goodness in congregations. They need to be loved and nurtured. They need to be led toward greatness of faithfulness and service. They deserve our lives and our best energies. As we come to look at the patterns of leadership and followership in public church we will see that both lay and pastoral leadership have to be open to transformation in ways that closely parallel our reworking of the doctrine of the sovereignty of God in the new paradigm.

PUBLIC CHURCH: A COMPOSITE PICTURE

"Public church" points to a vision of ecclesial *praxis*, a proposal in practical theology. It seeks to be faithful to a biblical grounding in its claim that ecclesial community, formed by the presence and fellowship of Christ, points beyond itself to the *praxis* of God in the processes of history. It tries to point to and embody a transforming presence in human relations, in societies, and in care for embattled nature. That God's *praxis* transforms toward wholeness, justice, and peace finds witness in ecclesial community as congregations practice their principles of equality, partnership, and inclusiveness, as they welcome and extend hospitality to the stranger, and as they give their lives for transformed human community in particular contexts.

Some contemporary background needs to be sketched as groundwork if we are going to discuss this vision of public church. In 1977 the sociologist Richard Sennett published a book entitled *The Fall of Public Man*.[2] In a method he called historical "postholing" he studied in depth the relationship between the public and private domains in the lives of citizens of three world-class cities, New York, London, and Paris. His time periods were the middle decades of the eighteenth, nineteenth, and twentieth centuries. Sennett argued that across two centuries we have seen a steady but dramatic shift in which public life has been emptied of much of its significance as an arena for participation by the general populace. Increasingly public life has been turned over to the control of professional elites. Intimidated by the large size of our institutions, by the cost and risks of electoral politics, and absorbed by the all-consuming demands of work in the private sphere, many "amateurs" have withdrawn from public life. The political process, now mediated to the public by commercial television, is increasingly under the control of smaller and more insulated elites, with conventions and public debates falling into the category of entertainment for passive onlookers in the privacy of their own homes. The world of work in private corporations, professions, or institutions has claimed ever increasing amounts of people's time and energy. And many of us modern people, Sennett suggests, have come to place more and more weight on the private domains of family, marriage, friendship, and intimate relations as the contexts where our most important life meanings are worked out. We have fallen, Sennett suggests, into a kind of "tyranny of intimacy."[3]

One of the most insightful recent characterizations of the concept of "public" has been offered by William J. Everett. The public, he writes, "is a kind of discourse to which everyone has potentially equal access, whose content is people's common concerns, and whose outcomes are governed by reason and persuasion rather than by force or deception. . . . [T]his public demands some common world of basic cultural reference points as well as material bases and geographical space in order to exist. A public is a peculiar pattern of relationships among people inhabiting this world together."[4]

The sociologist Daniel Bell, writing in 1978, called our attention to the danger of emptying the public square in a different way. In *The Cultural Contradictions of Capitalism*[5] Bell argued that our lives in contemporary society manifest a kind of trifurcation, a division into three separate spheres. The dominant sphere for many of us—the sphere that can move us around the country or, indeed, around the world, and the sphere that takes most of our time and energy—is the "techno-economic order." This is where we work and make a living, and where we contribute to the economy. The techno-economic order has its own ethos of values, its own professional or ethical codes. It is an important crucible in which our fundamental worldviews are shaped and changed.

The second sphere is that which Bell calls the "polity" or "governance." All of us are citizens, and in a democracy we technically have access to participation in governance. As we have already pointed out, however, the domain of polity has increasingly come under the control of professionals. The money required to mount a serious campaign for public office today means that the moment one election is over, major energies must be mounted to prepare the "war chest" for the next campaign. "Citizen" politicians are an increasingly rare and endangered species today. The polity has become a separate sphere with its own professional standards, its own world of significance and meaning, and its own professional elite.

Bell's third sphere in our trifurcated lives he refers to as "culture." By culture he means all those dimensions of our lives where we have discretionary time and where we can use the money we have left over from the struggle for economic survival and well-being. This is the world of family, of friendship, of volunteer service, of the arts, of sports and leisure, and the like. It is interesting to note that Bell also puts religion squarely in this privatized sphere. He claims that religion and other traditional sources of ethics and normative standards no longer have much impact in the more public worlds of the techno-economic order and the domain of polity. Religion, like the symphony, is something one participates in if one has a "taste" for such things. Culture—including religious participation—becomes more and more a matter of voluntary and privatized meanings and relations in which we associate with persons very much like ourselves. Our participation in the privatized activities that constitute "culture" may provide encouragement and support for our lives, but it makes very little impact on our participation in the techno-economic and political worlds. This is the disjunction of spheres in our lives.

It was against the backdrop of analyses like those of Sennett and Bell that the New Religious Right emerged and began to gain prominence in the late seventies in the United States. Organizations like Jerry Falwell's "Moral Majority" sought, through education, television, and participation in the political process, to offer a version of fundamentalist or evangelical Christian faith intended to reknit the divided spheres of our lives under the integrating power of faith. In passing it is interesting to note that the religious Right was more assiduous in pursuing influence in legislatures, in the courts, and in the polity—and that in regard to issues affecting family life—than in addressing increasingly disturbing patterns of maldistribution of resources in the techno-economic order.

Martin Marty coined the term *public church* in a book by that title published in 1981. Marty's discussion stands in the spirit of Alexis de Tocqueville, who worried that democracy could not function without institutions mediating between the individual and government, on the one hand, and between the individual and the masses, on the other. Voluntary associations as well as churches he saw as critical for this kind of mediation. Marty's concerns go beyond Tocqueville's, however, to focus on the contributions churches can make from Christian tradition to the "ordering faith" of the public toward clarification of and care for the "common good."[6]

Parker Palmer in *The Company of Strangers*, also published in 1981, lamented the loss of public space in modern societies, space where strangers can interact, thus exchanging the richness of their diverse racial, ethnic, and religious backgrounds. He called for churches to become communities in which diversity can be included and people can practice the arts of exchange and persuasion that are requisite for life in public.[7]

I have already mentioned the response of some fundamentalists and evangelicals to the decline in the cultural and political influence of religion and religious communities in North American society. Leaders are diverse as Falwell, the Luthern pastor Richard John Neuhaus, and the Catholic political theologian Michael Novak, in addition to the bishops of the American Catholic church and of other communions, have helped shape competing notions of the public church by their urging that the churches engage issues affecting the common good in public discourse and through visible actions of witness.[8]

Collections of essays edited by Mary Boys on *Education for Citizenship and Discipleship*, along with my own writing, have sought to address the role of the churches in reconstituting ethical and moral foundations in the education of the public.[9] In addition, I have sought to address, in preliminary ways, the question of formation for public Christians that takes seriously the reknitting of the spheres in and through their vocations. I have argued that if the Church is going to regain influence in the future, it must take more seriously the awakening and forming of the covenantal identities and vocations of its members.[10]

The following description of congregations of public church represents an effort at "characterization." It is an effort to give specificity to a vision and model that has evolved from practical theological construction and from preliminary observations of particular congregations. Here I offer seven clusters of the characteristics of public church:

1. Public Church Fosters a Clear Sense of Christian Identity and Commitment

Public church congregations have "boundaries" and criteria for inclusion. They require grounding in Christian tradition, including denominational or confessional particularity. They take "joining" and assimilation seriously. They value preaching that combines solid grounding in and interpretation of scripture and tradition with specific address to contemporary issues of personal and public responsibility.

Public church is not to be confused with some version of an American "civil religion." This is not a bland, lowest common denominator, watered down "faith in general." There is a way of being inclusive that takes in anything. We have in mind here a different kind of inclusiveness. Public churches, whether Evangelical, Orthodox, Catholic, or "mainline," have a spine of identity grounded in scripture and tradition, in proclamation and the sacraments. They are praying, praising, proclaiming, and practicing congregations. They take the reception and formation of new members seriously and typically have determinative covenants, whether explicit or implicit, embodying standards and expectations for membership accountability.

For a congregation to be deeply and particularly Christian means that its identity derives from a relation with Jesus Christ. Dietrich Bonhoeffer once wrote, "The Church is nothing else but a sector of humanity where Christ is really taking form." Identity in Christ means participating in the story opened up by God's self-offering in the Christ event. It means being grafted into the mission of Jesus to point to and help to bring the commonwealth of love and justice that Jesus announced and embodied. To form this identity public church helps prospective members to find linkages between the motives, hungers, and life experiences that draw them toward church and the healing and empowering movement of God's grace.

The identity of public church coheres in either an explicit or a functional covenant regarding the *praxis* of Christian life and community. This involves not so much a lock-step of belief or consensus on the *content* of faith, but rather, a shared agreement about where authority for community life and faithfulness is located, and how the community faithfully can live between its memory and hope and the horizons of challenge and calling in the present era. Public churches agree about the main directions of God's story and involvement in creation and history. As congregations they exhibit a clear and deep sense of Christian identity.

2. Congregations of Public Church Manifest a Diversity of Membership

"Diversity" means racial, ethnic, class, and within confessional bounds, theological differences. Public church congregations make clear by policy, program, and personnel that diversity is valued. Through liturgy, program, and/or preaching public churches provide centripetal pulls toward unity without compromising diversity. In part, public church's receptiveness to strangers arises from its welcoming of diversity within its community.

Public church Christians can relate nondefensively to persons and groups of other or no religious backgrounds in the larger public because of an openness born of identity and conviction. My colleague Walter Lowe once reminded us that "openness" is a second-level virtue. Often we speak of openness as though it were a primary virtue like faith, hope, love, prudence, or courage. But it is not; it is derivative. When you have only openness you don't have much. A window stuck *open* is as useless as a window stuck *shut*. In either case you have lost the use of the window. Openness is an attribute of a system or organism that has significant structure and integrity in itself. Openness is possible for persons or communities who know who they are. When the spine of identity is well established, it is possible to risk relating in depth to those who are different from the self. Public church exhibits a principled openness in the midst of pluralism, born of its clarity about its convictional grounding and its own practice of inclusiveness.

The covenant unity that makes true diversity possible, and that keeps struggle and controversy nondestructive, centers in the core activities that exert centripetal drawing power in the congregation: *kerygma, leitourgia, koinonia, diakonia,* and *paideia,* about which there will be more later in this book. Public church manifests a diversity in membership and an openness born of conviction and identity.

3. Public Church Consciously Prepares and Supports Members for Vocation and Witness in a Pluralistic Society

As churches committed to Jesus Christ under the sovereignty of God, public congregations are prepared to pursue their missions in the context of pluralistic societies. With a Trinitarian conception of God's being and action that excludes no dimension of the universe, public Christians try to be alert for the signature of Spirit in the variety of publics with whom they interact. They do not believe that the only faithful way to relate to their variety of Christian and non-Christian neighbors is through proselytization, on the one hand, or the anathema of judgment, on the other. Such churches invite the stranger to life-transforming faith in Jesus Christ. They also recognize that other folk than Christians experience and recognize the presence of God in creation and history.

Diversity within the congregation and the learning of skills of conflict and struggle while staying in fellowship constitute experience in a "little public" that provides training for interaction within the larger sphere of pluralistic public life.[11]

Congregations of public church are committed to civility. Civility involves effective commitment to the kind of dialogue and engagement in public that allows persons to express deep convictions, to address controversial concerns, and to differ with others deeply, yet without having either to decimate the opponent, control the arena, or withdraw from the encounter. Such civility requires confidence in the possibility of finding common ground underlying a multiplicity of discourses. It calls for reliance upon conflict mediation and the skills and disciplines of persuasion. It means a commitment to creating and maintaining "public space"—campuses. The Jesuit philosopher Walter Ong reminds us of the original meaning of the term *campus*, a field where people engage in struggle but without resort to arms. Public churches are committed to joining with others to create campuses, where the stranger can be met humanely and where we can struggle over issues that matter without resort to arms. Public church congregations consciously prepare and support members for vocation and witness in a pluralistic society.

4. Public Church Balances Nurture and Group Solidarity Within with Forming and Accountability in Vocation in Work and Public Life Beyond the Walls of the Church

Public church congregations balance the encouragement of intimacy within the community and concern for a family-like feeling with care about the more impersonal and structural domains of public life. An effort to retrieve a strong doctrine of *vocation* underlies this vision of church. The concept of vocation, derived from biblical sources, has rich and deep rootage in Jewish and Christian traditions.[12] As stated in chapter 5, vocation refers to the ontological calling all persons and communities have to be in partnership with God. We must reclaim the term *vocation* from guidance counsellors and occupational therapists and from a too-narrow association with the world of work. Nor may we continue to allow it to refer only to the callings of priests, nuns, ministers, and those pursuing "full-time Christian (meaning professional) service." Vocation is a larger concept than career, occupation, or profession. If it were not, children would not have vocations; persons whose lives are spent primarily in volunteer service would not have vocations; and that most rapidly growing group of people in U.S. society, those who are in or near retirement, would not have vocations. In terms I developed in chapter 5, vocation is the response a person makes with his or her total life to the call of God to partnership. This means that vocation includes our leisure, our relational life, our roles as citizens, our roles as members of families; it includes our religious activities and our work, paid or volunteer. Vocation is a way of pointing to what gives coherence, meaning, and purpose to our lives, to what links us and our labors to some center of value and power upon whom we recognize ourselves to be dependent.

Public churches encourage and support their members in the development of vocations in which partnership with God is carried into the large-scale economic, technical, political, commercial, and religious structures that shape our lives. Such churches support Christian thinking and action in the context of the complexity and ambiguity of our world. Much of the time and energy in most churches is spent in internal administration and maintenance. How exciting it becomes when an equivalent or greater amount of effort is devoted to equipping people for their vocations in partnership with God in the world beyond the church's walls. Public churches try to free their members from many of the tasks of institutional maintenance and internal ministry for the sake of strengthening their vocations as Christians in the marketplace, the school, the law office, the legislative halls, the hospital, and the corridors and committees of peacemaking and ecological healing. Public churches call forth and empower the ministry of laypersons, not by telling them what they must do in the context of the complex systems in which they work and live, but by giving them access to and grounding in scriptures and tradition so that *they* can become informed practical theologians and ethicists in their roles as leaders and followers in their public lives.

Congregations of public church consistently seek to maintain a balance between *koinonia,* a warm, supportive fellowship of solidarity within the community, and *diakonia,* the personal and collective vocations that address and keep just the systems and structures of society. To this end public church congregations involve members in ongoing study and continuous mission. They work to maintain a balance between spiritual deepening and renewal and the sustainment and accountability of members in vocation in public life. Public churches balance nurture and group solidarity within with forming and accountability in vocation in work and public life beyond the walls of the church.

5. Public Church Evolves a Pattern of Authority and Governance That Keeps Pastoral and Lay Leadership Initiatives in a Fruitful Balance

Such congregations rely upon scripture and tradition as sources of principled norms for adjudicating theological and practical differences. They resist "personalizing" issues and evolve procedures and skills in leadership that allow for conflict and struggle in the context of covenant faithfulness. They include diverse "voices" in dialogue prior to decision making; they strive for consensus; and they seriously attempt to provide seeds for reconciliation in the process of argumentation and decision.

This vision of public church, I contend, is incompatible with "mystery-mastery" models of clercial authority. In the mystery-mastery approach the minister, by virtue of ordination, formal theological training, and presumed spiritual seniority, assumes the responsibility for being the sole source and arbiter of all religious truth in the congregation. He or she (though usually he) carefully prepares and regularly offers well-crafted, polished sermons and teaching, the purpose of which is to provide definitive interpretation and guidance for the community. However, such a minister seldom gives the congregation access to his sources. His hearers are never invited into the "kitchen" to be part of a dialogue of interpretation and application of scripture and tradition. In contrast, authority in the ministry of public church depends not only upon ordination and training but upon the skill, willingness, and imagination of pastors in empowering lay members for able participation in the practical theological and ethical guidance of the church in its mission. The reimaging of God as sovereign that we undertook in chapters 2 and 3 has direct implications for a reimaging of ministerial authority in churches of the new paradigm. Such ministers invite participation in the discernment and interpretation of God's *praxis*. They risk vulnerability in order to be part of the empowerment of lay ministry and vocations. Public church has a pattern of authority and governance that keeps pastoral and lay leadership initiatives in a frutiful balance.

6. *Public Church Offers Its Witness in Publicly Visible and Publicly Intelligible Ways*

The congregation's use of money and influence and the setting of mission "priorities" are evangelical in the sense that they *demonstrate* Christian love and commitment to justice. The church and its leadership seek to find publicly accessible language in which to offer the witness and vision and the imperatives to which its Christian faith gives rise.

The principled openness and commitment to the common good characterizing a public church congregation is made manifest in its budget and in the presence and activities of its members—as persons and as a corpora. Through witness, service, advocacy, lobbying, and, if needed, protest, the congregations of public church try to live their version of the gospel story. To the degree they are faithful their witness communicates the promises and imperatives of the gospel as the community has been grasped by them. They seek to offer the wisdom of Christian faith in publicly comprehensible language and imagery.

When the American Roman Catholic bishops wrote their two pastoral letters on the nuclear situation and the United States economy, they offered a strong model for this challenge of giving our witness in public language. A passage from an early draft of their letter on the economy puts it well:

> We write with two purposes: the first is to provide guidance for the members of our own church as they seek to form their consciences and reach moral decisions about economic matters. The second is to add our voice to the public debate about United States economic policies. In pursuing the first of these purposes, we argue from a distinctvely Christian perspective that has been shaped by the Bible and by the content of Christian tradition and from a standpoint that reflects our faith in God: Father, Son, and Holy Spirit. The second purpose demands that our arguments be developed in a reasoned manner that will be persuasive to those who do not share our faith or our tradition.[13]

Public church offers its witness in publicly visible and publicly intelligible ways.

7. Public Church Shapes a Pattern of Paideia for Children, Youth, and Adults that Works Toward the Combining of Christian Commitment with Vocation in "Public"

Such a congregation exhibits clarity about the virtues, passions, and deep emotions it needs to form in members. It involves members in the disciplines of prayer, liturgical and sacramental participation, study, and missional action required for the formation and growth of "public Christians." It nurtures a certain robustness of commitment and identity capable of sustaining the initiatives and ambiguities of public Christian vocation and witness.

Virtues arise out of and are shaped by the "practices" in which communities engage. Intentionality about becoming and being public church requires practical clarity about the knowledge, skills, and attitudes necessary for the demands of ecclesial practice in such communities. Christian formation or *paideia* is broader than merely instruction and education in the schooling sense— though it includes these. Through liturgy, through proclamation, through the *ascesis* of spiritual disciplines, through the awakening and nurture of a sense of *vocation*, through participation in community discernment and decision making, and through apprenticeship involvement in mission, congregations of public church engage in systematic formation. Such congregations foster ongoing development in faith, providing support and challenge for continuing *metanoia* and transformation. Public churches work at shaping a pattern of *paideia* for children, youth, and adults that aims toward combining Christian commitment with vocation in public. In chapter 7 we will return to these themes in greater depth.

PUBLIC CHURCH IN ACTUALITY: PRELIMINARY PORTRAITS

In the research project The Faith and Practice of the Congregation, our team used an earlier version of the foregoing seven characteristics of public church as the basis for identifying congregations for our study. Recommendations from civic and church leaders in our city brought some seventeen congregations to our attention based on their reputations. From these we chose three churches for in-depth inquiry. We did not presume to test these churches against our abstract criteria. Instead, we put our model of public church "at risk" in relation to actual congregations that knowledgeable observers judged had many of the qualities of public church. We did not expect that any particular congregation would exhibit all the characteristics of the model; nor did we assume that only the characteristics we had identified would be relevant for characterizing these churches. Though this is not the place for a full review of the results of our two years' work, I offer some reflections on the three actual public churches we, with the help of eight part-time researchers, came to know in some depth.[14] First is a brief description of the three faith communities.

CORNERSTONE AFRICAN METHODIST EPISCOPAL CHURCH

The story of Cornerstone Church is inseparable from the development of the African-American community in Atlanta. As one of the oldest congregations in the city, Cornerstone has been for every generation of African Americans a focal point for community meetings, social and religious support, and racial pride. It embodies in its own story both the pain of race relations in the

United States and the possibility for achievement of racial justice in a rapidly changing urban environment.

A sense of history and presence is a common bond for participants in Cornerstone's congregation. Their forebears had to stretch their "nickels and dimes" as far as they could "to make sure that there was a place of worship here." They built a sturdy stone structure of grand design for its neighborhood as a focal expression of racial and community pride. "We want this to last through generations," one member put it, just as those did who had the "love and commitment, that kind of hard work, going the third and fourth miles of the way," to build and maintain the church.

Cornerstone played the lead role in its denomination's founding of a college in the city. For many years it has consistently been a spearhead in the fight for the civil and human rights of minority persons. It built and operates a high-rise, low-cost retirement center for elders in the community. Volunteers from Cornerstone's membership carry out ministries of feeding street people, working with neighborhood youth, and managing a drug hotline. The church is playing a key role in the movement to reestablish the economic and aesthetic health of the famous avenue on which the church is located.

The six to eight hundred regular worshipers at Cornerstone are led by a pastor who grew up in the congregation and who now, at age fifty, has emerged as a visible, active leader for Atlanta's African-American community as a whole. Through his example and the themes he strikes in his worship leadership, they are continually reminded of their responsibility as a congregation to stand in solidarity with fellow African Americans, especially those less fortunate, to ensure their civil rights, economic opportunity, and social justice in a society in which they have had to fight for a place.

SAINT STEPHEN'S EPISCOPAL CHURCH

On April 21, 1989, the *Atlanta Constitution* ran an editorial marking the 125th anniversary of Saint Stephen's. Contrasting the church with downtown churches of Boston, Chicago, and other cities that had lost members to the suburbs, the article declared Saint Stephen's "an oddity" for thriving in an urban setting.

A list of the social ministries of the parish took up an entire paragraph—the soup kitchen, medical clinic, and post office for the homeless, the street academy, the ministry to the Hispanic community, the theater company—and the diversity of the people was celebrated as well. Saint Stephen's was "the most heterogeneous parish in town," the paper sang, and "a lot more than a church to its neighbors." For the vision of this church was "a place where black, white, rich, and poor" could, in the words of the new rector, "come together in strictly human ways, something that does not occur in very many places in this city."

Saint Stephen's has always been entwined in the public life of the city, though the nature of that public has changed drastically over the years. Until relatively recently, Atlanta was a city of completely different scale, with about 90,000 residents in 1900 and only about 270,000 as late as 1930. Today the metropolitan area has a growing population of 2.3 million.

When a group of parishioners created a time-line story of the church in the fall of 1988, they filled the newsprint to overflowing with descriptions of the early 1970s; soup kitchen, academy, television broadcast, counseling center, to mention only a few ministries that took form in this time. Such a proliferation of interests mirrored Atlanta's "yuppie" expansion. Saint Stephen's acquired a reputation as an open space where people with innovative ideas could find support and give them a try. Close to a thousand people, in the four services combined, worship at Saint Stephen's each Sunday, and the budget has grown well beyond the million-dollar mark.

Boasting that no powerful person or group in the city is more than a phone call away from Saint Stephen's, the church owns much of the extremely valuable real estate around it and will be a major player in this decade's redevelopment of that area. With upscale housing for ten to twelve thousand people to be built within a mile's radius of the church, Saint Stephen's faces difficult and wonderful challenges as it wrestles with how to reconcile its commitments to serve both the lowest of the low and the highest of the high in the city.

COVENANT BAPTIST CHURCH

Covenant Baptist Church celebrated its seventy-fifth anniversary in 1988. For the first fifty years of the congregation's life it followed almost perfectly the trajectory of development for successful near surburban congregations in the Southern Baptist denomination. Given the award as the "outstanding church in the Southern Baptist Convention" in 1963, Covenant's congregation already felt the shock waves of neighborhood racial change that would bring the resignation of their pastor and the challenge of a new era. While similar Protestant churches facing community change sold their property and relocated in more distant suburbs, Covenant, guided by a strong team of lay leaders and a new pastor of unusual biblical grounding and theological gifts, chose to stay. Whenever asked by the press or by members about Covenant's policy regarding racial inclusiveness, this pastor answered, "To vote on whether or not to accept Negroes as members would be in reality to vote on whether or not we are to be a church of Jesus Christ, and that's not up for votes."

Through the struggles of this era this church redefined its covenant and mission. New members hear the stories of the reformative years from 1965 to the mid 1970s and are asked if they can subscribe to the church's covenant:

WE COVENANT TOGETHER

We are together to be the church of God in Christ. We are not here by chance, but God through His grace is making of us a fellowship to embody and to express the Spirit of Christ.

In this fellowship, "we are no longer Jews or Greeks or slaves or free men or even merely men or women, but we are all the same—we are one in Christ Jesus" (Galatians 3:28, Living Bible). Therefore, we reject any status in this fellowship in terms of church office, wealth, race, age, sex, education, or other distinctions.

As a member of such a fellowship, I intend to live under the following commitments:

- I will gather regularly with the church to worship God, share the good news, and continually examine its implications for my life.

- I will study the Bible, meditate, and pray so that I will more fully experience the presence of God.

- I will also be sensitive to God's message as it comes to me from persons, history, the arts, nature, current happenings in the world, and other sources.

- I will be responsible to God through the creative use of all my income and possessions. I will give systematically and even sacrificially to the financial support of our church's ministry.

- I will try to discover and affirm the gifts God has given me and use them in His service; I will try to evoke, affirm, and celebrate the gifts He has given to others.

- I will intentionally give myself as Christ's servant through participation in His mission in the world.

- I will offer to know and love my sisters and brothers in this fellowship, and I am willing to be known and loved by them.

- With God's help and the help of my brothers and sisters in this fellowship, I make this covenant.

In 1972 members of the church placed the granite "covenant rock" in front of the church as a witness to the church's commitment to staying there in ministry and mission. Between 1966 and 1979 Covenant's membership shrank from 1,347 to 598. It has remained about constant since then. In that creative era, however, it hired a full-time African-American community minister, began and staffed a coffee house ministry downtown, carried on a ministry with Cuban prisoners in the Atlanta federal prison, and brought about the integration of the Baptist children's home. In addition, since the early 1970s at least five women have been ordained by Covenant in an era in which hostility to the idea of women as clergy has stiffened in the Southern Baptist Convention. In the 1980s Covenant spawned a publication on world hunger and food that has gained international recognition, a national newpaper for Southern Baptists setting forth an alternative to the fundamentalist vision, a ministry to the homeless aimed at long-term rehabilitation, and a group home for retarded adults.

PUBLIC CHURCH CONGREGATIONS: FIRST REFLECTIONS

In concluding this chapter on public church I draw a few observations of my own setting forth what I think we are learning about congregations of public church from this study. Much of the work of interpreting the voluminous data generated in our multifocus study of these three congregations remains yet to be done. Though Tom Frank's thinking and writing have been drawn upon in formulating these first observations, our joint conclusions, based on the more complete analysis of our richly layered data, will come later and will supersede these initial assessments. At this early point the following reflections stand out for me:

1. Each of the three congregations we studied has a clear profile in its community and in the larger city. They are known for their commitment to social ministries. They are known for their political and economic presence and involvement. They are recognized, in each case, by virtue of landmark physical features (not grandiose, but unique and distinctive). They each have strong traditions in worship and music. They have become, by virtue of these clear profiles, *magnet* churches, drawing members and participants from all across the metropolitan area. People drive twenty to thirty minutes or longer to worship in and be part of these communities of faith.

2. Though none of the three congregations exhibits diversity of membership in what might be considered "ideal" proportions, they do span the range of rich and poor, well educated and poorly educated, and exhibit some racial, ethnic, and social-class hetero-geneity. Each congregation is known for its hospitality to the stranger—whether in the guise of persons and groups or political causes. They are not identified as "left-wing" or "right-wing" but as churches that take stands on the basis of their understanding of the imperatives of Christian faith.

3. Each church could look to some recent period of crisis in which the church's life and ministries seemed to be facing decline and death. All three, in different ways, exhibit today the fruits of seasons when dynamic and fearless clergy leaders matched with committed, dynamic, and courageous laity to open new eras in the congregations' history.

4. We observe that the transition toward being public churches does not happen overnight. It takes seven to fifteen years to "grow" such a church. The transition, in these congregations at least, has involved significant changes in governance patterns. These changes and maturing processes continue. In Saint Stephen's and Covenant, the change has been in the direction of expanding lay participation in governance and church leadership. In Cornerstone the pastor has maintained close control of

leadership, but his insistence that all elected leaders of the church be tithers has had the effect of widening and opening up the ranks of leaders and of making place for many younger or more dynamic persons to emerge into leadership roles. These changes have resulted, in each case, in there being two congregations, one older and socialized into the earlier patterns of congregational life, and the other younger and formed by the newer patterns.

5. These congregations of public church are fermentive and filled with internal tensions. Far from being placid and tranquil, they have vigorous arguments and heated discussions about matters of congregational mission. As a norm, it seems that public churches have evolved better skills at managing conflict and at practicing the arts of good politicians than nonpublic churches— that is, avoiding the personalizing of issues, with the fall into *ad hominem* accusations and debate, and engaging in the practice of forgiving and asking for forgiveness when deep differences on issues have led to loss of balance in argumentation and decision making.

6. Each of the congregations has certain symbolic, ritual, or verbal practices that seem expressive of the sense of identity in the congregation and seem to provide the basis from which resolution of differences within or without can be undertaken. For Covenant the statement of covenant worked out by congregation members and the "covenant rock" provide a highly verbal and powerful visual symbolic statement of identity and purpose, whereas congregational meetings express a "family" commitment to include all voices in making decisions. The Saint Stephen's congregation repeats the Nicene Creed with an unmistakable lilt and definiteness, and the weekly Eucharist is clearly their unifying center of piety. At Cornerstone the congregation reads out the Decalogue followed by the gentle sway of a verse of "Nearer My God to Thee" in a determined harmonizing of law and gospel. And on the first Sunday of every month, the altar completely covered in white, the pastor, attended by women in white uniforms, celebrates Holy Communion clad completely in white clothing. These are holy moments and movements, symbolic of the identity and callings of these congregations.

7. Each of our congregations experienced difficulties in ministering with their youth, and each has faced some struggle in providing a comprehensive program of formation for children.

Geographical dispersion, busy schedules, and, perhaps, the inherent difficulty of translating adult faith into a nurturing narrative for children and youth partially explain these difficulties. Efforts are made in each community to offset these deficiencies by offering volunteer service programs, retreats, and mission trips for the youth and consistent Sunday classes for the younger children.

8. The congregations all have significant membership orientation processes. They attract persons from many different denominational backgrounds and thus have a sense of imperative to convey the tenets and practices of their given heritage and their respective formative congregational stories. Classes are led by both clergy and laity, normally in anticipation of reception into membership. Covenant, with its Baptist tradition of believers' baptism by immersion, has a category of "Friends of Covenant" for youth or adults who want to affiliate with the community but have either not been baptized or have received it at the hands of another (non-Baptist) congregation.

9. As we began our study we hypothesized that the "modal level" of faith development (the average expectable stage of faith for adults) in public church congregations would be postconventional (i.e., Individuative-Reflective or beyond). Of the twenty-two (thirteen males, nine females) randomly selected adults interviewed at Saint Stephen's and the fourteen (seven males, seven females) interviewed at Covenant we found the following: *eleven* whose way of being in faith can be called *conventional*, and *twenty-five* whose way of being in faith can be designated *postconventional*. In a broad sense these data support the assumption that the ethos of public church congregations will be dominantly postconventional. We also find in this data, limited though it is, some support for the observation (mentioned in point 4 above) that there seem to be two congregations at both these churches. Of the eleven conventional respondents, four were male and seven were female. Five were over the age of sixty. Of the twenty-five postconventional respondents, sixteen were male and nine were female, and only four of them were sixty or above.[15]

In a rhapsodic beginning to this chapter I expressed love for congregations and a sense of their specialness. We looked at the background in the 1970s out of which concern for the public role of religion and the churches arose. Attention then focused on seven characteristics of public church—an effort at a kind of composite portrait on the basis of impressionistic descriptions. The chapter concluded with snapshots of three actual public church congregations, with preliminary reflections upon the data from our studies among them. Next, we turn from the task of description to that of prescription. Are there normative theological foundations for public church? What bases in biblical faith provide the generative guidelines for congregational formation and re-formation toward public church? Can we identify theological resources for ecclesial re-formation as we live into the emerging new cultural paradigm and the challenges of the twenty-first century?

NOTES

1. I emphasize that the formulations on our project and its findings in this chapter are *partial* and *preliminary*. Presentation of the data from this intensive two-year research will come in the form of a book that Thomas E. Frank and I are writing together. I gratefully acknowledge that some of the prose and many of the ideas expressed, especially in the parts entitled "Public Church in Actuality" and "Public Church Congregations: First Reflections," are the product of our joint work. We both are indebted to the contributions of the research staff who worked with us and to the churches—given fictional names here—who generously shared their lives with us. We also acknowledge with gratitude support for the project from the Pew Charitable Trusts.
2. Richard Sennett, *The Fall of Public Man* (New York: Alfred A. Knopf, 1977).
3. Though "public life" here includes governmental service in elective or appointive offices, it is not limited to that sphere. Public life includes all the ways persons participate in the discourse that shapes awareness and attitudes toward issues that affect the common good. It can include such things as actively belonging to some of the wide range of voluntary associations that mediate between large-scale institutions and the masses of the population. It can also include such activities as writing letters to a newspaper, writing books or articles, lecturing, appearing on television, or participating in civic committees dealing with everything from the environment to the arts. For a distinction between the public and government, see John Dewey, *The Public and Its Problems* (New York: Henry Holt, 1927).
4. William J. Everett, *God's Federal Republic* (New York: Paulist Press, 1988), pp. 129–30.
5. Daniel Bell, *The Cultural Contradictions of Capitalism* (New York: Basic Books, 1978).
6. Martin E. Marty, *The Public Church* (New York: Crossroad, 1981).
7. Parker J. Palmer, *The Company of Strangers* (New York: Crossroad, 1981).
8. See Jerry Falwell, *Listen America* (New York: Bantam Books, 1980); Richard John Neuhaus, *The Naked Public Square* (Grand Rapids: Eerdmans, 1984); Michael Novak, *The Spirit of Democratic Capitalism* (New York: Simon & Schuster, Touchstone, 1982).

9. Mary Boys, ed., *Education for Citizenship and Discipleship*, 2 vols. (Philadelphia: Pilgrim Press, 1989); James W. Fowler, "Pluralism, Particularity and Paideia," in *Journal of Law and Religion* 2/2 (1984): 263–307; and "Reconstituting Paideia in American Public Education," in *Caring for the Commonweal*, Parker Palmer, Barbara Wheeler, and James W. Fowler, eds. (Macon, GA: Mercer Univ. Press, 1990).

10. See James W. Fowler, *Becoming Adult, Becoming Christian* (San Francisco, Harper & Row, 1984), chaps. 4 and 5; and *Faith Development and Pastoral Care* (Philadelphia: Fortress Press, 1987), chaps. 1 and 3.

11. See Everett, *God's Federal Republic*, p. 157.

12. See Fowler, *Becoming Adult, Becoming Christian*, chap. 5; and *Faith Development and Pastoral Care*, chaps 2 and 3.

13. From "Catholic Social Teaching and the U.S. Economy," in *Origins: NC Documentary Service*, vol. 14, no. 22/23 (Nov. 15, 1984): 343. The role of communicating the church's witness in public language is obscured, however, by the bishops' decision, in Spring 1990, to hire an advertising agency and a polling firm to propagate the church's teaching against abortion. This is no longer a contribution "to help Catholic Christians form their consciences" and to invite non-Catholics to rational debate. Rather, it becomes more nearly an effort to commend a partisan stance and directly to influence judicial and legislative processes. The church risks its integrity in their moving from teaching and fostering public debate to direct partisan political activity.

14. See the preliminary version of our findings in the unpublished research monograph by Thomas E. Frank and James W. Fowler, *Living Toward Public Church: Three Congregations*. The descriptions here of "Cornerstone" and "Saint Stephen's" churches are excerpted from writing by Frank and are used here with his permission.

15. At this writing interviews from Cornerstone, which were conducted most recently in our study, are being transcribed and are not yet available for analysis.

7. Ecclesiogenesis: Forming Personal and Public Faith

Alleluia! Praise Yahweh, my soul! . . .
Do not put your trust in princes,
in any child of Adam, who has no power to save.
When their spirits go forth they return to the earth,
on that very day all their plans come to nothing.
How blessed are those who have Jacob's God to help them. . . .
Yahweh gives sight to the blind, lifts up those who are bowed down.
Yahweh protects the stranger, and sustains the orphan and the widow.
Yahweh loves the upright, but frustrates the wicked.
Yahweh reigns forever.

FROM PSALM 146:1, 3, 5, 8–10, NJB

Make your own the mind of Christ Jesus:
Who, being in the form of God, did not count equality with God
Something to be grasped.
But emptied himself, taking the form of a slave,
becoming as human beings are;
and being in every way like a human being, he was humbler yet,
even to accepting death, death on a cross.
For this God raised him high, and gave him the name
which is above all other names;
so that *all beings* in the heavens, on earth and in the underworld,
should bend the knee at the name of Jesus
and that *every tongue should acknowledge* Jesus Christ as Lord,
to the glory of God the Father.

FROM PHILIPPIANS 2:5–11, NJB

The weaving of this book is almost at an end. We began with a framing of promises and perils of this decade and the new millennium. We examined the thesis that we are experiencing a paradigm shift in cultural consciousness. Then we turned to theological chapters including biography, narrative, and metaphorical reconstruction. There we sought to evoke new sensibilities and responsiveness to God's pervasive participation in our universe's becoming. We explored two dynamics of faith in chapters 4 and 5. One explored in more depth the stage theory of faith development. The other made explicit the themes of story and vocation, themes that have been part of the deep warp and woof of our weaving. The previous chapter's exploration of public church as vision and actuality aimed to address our initial questions regarding the kind of churches we are called to be and nurture for the twenty-first century. Now, in conclusion, we have an opportunity to consider something about how to get from here to there—how, in congregations, to respond to the Spirit as weaver in the process of awakening and nurturing the new creation.

SCRIPTURE, SIGN, AND CONGREGATIONAL (RE-)FORMATION

We turn now to congregational (re-)formation. The Latin American liberation theologian Leonardo Boff introduces a thought-provoking term in the title of his 1986 book: *ecclesiogenesis*. By *ecclesiogenesis* he refers to a process of rebirth in the church from *below* and from *outside* the established structures.[1] In this section I intend to inquire into the sources and guiding norms from the Bible for ecclesiogenesis and to show in what ways they point to and shape the character of public church.

The New Testament and hermeneutics scholar Lewis Mudge proposes an approach to ecclesial practical theology that promises to help us at this juncture. Mudge's proposal draws on the discipline of *semiotics*. *Semion* is the Greek word for "sign." Semiotics, as a discipline, is employed to study the underlying rules or signs that operate to guide actions or form meanings in accordance with a community's or a culture's deepest values. For example, writers or speakers in the course of producing a written or spoken paragraph do not usually pause or reflect over each word or word combination. Instead, they engage the internal images guiding the communication, interrogating them for meanings. Then, in accordance with their evolved "style," they utter or write the sentences, one after the other. If semiotically trained analysts examine enough of a communicator's writing, they will be able to identify patterns and rhythms by which the author's words are combined. Analysts will be able to discern the underlying *rules*—the "signs" —by which the speaker or author produces her or his prose. So we say of a piece of writing: "It reads like Hemingway," "it sounds like John Donne," or "it is like Willa Cather." Or we might say of a speech, "It reads like Martin Luther King, Jr." A semiotic analyst could identify for us the largely unconscious cluster of rules that guide each of those writers and speakers in their creative choices of words, their distinctive uses of imagery, as well as the rhythm and pitch of their rhetoric.

Cultures can also be analyzed semiotically. A culture has a shared semiotics or system of signs that link people with shared meanings and values and make possible communication at widely varying levels and through a wide range of gestures and symbolic actions, as well as language. From this standpoint, "a culture consists of signs functioning within a silent syntax so that its members can not only speak, but act understandably in a vast variety of ways. The task of semiotics is to describe and explain these signs, their interaction, and the rules that govern these interactions, thereby delineating the cultural complex that emerges as a result."[2]

Consider, for example, the semiotics or underlying signs by which members of our society communicate success. We all know that there are visible signifiers of status, wealth, power, and political influence in this society. Such signs are both massive and subtle. Public life-styles make unmistakable statements. In the decade of the eighties a figure such as Donald Trump became a kind of caricature of this point in particularly visible ways. But even if a person is more subtle and provides no such overt clues, we still look for more subtle indicators of manner, dress, accent, and the like that tell us how a person or his or her family have fared in the struggle for "success." A systematic study of such sets of signs will reveal the manner in which they convey and maintain an imaginatively construed syntax of power.[3]

From this semiotic standpoint, congregations can be seen as cultures shaped by signifiers that determine both how they shape their life together and how they read and interact with the larger world of which they are a part. Congregations can "read" society's signs in their own ways, either *legitimating* or *countercultural*. The congregation's readings of the culture around it are correlated with the sign system that the *ecclesia* forms in its members. This syntax of covenant and calling encodes Scripture and tradition and the congregation's particular vernacular of spirit and mission.

For *ecclesiogenesis*—for the rebirth of the Church from below or outside its established structures—it is essential to identify the semiotic sets that the Bible offers us for the church's distinctive "readings" of culture and shaping of its life. The biblical texts I placed at the beginning of this chapter, added with another I will offer later in the chapter, seem to me to connect us with three interrelated semiotic sets that are essential to grasping and being grasped by the "reading" of the world, the response to its power, and the shaping of lives to which the Christian church is called.[4] Please notice that with each text there is a semiotics that begins with a *destabilizing* or a *deconstruction* of the world's sign system dealing with power. In a way that is analogous to our discussion of paradigm shift in chapter 1, this destabilizing is then followed by a *reconstruction*. The revisioning of power, in each case, gives rise to an alternative way of being in the world and in ecclesial community. Let's examine each of these texts and the semiotic sets they point to, if only briefly.

First is Psalm 146. Refer back, for a full reading, to the opening of this chapter. The psalm begins with destabilization.

"Alleluia! Praise Yahweh, my soul!" The semiotics of praise draws us out from self-absorption and detaches us from centers of value and power other than the Holy One. The address from "my soul" bids to connect us to the deepest seat of knowing and clear discernment and responsiveness within us. Then we turn to a semiotics directing us away from idols and idolatry. *"Do not put your trust in princes, in any child of Adam, who has no power to save."* The signs here encode negation of the culture's semiotics of power and privilege. There are no "special" people in the sense of being exempt from finite mentality and understanding. There are none who are exempt from self-deception and self-serving distortions. There are no people who deserve to claim godlike prerogatives, whether under the illusion of benevolence or under some ideology of the divine right of kings, or presidents, popes, bishops, or premiers.

After this deconstruction of aspects of the world's syntax of power, our attention is directed to the emergent pattern of the divine *praxis*. The character of God's power and its purposes emerge through the text:

How blest are those who have Jacob's God to help them,
whose hope is in Yahweh . . .
Yahweh keeps faith forever,
gives justice to the oppressed,
gives food to the hungry;
Yahweh sets prisoners free . . .
> *gives sight to the blind . . .*
> *lifts up the bowed down . . .*
> *protects the stranger . . .*
> *sustains the orphan and the widow . . .*
> *loves the upright . . .*
> *frustrates the wicked . . .*
Yahweh reigns forever. . . .

Does this passage sound familiar? Its semiotics seem to be of a piece with Isaiah 42 and 61 and with Luke 4:16–20. Yahweh is like that. This syntax of power illumines the character of God. This semiotic set provides the strongest clues to the passions that formed and directed Jesus as the Christ. He is like that. The Church, in ecclesiogenesis, is called to partnership in the *praxis* of this God committed to saving justice, to this God who brings eyesight to the blind, release to captives, light to those in darkness, and who makes covenant with people that they may bring light and life to the nations (Is. 42:6–7).

For our second semiotic cluster I direct you to the passage at this chapter's beginning from Philippians 2:5–11:

Make your own the mind of Christ Jesus, who,
being in the form of God . . .
did not grasp for equality with God,
but emptied himself . . .
entered into full solidarity with humankind . . .
accepted death on the cross
showing in that act the love, grace and glory of God.

This text belongs to a semiotic set that includes, among other passages, the suffering servant texts of Isaiah 42 and following chapters. Here again there is a deconstruction of the power world *before* the text, and a reconstruction of power relations in accordance with the community intended in the semiotics of the text. Mudge says it well:

The Philippians are to do their practical reasoning understanding that, because they are in Christ, the power relationships characteristic of the Roman world will no longer control the forms of imagination of each other that give rise to interpersonal conduct. Factionalism, vainglory, selfishness are symptoms of the old power world. They are to be replaced by love, mercy, compassion, concern for others, the sharing of suffering. . . . The community is to be "of one mind" on these matters. . . . The Philippian community is to embody in its currrent form of life the situation that will exist when all the principalities and powers bow the knee to the name of Jesus. . . . "Every tongue" will then "confess" *homologein*, that the world's scheme of identities and values has been rearranged in accordance with a new power geometry.[5]

Here we find ourselves in a semiotic set that includes 1 Corinthians 12, Romans 12, and Galatians 3:28.

Third, I refer you to Matthew 9:9–17:

Now while [Jesus] was at table in the house it happened that a number of tax collectors and sinners came to sit at table with him and his disciples. When the Pharisees saw this, they said to his disciples, "Why does your master eat with tax collectors and sinners?" When he heard this he replied, "It is not the healthy who need the doctor, but the sick. Go and learn the meaning of the words: *Mercy is what pleases me, not sacrifice.* And indeed I came to call not the upright, but sinners."

Then John's disciples came to him and said, "Why is it that we and the Pharisees fast, but your disciples do not?" Jesus replied, "Surely the bridegroom's attendants cannot mourn as long as the bridegroom is still with them? But the time will come when the bridegroom is taken away from them, and then they will fast. No one puts a piece of unshrunken cloth onto an old cloak, because the patch pulls away from the cloak and the tear gets worse. Nor do people put new wine into old wineskins; otherwise, the skins burst, the wine runs out, and the skins are lost. No; they put new wine in fresh skins and both are preserved." (NJB)

These verses bring to expression a semiotics of discipleship that destabilizes the old syntax of ethnic restriction regarding the covenant. It directs the Church to reach out to and receive the stranger. It calls upon the Church to direct its message of liberation and redemption to those persons and those situations wherein distortion prevails. Then, in accord with the syntax of the new age inaugurated by the living Christ among us, it calls us to serve and love with motives of joy, not moralism. The Bridegroom *is* among us. Let us put new wine into new wineskins.

Congregations shaped by the semiotics of texts like these offer a distinctive reading of our culture and our times. At the same time they embody a distinctive formation of life within the community and beyond it in vocation in the world. To the degree and in the manner that they show forth the semiotics of new creation in Christ, congregations themselves become signs of this present world's future possibility. In our exploration of the vision and actuality of public church we sought to describe and test characteristics of congregations engaged in processes of ecclesiogenesis. By their *praxis* they are endeavoring to shape their common life and to read and respond to the world through a semiotics that anticipates and lives toward God's future and the commonwealth of love and justice.

FORMING PERSONAL AND PUBLIC FAITH

In order to deepen our sense of how congregations can proceed in ecclesiogenesis for the present emergent age, we turn to the dynamics of congregational formation and transformation in faith. I want to engage with you in an effort to see the work of congregational formation in holistic, systemic ways.

Here I will rely upon a way of naming the dimensions of the congregation's life and mission that draws on key concepts from the Greek of the New Testament. Recently Maria Harris has retrieved a very similar way of speaking about the congregation as ecology of care and vocation in her book *Fashion Me A People.*[6] My use of this approach antedates my reading of Harris's fine book and differs from hers in some important ways. Here I will speak of *kerygma, leitourgia, koinonia, diakonia,* and *paideia.*[7]

Many observers of congregational life have testified that there is a systolic and a diastolic rhythm to the life of the Church. There is a heartbeat of alternation between the *centripetal,* the in-drawing, centering, and grounding movements of the community's life, and the *centrifugal,* the outflowing, missional movements of the congregation. This is Elizabeth O'Connor's "journey inward" and "journey outward." As we consider this heartbeat rhythm we see that formation and re-formation of the *body* of Christ, and of the persons it constitutes, occurs in the context of five interpenetrating dimensions of the congregation's life. Through participation in these dimensions of ecclesial being and action persons form the semiotic sets by which they "read" their surrounding cultures and by which, corporately, they are constituted for liberating and redeeming presence and witness in the world.

KERYGMA

The first of these five dimensions is *kerygma*—proclamation, teaching. *Kerygma* is the telling of the story of God's self-disclosure and self-giving. It means bringing to expression, through preaching and teaching, the pattern of the divine *praxis*. Chapters 2, 3, and 5 represent efforts in several modes to present *kerygma*. Most of us have neither the arrogance nor the artistry to do what the young Karl Barth set out to do in his Saffenwill parish in Switzerland. He determined so to immerse himself in the letters of Paul that he could, in his preaching and teaching, proclaim what Paul, were he writing here and now, would proclaim. Most of us are more modest in our claims, and for good reason. But perhaps we should be no less audacious in our aims. Preaching and teaching, empowered by the Spirit, open hearts to the word and working of God. Where the preacher-teacher faithfully mediates the relation between congregation and text and between text and surrounding culture, and where both focus on the callings of the congregation, hearts are touched, horizons are changed, possibilities are opened, callings are awakened, and imperatives of the heart take form. Pettiness and pettifoggery dissolve. A semiotics of the soul, shaped by the Spirit of God, works like leaven in lumpy hearts, like salt in flavorless fare, like seeds growing silently. "New creation" happens.

Preaching and teaching the gospel requires a unique form of communication. No other mode of discourse attempts, through speech event, to be the vehicle for present, local *revelation*. Its success depends less on the native gifts of the interpreter—and far less on his or her "winsomeness"—than upon his or her intercourse with the texts and availability to the Spirit. In a world of flim-flam communication in which the most artful uses of language and imagery are often put in the service of commercial seduction, it is a remarkable thing to encounter courageous and well-formed efforts to tell the truth. Though it is increasingly hard to do, preaching is something to which people—when they encounter an honest truth seeker and sharer—will give a quality of attention reserved for no other. There is no more important work in the world than honest, hard-working artistry in the service of proclaiming the word of God. Romans 10 puts it rightly:

> The word is very near to you, it is in your mouth and in your heart, that is, the word of faith, the faith which we preach. . . . All who call on the name of the Lord will be saved. But how are they to call on the Lord if they have not come to believe? And how will they come to believe if they have never heard? And how shall they hear unless there are preachers (and teachers)? (3–14, NJB)

LEITOURGIA

Leitourgia constitutes the second dimension of ecclesial being and re-formation. *Leitourgia* is liturgy, the work of the people in worship. Sometimes we fail to take seriously enough the formative power—the teaching power—of worship and sacrament. The essayist Annie Dillard focuses this lack of seriousness in a piece included in her book *Teaching a Stone to Talk.*[8] In "An Expedition to the Pole" Dillard draws an extended parallel between eighteenth- and nineteenth-century expeditions to reach the North Pole and a contemporary's search for encounter with the Absolute in Christian worship. One senses that this essay derives its energy and power from Dillard's own struggle to find a community of celebration alert, attentive, and disciplined enough to help her respond to the penetration of the Absolute in their midst.

Dillard begins by chronicling the ill-conceived and tragic expeditions of a number of early Arctic explorers. In her moving vignettes of their often disastrous ventures she succeeds in etching for us the mystical and spiritual magnetism exerted upon those early explorers by the concept of the pole—the place of convergence for all longitudinal vectors in a kind of absolute zero. Her descriptions give us vivid images of the dark black waters contrasted with the white and green ice of the vast, empty, and silent Arctic spaces.

Alongside this narrative of explorers on a dangerous spiritual quest, as well as a quest for fame and fortune, Dillard juxtaposes her search, in church, for the presence of the Absolute:

Why do people in churches seem like cheerful, brainless tourists on a packaged tour of the Absolute?

The tourists are having coffee and doughnuts on Deck C. Presumably someone is minding the ship, correcting the course, avoiding icebergs and shoals, fueling the engines, watching the radar screen, noting weather reports radioed in from shore. No one would dream of asking tourists to do these things. Alas, among the tourists on Deck C, drinking coffee and eating doughnuts, we find the captain, and all the ship's officers, and all the ship's crew. The officers chat; they swear; they wink a bit at slightly raw jokes, just like regular people. The crew members have funny accents. The wind seems to be picking up. . . .

On the whole, I do not find Christians, outside of the catacombs, sufficiently sensible of conditions. Does anyone have the foggiest idea what sort of power we so blithely invoke? Or, as I suspect, does not one believe a word of it? The churches are children playing on the floor with their chemistry sets, mixing up a batch of TNT to kill a Sunday morning. It is madness to wear ladies' straw hats and velvet hats to church; we should all be wearing crash helmets. Ushers should issue life preservers and signal flares; they should lash us to our pews. For the sleeping god may wake someday and take offense, or the waking god may draw us out to where we can never return.[9]

Any proper appreciation of the power of *leitourgia* begins with the recognition that prayer, praise, sacrament, and worship form deep emotions within us. With liturgy we deal with the *kinesthetics* of faith. Through the teaching power of sacrament and worship, faith gets into our bodies and bone marrow. You may have noticed, as I have, that frequently persons who have had severe strokes and can no longer speak are still able to sing hymns, say the Lord's Prayer, or recite the Twenty-third Psalm. How can that happen? What is it about our brains and our emotional systems that makes that possible?

Let me try to explain it. As is becoming well known, the human brain and body are divided into two roughly symmetrical halves. Each half of the brain receives input from nerves and issues commands to nerves on one side of the body. However, for reasons that are not well understood, there is a crossover of nerves going in and out of the brain such that nerves belonging to the right side of the body connect with the left brain and nerves belonging to the left side of the body connect with the right brain. We say that nervous organization is essentially contralateral, literally, "opposite-sided." The part of the brain that seems most deeply implicated in learned cognitive skills is the cerebral cortex, which in human beings is the largest part of the brain. The cortex surrounds the rest of the brain like a thick cap, but it is divided down the midline into two cerebral hemispheres. Although the two hemispheres are to be a certain extent capable of independent operation, they are connected by a fat bundle of nerve fibers called the corpus collosum. When this is intact, information can be transferred from one side of the cortex to the other. In most animals, each cerebral hemisphere seems to do roughly the same job. There is now incontrovertible evidence that in some higher mammals, however, especially human beings, each hemisphere is or becomes specialized to some degree. For most people, the 90 percent or so who are unambiguously right-handed, the mechanisms controlling language behavior seem to be primarily concentrated in the left hemisphere, and those controlling spatial orientation and other nonverbal skills in the right hemisphere. There are suggestions that the right hemisphere is more "emotional" than the left. Patients with right hemisphere damage are often strangely nonchalant about their condition, even when one side of the body is completely paralyzed.

In 1982, noticing that victims of right-hemisphere strokes typically speak in flat monotones, even about the most emotionally charged matters, a University of Texas researcher named Eliot Ross coined the term "aprosodia," from the word *prosody*, referring to pitch, melody, rhythm, and intonation. He used aprosodia to describe a sort of right-hemisphere version of aphasia, the loss of speech. The damage, he says, is to the emotional centers in the right hemisphere that are mirror images of the left-brain speech centers. There is one center on the right for the *perception* of feelings. Then he hypothesizes that there is another center in the right brain for *emotional expression*. Emotions and feelings—deep dispositions and images of the heart—use different neural configurations than do our discursive verbal and conceptual communications.[10]

I am convinced that much of what we know, especially our convictional knowing, forms and operates within us as images. Images are by no means always visual. Images are internal representations, and they range from vague and barely noticeable patterns of feeling to sharply defined forms. Images hold together our conscious and our unconscious knowing. Images hold, in fused forms, both what we know and how we feel about what we know. Our convictional images involve both left and right hemispheric patterning. Music and nonverbal dimensions of the liturgy, as well as the poetry of liturgy, address the wombs of images within us. They evoke and direct our convictions. They guide and confirm the resting of our hearts.

Christian worship and sacrament form in us deep dispositions of the heart—the strong emotions that give purpose, courage, tone, and passion to our faith. My colleague Don Saliers has identified four such clusters of Christian emotions.[11] First Saliers speaks of *gratitude and giving thanks.* Probably each of us can testify to how different a day is if we begin it with, and maintain throughout the day, the sense that life is gift, that creation shows forth the love and grandeur of God, and that other persons are extraordinary, mysterious treasures. Second, Saliers points to the emotions of *holy awe and the fear of God.* Isaiah in the temple, in Isaiah 6:1,5 is a prototype here: "In the year that King Uzziah died, I saw the Lord high and lifted up. . . . And I said, I am a man of unclean lips and I dwell among a people of unclean lips. . . . My eyes have seen the Lord, Yahweh Sabbaoth." Such wonder and amazement overcome *us* when we begin to grasp the fact that the Creator of a universe 13 billion light years in extent and still expanding should address us as persons and should call us to service and praise: "Oh Lord, our Lord, how excellent is thy name in *all* the earth!"

Third, there are the emotions of *joy* and *suffering.* Saliers reminds us that "Christian faith is born in the tension of suffering and joy, of cross and resurrection. The language of joy and of rejoicing we receive in Scripture must always be read against the backdrop of the life of suffering."[12] It is utterly authentic, therefore, when, in the middle of his joyous and celebrative Christmas oratorio, Johann Sebastian Bach includes the sonorous (and otherwise ominous) strains of "O Sacred Head Now Wounded." A poem by J. Lowell Smith, a lay Christian from my congregation in Atlanta, who was dying of congestive heart failure, vividly expresses this love and joy:

Grieve not for me
But have a ball—
From earthly life
I've had a call.

I'm going home:
My Lord has said
Who believes in Me
Is never dead.

So have some fun—
Remember me
Not with grief
But Christian glee!

Not great poetry, but great piety—joy and suffering.

A final cluster of Christian emotions Saliers identifies as "the *love of God and neighbor.*" It is sometimes tempting to think of the command to love as a religious version of Kant's categorical imperative—as an ethical principle by which to live. How much more powerful it is, when, through worship and sacrament, these dispositions have begun to take deep root in our hearts as the very emotional wellspring of our motives and motions.

KOINONIA

We come now to *koinonia,* the third dimension of ecclesial being and re-formation. In the Greek New Testament *koinonia* means, literally, "partnership." It has come to stand for the spiritual fellowship of the community of faith. As regards the formative and re-formative power of the koinonia I want to emphasize that we form *conscience* and *consciousness* through participation in community. Thomas Green, a philosopher of education at Syracuse University, has identified five voices by which conscience speaks within us.[13] These voices do not always harmonize within us, Green points out; they may give rise to tension and the struggle of internal dialogue. What are these five voices of conscience formed in Christian community—in *koinonia?*

The first voice Green identifies is that of the conscience of *craft.* How old were you when someone, for the first time, said to you, "If you are going to do it at all, *do it right*"? From early on—as early as two years of age, say the developmental psychologists—we begin to pay attention to the standards and requirements for doing things well that are held up by those who matter to us. The Greek word *homartia*, one of the terms the New Testament uses for sin, means, literally, "missing the mark." It reflects an action, an attitude, or a pattern of living that demonstrates a failure to live well. Christian community provides both models and teaching that precipitate in us the desire to live in accordance with the goodness in persons, the virtues befitting discipleship. Through the encounter with such models and teachers we form the voice of the conscience of craft.

Closer to what we normally think of when we speak of conscience, perhaps, is the voice of the conscience of *responsibility*.[14] This is the voice of duty, of fidelity. Duty as it is understood here is particularly related to promises freely made and conscientiously kept. Our freely made promises and covenants are among the only ways we can give dependability and structure to the unknown future. Promise making and promise keeping are among the most distinctively human activities we can name. Our promises, freely given, create structures of duty and commitment that may require that we be ready to set aside the moment by moment pursuit of pleasure or our own narrow conceptions of the good in order to fulfill them. The conscience of responsibility particularly responds to the congregation's call to disciplined life—life shaped faithfully in accordance with the use of the gifts God has given us for partnership in our vocations and for building up the covenant community. This is the conscience of responsibility.

Koinonia also helps to form in us the conscience of *membership*. This voice of conscience presumes a disposition of solidarity with the community in which one enters into the tasks of nurturing and caring for the network of relations that constitute the community. When the community is trying to make decisions or solve problems, therefore, it is never enough for one who claims to be a member simply to say no when another makes a serious proposal about what the community should do. The conscience of membership requires that all persons should enter deeply and imaginatively into the proposal and look for its strengths before declaring it inadequate. And that step cannot be taken unless and until the critic has something to offer that potentially better addresses the matter at hand. This is the conscience of membership.

Next Tom Green speaks of the conscience of *memory*. *Koinonia* extends to the communion of saints. Nearly six feet one, graceful and forceful, beautiful of face and voice, the author, singer, and dancer Maya Angelou addressed a packed audience of black people and white people in Glenn Memorial Auditorium at Emory. She thrilled us as she recited and sang the poetry and prose of African-American forebears of the eighteenth and nineteenth centuries. Then she said to *all* of us: "If you do not make your own the precious treasures of those who have gone before you, and who transmuted into this art and literature their sufferings, their abuse, their faith, and their claiming of freedom, you do not deserve the community of freedom and inclusiveness you now enjoy." Keeping faith with the memory and the hope, the sufferings and greatness of those who have preceded us in the community—the "communion of saints"—in the *koinonia* we form the conscience of memory.

The fifth voice of conscience formed in community is that of the conscience of *imagination*. In community, we learn something about thinking through the consequences of our actions and policies today for persons and generations not yet born. One native American tribe taught that a policy was right for that tribal group only if it could be justified as being beneficial and not harmful for six generations to come. This is a conscience of imagination. For Christians in the Christian context, this means taking seriously the in-breaking commonwealth of love and justice and that reversal of time mentioned earlier. It means seeing our present practice and our present choices in the light of God's promised future. And that awareness gives us freedom and responsibility in each moment in the present. The conscience of imagination is precisely that place where we learn in community to be open, vulnerable, and accountable to what God is calling us to do in the present and in the future, not just faithful to the memory. Doing this enables us to avoid getting trapped in the conscience of the memory, making of tradition an idol.

These five senses of conscience, it seems to me, are part of what *koinonia*, as a dimension of ecclesial *praxis*, teaches us.

DIAKONIA

The fourth dimension of ecclesial *praxis* that serves to form Christians can be referred to as *diakonia*, which is the term for *service, mission, vocation* in the world. In the systolic and diastolic rhythm of alternately moving toward center and then dispersing into the larger world, *diakonia* as vocation, service, and mission is how we move out, carrying vocation into corporate structures, into our common life, with concern for the renewal of the common good. John Westerhoff may have been echoing Twelve Step programs when he said that often we *act* our way into new ways of believing more readily than we *believe* our way into new ways of acting. My Methodist forebear John Wesley was well aware of this truth. When people responded to the preaching of John and Charles Wesley and other Methodist preachers, they were invited into societies that might include several hundred people. Soon, however, they were assigned to neighborhood "class meetings" of sixteen men and women where they were held accountable each week for the way they were walking the Christian walk. Diaries of some five hundred early English Methodists show that their heartwarming experiences—the affective confirmation of their commitments or recommitments to God—occurred, on the average, two years after they began to attend the class meetings and to learn and practice Christian attitudes and behavior.[15] So we learn faith and the posture and the movements of faith by doing them and by being apprenticed in a community that provides us examples and gives us contexts in which to do mission. "Get the motions right; motives will follow." This is *diakonia*.

PAIDEIA

As the final of these five dimensions of formation and transformation in the congregation we come to *paideia*, the Greek term for the comprehensive process of intentional and indirect formation by which men and women were prepared for participating roles in the *praxis* of the city-state. It involved attention to learning the stories and myths of one's people. These were learned through study of the epic poetry of classic literature, through participation in plays and rituals, through listening to debate and advocacy in the processes of governance in the public square. *Paideia* involved training in the disciplines and skills required for citizenship. Through athletics, coordination and physical skills were taught. Men and women learned how to care for the conditioning of their bodies even as they formed the virtues of courage and loyalty. Music and mathematics were part of the *paideia*, for the inherent pleasure of the former and utility of the latter. But both music and mathematics were employed for deeper purposes: they contributed to the ordering of the soul through the aesthetic structures of the music and the rational structures of the math. *Paideia*, in this sense, then, is the comprehensive approach taken in the *polis* to preparing the young for full participation in and contribution to the common life and common good of the city-state.

Our discussion of the dimensions of ecclesial *praxis* in this section have meant to suggest that Christian living—the practical knowing, the grounding in the story, the development of virtues, passions, affections—take form in the Church in ways analogous to the *paideia* of the *polis*. Thus the task of *paideia* in the congregation, I would suggest, is twofold. The first task lies in the necessity for providing some systematic grounding in the teachings, history, and practices of the community. Here the task properly is *didache*, "instruction, teaching, catechesis." The second task, however, involves care for the orchestration and faithfulness of the community in providing and involving each member in the dimensions of *kerygma, leitourgia, koinonia,* and *diakonia.* This combination of formal and focused instruction with full participation in the communal and missional life of the congregation encourages formation of faith that can develop the stability and strength of maturity and can awaken and form persons for faithfulness in vocation.

George Lindbeck has written an influential book called *The Nature of Doctrine* that is very pertinent here.[16] Lindbeck says that we learn and form the deep structure of faith in our minds and hearts through our participation in the language and life of the Christian community, as I've been describing it. Doctrine becomes important, like the rules of grammar, when we come to the point where we have to determine whether what has been and is being formed in us, and the community, is authentic and true. In this sense, doctrine formulates the semiotic system of authentic faith for the community. *Paideia*, in its instructional mode, helps us become aware of the rules, of the grammar, of Christian living. We need to be systematic about that; we need to be comprehensive about that; we need to be creative about that. As we undertook in chapters 2, 3, and 5, the Church must rework its formulations of doctrine as the community engages new eras and their challenges and as new forms of consciousness are required. *Paideia*, we might say in summary, has the responsibility for preparing and keeping people competent to participate in the congregation's ongoing work of practical theology, for shaping their vocations, and for helping to guide the congregation's witness and mission in public.

PUBLIC CHURCH AS AN ECOLOGY OF FAITH NURTURE

To look at the dimensions of congregational *praxis* and their contributions to faith formation and transformation is to look at congregations as ecologies of nurture and vocation. In this book we have given attention to the task of theological reconstruction for the twenty-first century. We have examined the developmental and transformational dynamics of growth and change in faith. The vision and actuality of public church congregations have been characterized. In this present chapter we have thought both normatively and functionally about how the congregation shapes the faith and vocations of its members. Here I propose to offer a few thoughts about congregations of public church as ecologies of faith nurture. By now readers are familiar with the theory of stages of faith. Here we will consider how, in the inter-living of persons who may be described by all of the different stages of faith, congregations of the public church can try to minister to the particular needs and strengths of persons in each of the stages.

The diagram "Congregational Formation: The Ecology of Faith Stages" portrays in circular fashion the inter-living of persons of different stages of faith consciousness in congregations. At center the unifying and forming powers of congregational life are represented. In contrast to linear or "stair step" understandings of the faith stages, this depiction shows that the inter-living of persons of several stages is part of the dynamic richness of congregational life. The systolic/diastolic "heartbeat" involves this inter-living and the dialectic of the journeys inward and outward that make it up.

Congregations of public church aim not for internal homogeneity but for a corporate unity that can include a robust pluralism within. Such churches are places where, as we said earlier, we come to learn to "stand each other." This means the community learning to understand itself as a covenant community—called by God from beyond itself. It is not called, at least initially, for warm

Congregational Formation: The Ecology of Faith Stages

PRIMAL   UNIVERSALIZING

INTUITIVE-PROJECTIVE   CONJUNCTIVE

KERYGMA—Story, Preaching
LEITOURGIA—Worship, Sacrament
DIAKONIA—Mission, Service
KOINONIA—Community, Body of Christ
PAIDEIA—Instruction, Formation

                                INDIVIDUATIVE-
MYTHIC-LITERAL   REFLECTIVE

SYNTHETIC-CONVENTIONAL

compatibility and harmony. Rather, members are called into honest struggle with each other, and in dialogue with Scripture and tradition, to be formed into persons and a community that God can use for partnership in their vocations and covenant faithfulness in the world.

Public churches require a coherent approach to the formation of their members across the span of ages and stages. As we have said, this involves the five dimensions of ecclesial *praxis* elaborated in the previous section: (1) preaching and teaching, (2) participation in worship and sacraments, (3) personal and group prayer and study, (4) involvement in mission, and (5) practical theological reflection on vocation. Public churches also take very seriously the process of initiation and inclusion into the community.

One distinctive character of educating public Christians derives from the commitment to aim, in all dimensions of its education and congregational life, toward a postconventional modal level of faith development. By "modal level" I mean the average expectable level of development for adults in the community.[17] The public church requires a substantial number of adults who appropriate the tradition in the Individuative-Reflective and Conjunctive stages of faith.[18] Such communities will make careful provision for forming children and youth and other adults in ways that effectively meet them in their respective stages. However, basic Christian nurture must be undertaken in very intentional ways if the hoped-for developmental trajectory is to lead beyond conventional appropriation. Though space here does not allow for discussion of educational nurture in detail, we can close with a brief description of principles pertinent to each of the stages that might guide congregations that intend to grow in the characteristics of public church.[19]

Primal Faith

Recent research offers profound new insights into the importance of prelanguage experiences and relations for the roots of faith and selfhood in infancy.[20] Parents need prenatal education to heighten awareness of these matters, to provide models of relating, interaction, and care that are productive of optimal patterns of mutuality, and to clarify the faith they want to share and in which they want to nurture their child(ren).[21] Strong grounding in basic trust is required for the engagement with "strangers" involved in being public Christians.

Intuitive-Projective Faith

Faith nurture for public churches requires early childhood experiences of Christian community. This includes interaction with adults who are able to certify and honor children's experiences and interpretations, thus avoiding shame and the construction of "false selves," while gifting their imaginations and enriching their base of experience.[22] As is the case in each subsequent stage, the spine of identity is built by providing stories from the tradition to awaken the horizon of moral and Christian meanings and communicate images of the love of God, while portraying the world honestly as a mixture of good and evil. I encourage participation in the Eucharist for young children as they express interest and the desire to partake. This gives them access to the taste and feel of participation in the community of faith (the kinesthetics of faith). In the next stage they can be given special instruction, along with their parents, to help them understand and connect what they have experienced with the Christian story. We also urge adults to pray in classes with children, in terms meaningful to the children, while inviting them to pray orally with and for each other, and for the needs and issues of their experience worlds. Young children should have regular experiences of interaction with children and their parents from religious, ethnic, and racial groups other than their own. Stress should not be placed upon differences or upon detailed understandings of other religious traditions but rather upon inclusiveness and the naturalness of children and their families interacting together.

Mythic-Literal Faith

Stories and experiences of belonging to the community are of paramount importance in the Mythic-Literal stage. Worship-readiness classes for six- to nine-year-olds provide important opportunities to link biblical narratives with sacraments, symbols, and the church year. Stories of the men and women who are heroes of the faith (including preeminently, Jesus as the Christ) should include many who, for the love of God, cared for or struggled for the rights of persons from very different religious communities, classes, or racial or ethnic backgrounds. As their identity and knowledge about their Christian community deepens, opportunities should be provided for them to visit or receive visits from persons or groups from other religious communities. While avoiding judgmental comparisons, the encounter with other traditions should both widen their horizons and deepen their awareness of and commitment to their own faith. With adults and older youth, school-aged children should be involved in missions of care for homeless persons, refugees, elderly persons, or victims of disasters. This is the *praxis* of *diakonia*. They continue to need times of prayer and discussion of faith with adults who are confident and committed public Christians.

Synthetic-Conventional Faith

Traditionally confirmation comes at about the time of full-scale transition into the Synthetic-Conventional stage. For young persons dealing with new issues of identity, the religious hunger (often unrecognized) is for a more personal relation to God in which they know themeselves to be known and loved, despite awkwardness and the beginnings of distancing from their parent(s). Confirmation needs to be a true rite of passage, not to adulthood, but rather to the status of one who has begun to be responsible in new ways for the forming and extending of her or his faith. It is an important time to provide opportunities for practice in taking the perspectives of others and learning the skills and motives of care for others in community. Youth being prepared for full membership in public church congregations should also be given opportunities and challenges to take the perspectives of persons from different national, racial, or social class backgrounds and the contexts in which they live.

Good ministry for persons at this stage will also provide regularly (as well as on retreats) for development and practice of new forms of prayer and spirituality. These should help deepen the youth's personal relation with God and help the youth begin to attend to the shape of God's call to him or her for vocational partnership. The congregation's goal should be to provide its young people with a coherent, persuasive version of the Christian story, one that constitutes a viable conventional faith ethos. We should not avoid ideological critique when it comes authentically. Nor should we shy away from issues of injustice or theodicy that arise in the course of living. But the emphasis should be on transmitting a lively and authentic Christian orthodoxy, coupled with truly challenging opportunities for mission and service in areas and contexts where there are certain to be in-depth interactions with "strangers." A creed worked out by twelve sixth graders in the spring of 1990 on a retreat culminating their confirmation preparation provides a good example of the Church's helping to ground youth in a creative orthodoxy:

WE BELIEVE

In God as the creator of the heavens and the earth and every good thing therein.

That God is like a parent who loves us all equally and whose love is unconditional.

That God is with us always, in troubled and in happy times.

WE BELIEVE

In Jesus, God's son, who was born in a stable in Bethlehem to Mary and Joseph.

That he came to love us and show us how to love each other.

That out of love, Jesus died on the cross, and through his resurrection, has given us hope for living.

WE BELIEVE

In the Holy Spirit as God's presence with us in the world.

That the Holy Spirit helps us understand God's will, and gives us the encouragement and power to be God's people.

WE BELIEVE

That every person is created equal.

That everyone should work together to improve our world and care for all that the Lord created.

We are all called to help those in need: the hungry, the sick, the poor, and the homeless.

World peace can be accomplished if we help one another, living together in love and fellowship in the presence and wonderful ways of God.[23]

Individuative-Reflective Faith

The mid- to late teen years mark the usual transition to the Individuative-Reflective stage, in which young adults must take responsibility in a new way for their own life course. It is also a stage that requires critical reflection upon the contents of beliefs and values and attention to the constructing of a more explicit ideological orientation for one's life. Here the question of vocation as a grounding for identity can be fruitfully addressed. It is also the stage at which the distinctive theological foundations of the public church can be taught and at which young adults can become involved in the critical and constructive tasks of practical theological guidance in the Church's mission and work. Preaching and teaching must anticipate and honor the colleagueship of young adults, while making clear the call to vocational commitment. Vocation, here, as throughout this book, means "finding a purpose for one's life that is part of the purposes of God." Public church congregations depend upon having a strong core of persons, young adult and beyond, who have the requisite faith development to contribute to the critical analysis of societal systems and meanings and to be part of relating the norms and vision of Christian faith to them. Mission to and with the disenfranchised and the oppressed, coupled with critical reflection on social and economic relations, can help prevent persons in this stage from getting seduced into the individualistic values and numbness of affluent postindustrial capitalist societies.

Conjunctive Faith

Persons at the Conjunctive stage are required as senior members and leaders in public congregations. They provide examples of deep and passionate commitment to the Christian story combined with principled openness to the truths of others. They are the members of the congregation who have struggled (and are struggling) for freedom from false, oversimple images of faith. They are working toward the integration of the high and the low, in human life—the conscious and the unconscious. They are learning to live the paradoxical truths of the gospel, that it is in giving that we receive; it is in dying to the striving of the false self that we, by grace, are born to the seeds of a new being. They need support and nurture in their roles as models of postcritical commitment and mid-life vocation.

Approaches to spirituality for mid-life and beyond are needed to strengthen these persons for living the paradoxical character of public Christian faith in a pluralistic world. At a time when life roles can bring the more isolating burdens of institutional leadership, such persons need a community where they can relate in depth to others who are dealing with the polar tensions that mid-life involves. They need the passion and the energy of people in the earlier stages of faith to strengthen their courage and their sense of purpose in the midst of their engagement of the full ambiguity and complexity of contemporary life. As they encounter the stranger within, persons of Conjunctive faith may be able to help others embrace the strangers without to whom the public church is called to minister.

CONCLUSION

It is appropriate to end this chapter on ecclesiogenesis with reflections on ministry, support, and challenge for persons at

mid-life and beyond. Mid-life can be a time of deepening individuation—a time when one has come to terms with the roads not
taken, and come to measure the worth of those one chose instead.
It is a time of reckoning with the uniqueness of one's own life
cycle. It can also be a time of learning to value oneself in new
ways—no longer for the promises of what one may yet become or
for the reputation one may yet earn, but rather for the proven,
established pattern of strengths and vulnerabilities, of lovableness
and cussedness that one has discovered oneself honestly to be.
One comes to depend upon the grace of God, the grace of spouse
or partner, and the grace of institutions and of friends. Interdependence becomes an indispensable, felt reality, not just an
ideal.

Much the same is true of churches and congregations. Not all
churches are destined or meant to be "public churches." And for
those that are so destined, no one pattern will serve as a template
for their evolution toward public church characteristics. As my
rhapsody to the congregation suggested, there is much to value
and to devote ourselves to even in ordinary congregations. And as
our profiles of three very different public churches showed, there
are areas for growth and improvement in congregations that seem
to represent the vanguard.

It does seem clear to me, however, that we are in a time of
fundamental shifts in the ways we construct our relatedness—and
our imagining of that relatedness—to one another, to the systems
that knit us together in a global community, and to God. I hope
that the weavings of this book have begun to illumine some of the
dimensions of those shifts. And, of course, I hope that the pro-
posals I have tried to broker for new ways of imagining those
relations, and new ways of celebrating and serving them in
church, will prove to be helpful.

I am certain that "business as usual" in the old paradigms for
churches will continue to draw and involve significant numbers of
people. However, there are growing numbers of people who long
ago left their churches and have substituted for that involvement
active engagement in other kinds of "helping" institutions or
movements, or have simply claimed Sunday and other time that
would have been invested in church for leisure and other activities. There are many others who "hang in" our congregations with
half a lung and half a heart, who hope for new life and new

paradigms of church life. This book and its visional tapestries is intended for those who would work with and minister to people in these two kinds of groups.

In view of what has been written here about the divine *praxis*, a great deal is at stake in local church congregations. Talent and giftedness are democratically distributed in the world. The gifts God has given people are varied and many. Churches, when they are faithful, awaken and support people in claiming their giftedness and in finding ways to put it at the disposal of God's work in the world. Hindus have a phrase, *astikya buddhi*, which means, roughly, "alertness, or attentiveness to Transcendence." Churches, when they are faithful, call and form gifted persons to be *astikya buddhi*—to be alert and attentive to God's *praxis* and their part in it. This awakening can often bring astounding things from ordinary people. How many seemingly secular leaders, operating with great wisdom and sophistication in leadership roles in government, corporations, universities, and the arts and professions had their horizon of meaning and their moral sensibilities shaped in Protestant congregations or Catholic parishes, where family members gathered to worship and pray and ordinary people taught and shared their versions of faith?[24] A new paradigm of cultural consciousness will be vacuous indeed if it does not intentionally involve patterns of faith and community living that can serve powerfully to shape and support alertness and attentiveness to Transcendence and attachments of the heart to partnership with God.

In the absence or silence of Christian voice and participation in shaping the new creation the very stones *are* crying out. God's *praxis* is far wider then ecclesial *praxis;* the story of God's being and action in creation, evolution, and history is one great multidimensional story. It subsumes and transforms, while being disclosed and illumined by, the biblical and Christian stories. We are those who have been given the gift and the creative custodianship of the powerful story that centers in Jesus the Christ and that opens out toward the unfolding future of God's commonwealth of love and justice. It calls us—and should nerve us—to imagine God's future boldly, to labor for justice and love confidently, to offer the wisdom of God's promises faithfully, and to embrace the complexities of God's new creation on Gaia—Earth—with expectant joy and determined hope.

NOTES

1. Leonardo Boff, *Ecclesiogenesis: The Base Communities Reinvent the Church* (Maryknoll, NY: Orbis Books, 1986).
2. Lewis S. Mudge, "Toward an Ecclesial Hermeneutic," in Lewis S. Mudge and James N. Poling, eds., *Formation and Reflection: The Promise of Practical Theology* (Philadelphia: Fortress Press, 1987), p. 109. For a thorough discussion of the use of semiotic analysis in theology, see Robert J. Schreiter, *Constructing Local Theologies* (Maryknoll, NY: Orbis Books, 1985).
3. Mudge, "Toward an Ecclesial Hermeneutic," pp. 110–11.
4. This is not to imply that the three semiotic sets I will identify here *exhaust* the Bible's resources for ecclesiogenesis. Nor is it to imply that other semiotic sets from Scripture would not contradict or relativize these. My point, rather, is that these three sets have an important coherence and power; that their coherence envisions an ecclesial community with transforming potentials for their cultural contexts; and that they have particular relevance for forming and guiding public church congregations. Also note that I do not base my clues regarding these semiotic sets or clusters on the claim that the later texts have been directly influenced or shaped by dependence upon the earlier ones. My argument—or hints toward one—builds upon structuring similarities between the texts that constitute each of these clusters. By structuring similarities I mean the way they form an envisioning of the inner life of communities of faith, the "reading" and evaluation of their environing cultures, and the shaping of mission and responsibility within the larger society.
5. Mudge, "Toward an Ecclesial Hermeneutic," p. 114.
6. Maria Harris, *Fashion Me A People: Curriculum in the Church* (Louisville, KY: Westminster/John Knox Press, 1989).
7. For this last term, *paideia*, Maria Harris uses the more restrictive term *didache*, "teaching." The choice of the more comprehensive term *paideia*, or "formation," will be made clear farther on.
8. Annie Dillard, *Teaching a Stone to Talk: Expeditions and Encounters* (New York: Harper Colophon Books, 1983). This whole chapter's concern with ecclesiogenesis in the light of the passage from Luke 19:40 about the very stones crying out, can be said to be concerned with teaching stones to talk.
9. Ibid., pp. 40–41.
10. The foregoing is drawn from Judith Hooper and Dick Teresi, *The Three-Pound Universe* (New York: Macmillan, 1986), pp. 223ff.
11. See Don E. Saliers, *The Soul in Paraphrase: Prayer and the Religious Affections* (New York: Seabury, 1980), chap. 4.
12. Ibid., p. 68.
13. Thomas Green, *The Formation of Conscience in an Age of Technology*, the John Dewey Lecture, 1984 (Syracuse, NY: Syracuse Univ. Press, 1984).
14. The term Green uses for this is the conscience of *sacrifice*. The use of the term *sacrifice* in ethical thought has become, rightfully, a red flag for those doing ethics in ways that try to include and address women's experience. In my judgment the use of that term is not intrinsic to the meaning Green is trying to convey with this second voice of conscience. Though he clearly does want to imply that one should do one's duty, and that one should sacrifice one's desire to pursue other pleasures when duty conflicts with that desire, it is clear that Green sees duty as arising out of promises freely made, and not out of assuming and docilely fulfilling traditional roles that may have institutionalized dominance and subordination.

15. Oral communication from Thomas Alban, who has been studying these early Methodist journals in a large project reconstructing the practices of faith formation in the early Methodist movements in England.

16. George Lindbeck, *The Nature of Doctrine: Religion and Theology in a Postliberal Age* (Philadelphia: Westminster, 1984).

17. For the idea of the "modal level" of faith development, see Fowler, *Stages of Faith*, pp. 294 ff.

18. See Fowler, *Faith Development and Pastoral Care*, pp. 95–98.

19. See Richard R. Osmer, *A Teachable Spirit* (Louisville, KY: Westminster/John Knox Press, 1990), chap. 10, for a fuller discussion of goals and methods of Christian education based on the framework of the stages of faith.

20. See especially the important work of Daniel N. Stern, *The Interpersonal World of the Infant: A View from Psychoanalysis and Developmental Psychology* (New York: Basic Books, 1985). For a sustained reflection on the implications of Stern's work for understanding the dynamic roots of selfhood and faith, see Fowler, "Strength for the Journey: Early Childhood Development in Selfhood and Faith," in Doris Blazer, ed. *Faith Development in Early Childhood* (Kansas City: Sheed & Ward, 1989), pp. 1–36.

21. We might call this kind of covenantal work with expectant parents "Christian Lamaze."

22. The term "false self" comes from the work of the object-relations theorist D. W. Winnicott. See his *Playing and Reality* (New York: Basic Books, 1971). On this concept, see Alice Miller, *Thou Shalt Not Be Aware* (New York: Farrar, Straus, Giroux, 1984); M. A. Fossum and M. J. Mason, *Facing Shame: Families in Recovery* (New York: W. W. Norton, 1986).

23. Written by the 1990 confirmation class of the Glenn Memorial United Methodist Church, Atlanta, Georgia, and used here by permission. Ministers working with the youth were Lurline Fowler and Tom Shores.

24. And, of course, the same question can be raised with regard to persons with backgrounds in Jewish, Muslim, Buddhist, or other nurturing communities of faith.

INDEX